VOICES IN THE DARKNESS

The author (second from left) as an official of the United Nations Relief and Rehabilitation Administration in Greece following the Second World War.

VOICES IN THE DARKNESS
A Memoir

by Edgar M. Wahlberg

ROBERTS RINEHART PUBLISHERS
BOULDER, COLORADO

Copyright © 1983 by Edgar M. Wahlberg
Published by Roberts Rinehart, Inc. Publishers
Box 3161, Boulder Colorado 80303
International Standard Book Numbers 0-911797-01-7 (cloth) and
0-911797-02-5 (paper)
Library of Congress Card Catalog Number 82-062945
Printed in the United States of America

All rights reserved. No part of this book may be reproduced in any form or by any electronic or mechanical means including information storage and retrieval systems without permission in writing from the publisher, except by a reviewer who may quote brief passages in a review.

CONTENTS

1. BIRTH THROUGH HIGH SCHOOL, 1899-1917 1
2. UNIVERSITY THROUGH SEMINARY, 1917-1924 13
3. MINING CAMP, 1924-1926 22
4. GOODWILL RURAL PARISH, 1926-1930 31
5. DENVER, 1930-1944 43
6. UNITED NATIONS RELIEF AND REHABILITATION ADMINISTRATION, GREECE, 1944-1945 117
7. UNITED NATIONS RELIEF AND REHABILITATION ADMINISTRATION, CHINA, 1945-1946   142
8. MICHIGAN, 1947-1976 156

ACKNOWLEDGMENTS

I AM DEEPLY INDEBTED to many people who have helped make *Voices in the Darkness* a reality:

First of all to my wife Jimmie who helped recall events of the past and keep the record straight; to my children Lois, Bill and Lea for their loving encouragement; to Eddie Allen, one of many boys associated with Grace Community Church and Center; to Verna and Jim Hedlun who reviewed the early stages of the manuscript; to Bob and Zella Adell for analyzing a later copy; to Fritz Sterling, long-time friend and inspiration, for putting up the front money; to grandson James Wahlberg who designed the jacket; to Audrey Haerlin, revisionist; to Frederick R. Rinehart for his patient guidance as publisher; and to the thousands of people with whom it was a pleasure to be associated.

FOREWORD: BEHOLD A MAN

Many call him Reverend. Eleven call him Grandpa. Some call him fool, or "pink," or politically naive, or nigger lover. Three call him Dad. But most, with affection, call him Wallie. He prefers Wallie.

His personality allows no attitude of indifference, or of tolerance. All who know him are influenced by him. His word for life is Love. His position on any controversy of this day is explicit. His courage is never denied, and often respected by those who oppose him most.

His faith is slanted toward Christ and embodied in man. He gives up on no man. While turning the other cheek, he applies a stranglehold of love through perserverence and eloquence and logic. Discouraged by prejudice, shaken by ignorance, deeply hurt by slander, and scarred by accusation, he stumbles but never retreats. He has won more to love, or at least respect for his way, than he has lost. His faith in man is harrassed by hate and greed and discrimination. His perception of these hostilities is uncanny, and bold is his resistance. Love is his weapon, apathy and ignorance the batteground, and continuity of faith in man is his victory.

His abilities are many. He speaks and is understood. He writes and scratches deep into the heart. He argues and is heard. He protests not in vain. He leads and men follow. He relaxes in peace. He loves and is loved.

His ministry is more to torment than to tranquilize. He preaches Christianity as a social gospel. That fear, poverty, prejudice and hostility undergird sin. That sin is not of itself but the effect of a cause. That love is the only destroyer of these undergirding causes, yet, preached positively, Love is God. That Christian Living encompasses the First Commandment, but man's love for God can be achieved only by man's love for fellowman; and, further, man's love for man necessitates man's love for himself. That Christianity is practical and daily. That a man who respects himself, loves his fellowman, and worships his God, may not be perfect but his is the only way to successfully encounter each day of living.

Love is the key, each day is the lock, and man's salvation is the treasure.

He implements this theme by social action and concern, tempered by love. His ministry is demanding, irritating, provocative and true.

He fears as all men fear. Injustice, intolerance and war are his chief concerns. His failures are human. His grief is never hidden. He is sentimental and naive in family relationships. He seeks recognition immodestly. He forgives completely. His passion is fishing. He has been deceived by many more fish than men.

As love is his faith, his wife is his strength. She guides him, she organizes him, she resists him, she consoles him, she criticizes him, and sometimes misleads him, but she never forsakes him.

When Jesus was brought before Pilate in Judgment, Pilate, in his jowls of dissipation, surrounded by wealth and glory, yet perceived something about Jesus not recognized by the Pharisees. Even after scourging, wearing a crown of thorns, Jesus was ushered before Pilate, whose insight caused him to say, "Here is a Man!"

This man is no Christ, yet of all men I have known, I can say of him with conviction—"This is a Man."

Raymond Richmond Chase
(Rev. Wahlberg's Son-in-Law)
1923-1980

VOICES IN THE DARKNESS

One night I had a dream about a small town divided by railroad tracks—the poor living south of the tracks and the more affluent on the other side.

I saw a poor man ring the doorbell of a doctor's home, and heard him say, "My wife is very sick. Please come and help her." The doctor picked up his bag and followed the man. It wasn't far to his house, so they walked.

They passed rows of shelters with earth floors that had been built as temporary housing for sugar beet workers. Next they passed make-shift shacks lived in by the wretched poor. There were no conveniences in the houses. Water hydrants were outside and stinking toilets in back.

The doctor was too late. He found an emaciated corpse. There were three children dressed in rags. The doctor began to hear voices: the cries of little children, the sobbing of neighbors, and the mutterings of grown men.

He started back toward his home, but decided to walk around and listen. He heard people quarreling and complaining. He heard a young couple giggling and enjoying for a moment the only pleasure they could afford. He saw a fight between two enraged men. He heard wives yelling abusive words at their husbands and saw husbands rushing out into the night to a makeshift shanty where men were playing cards and drinking. Others were complaining about "no work for days now."

The doctor walked into the shanty, a gathering place for recreation and discontent. He sat by himself listening, and felt alone and confused. He had never experienced such unhappiness.

I wakened my wife and told her that I had the title for my book,
"VOICES IN THE DARKNESS."

1. BIRTH THROUGH HIGH SCHOOL, 1899-1917

Birth

I was born March 9, 1899, in a small three-room house in a working man's district in Denver, Colorado. We lived mostly in the kitchen except for sleeping. We had one stove, a kitchen stove which was supplied with coal and wood. Each house had an ash pit in the back, built like a large cone with a small top into which we dumped the ashes every morning except for a small amount reserved for the outhouse. The ashes in the pits were hot and a threat to children who climbed to the rim and sometimes fell into the smoldering ashes.

The city dump was a block away and was off limits to my brother and me. The dump is now a park and a high school is across the street. But the old house is still there and modernized, enlarged a bit to include a bathroom. We moved three times before we enjoyed this luxury, and then it was just a toilet in a damp and very small basement.

We used kerosene lamps for light and took our baths in the wash tub. This was a Saturday night ritual, whether we needed it or not. We had to be clean at all times but especially for church the next day. I never saw my father or mother taking a bath. Nudity was forbidden and shameful.

We moved four times before I was twelve years old. The last house was modern, having a bathroom. There were fearful enemies in each location—bedbugs, for the most part, and cockroaches. Mama was an immaculate housekeeper. She scrubbed and cleaned until the last enemy was gone—only to creep back. Mama worked on her knees with a hand scrub brush, using kerosene to fight the vermin. Our houses were not easily ventilated, especially in the winter. Then there were times when rats appeared in the alleys—the dump was not far away and there wasn't much that could be done.

Papa

We called him Papa. He was born in Smaland, Sweden, February 12, 1874. He followed his half-brother, Alfred, to the United States in 1896.

For a short while they remained together in Boulder, Colorado. Then Papa decided to try his fortune as a tailor in Denver. Uncle Alfred settled on a homestead near Durango, Colorado and arranged for a mail-order bride from Sweden. He prospered, but suddenly died. I liked this red-headed, red-whiskered man who was the first to encourage me to get an education. He promised financial help when I reached college, but this was not to be.

Papa was a journeyman tailor. He had learned his trade the hard way in Sweden, but could find no gainful employment there because everyone was impoverished. He left his homeland and family hoping to do better in America. Sweden was without trees and resources and hope. He returned to Sweden sixty-five years later to find Sweden covered with forests and enjoying relative prosperity. Papa confided to me, "I should have stayed in Sweden. Things are better there." His three brothers were alive, owners of small factories which had started as blacksmith shops. Papa survived his brothers, although he was the eldest. He lived to be ninety-three.

Papa was resourceful, a tireless, skilled workman. He kept up with the times. He loved discussions on almost any subject—the men gathered together separate from the ladies. Children were not allowed to participate, but some of us listened. Often Papa said to me, "Stanga munnen" (keep your mouth closed). None were unkind and no one felt shut out.

I recall many of these discussions which were part of my learning: relatives, the sick, Sweden, religion, politics, unemployment, ministers, Union leaders, William McKinley, Theodore Roosevelt, William Jennings Bryan, Samuel Gompers, Joe Hill, and more.

Joe Hill was Swedish. He changed his name from Hillstrom. A singer for the working class, a member of the International Workers of the World, he wrote parodies to popular church hymns. He was considered sacreligious and a dangerous radical. He was a gentle personality with a sincere devotion to the working people. One of his songs, to the tune of "In the Sweet By and Bye," follows:

> Long haired preachers come out every night
> To tell you what's wrong and what's right,
> But when asked for something to eat
> They reply with voices so sweet:
>
> Work and pray, live on hay,
> You'll eat pie in the sky when you die.

Eugene V. Debs was popular with labor and became the Socialist candidate for president. He was sentenced to prison for his opposition to the First World War. He didn't like the God of wrath portrayed in the Bible. He revered Jesus and had a large portrait of Jesus on the wall of his cell. He described Jesus as "the great Divine tramp who never had a dollar, but who loved and understood the common folk, the ordinary ruck of man, with an absorbing and abiding affection."

Papa was a charter member of the Journeymen Tailors Union in Denver. He had worked for years on piece work in a cubbyhole sweatshop for as long as twelve hours a day. In those days, there was no fund for workers who went on strike. The strikers, with the help of sympathetic Unions, helped each other. These were disturbing times for Papa, for his family, his fellow men and even the bosses. There was never a grudge in his mind. I became acquainted with one of his former employers who told me, "It grieved me and your dad when a strike was called. He would talk it over with me. I would say, 'John, it is what you have to do. Come back when it is over and I'll pay you more than they ask." Papa believed that a laborer was entitled to a fair day's pay and deserved his dignity as a man. He took great pride in his skill as a craftsman and resented the encroachments of "ready-made" goods.

His devotion to unionism and the needs of all workers was revealed in a street car strike. The Tramway Company had hired professional strike breakers and as a result won the strike and broke up the union. Papa vowed that he would never ride a street car again until the company came to terms with the demands of the union. He would allow Mama to ride and if the distance were far, his two sons. But he followed his outraged conscience and walked, regardless of distance—sometimes as far as eighteen miles. He started a habit which he continued for the rest of his life. He died at ninety-three and was ill only two weeks. He never relented even when I went to California to visit him. I would say, "That is a long way to walk." He would reprove me in a gallant and humorous manner, "Valking is gude fer you."

Papa was devoted to the Swedish Baptist Church of Denver, and was an articulate member for many years. It was "fundamentalist" in doctrine and creed. There was plenty of hell-fire and brimstone. I remember my baptism. I slipped from the minister's hand and I was wet inside and out.

I cannot recall the teachings, but I do remember the people. The church was vibrant with the problems and needs of many young men and women. Most had recently come from the "old country." They sought friendship and fellowship. They had to find work and a place to live. Sometimes their clothing was different and badly worn. Then came the hideous migration of the sick and helpless. Victims of undernourishment and tuberculosis, they were actually the casualties of working conditions and the exploitation of immigrant labor. Many of these people came under corporation-steamship contracts to provide cheap labor and to weaken the "danger of unionism."

New problems developed as their infections spread from home to home. A community structure was needed. Swedish people of all churches came together to launch the Swedish National Sanatorium. Land was purchased near Englewood, Colorado. Papa was one of the original trustees. The City of Denver allowed the Swedish people to have an annual collection day. I recall the cold and bleak Sunday when as a small boy I was present for the dedicacation of a brick house and perhaps a dozen tents which already housed some of the sickest. The first nurse was a victim of this dreaded disease and died.

There were many incidents of joy as Papa played with his boys, took them fishing, went sledding and skating. He amazed us with his ability to skate number eights—figure skating. Papa would buy an apple tree every fall and we would pick the apples and sack them and take them home. Expressman Carlson charged us only a dollar for a ten-mile trip. Most of our equipment was handmade. Papa raised rabbits and chickens to enliven our menu.

Papa had some advice for unions. He said, "It is bad for workers to fight

God and the bosses both. If the workers would go to church they could outvote the bosses and we could have God on our side instead of theirs."

Mama

We called her Mama. She was one of over one million Swedish people who fled the poverty of the homeland in the 19th century. They also sought a freedom proclaimed by our American democracy—often not available to the poor. Steerage passage was often paid by vested interests.

Mama was a beautiful creature with coal black hair and sparkling brown eyes. Her father had died at sea. She left a mother in Sweden with the promise to return. Her brother had preceded her to Kansas where he became a carpenter. He fell from a roof and was killed in 1917. She went to Denver to visit an aunt who earned her living by keeping boarders, many of whom were sick Swedes who could not stand up to the long hours and rigors of the menial jobs available to them. My mother hired out as a "chambermaid" and cook to an affluent family living on Capitol Hill, then a prosperous residential area.

She worked hard to please her employers and when she wanted to, made friends easily. She could be the life of the party and at times retire into herself, depending upon her mood.

She had a longing which was never fulfilled. I think she was disappointed in America. She loved attention and received recognition for the many delicacies she created in her life, what she cooked, the clothes and lacework she made, her housekeeping, and in the appearance of her boys. She loved to be appreciated and was disturbed when she was taken for granted. She was often quite ill, suffering from migraine headaches and undefined ailments. She was easily let down by disappointments and misunderstandings.

Mama was a perfectionist. She made her own drapes and lace curtains which adorned our homes. She knitted and sewed everything we used, including bed coverings and clothing. She did all the baking and cooking, counting on her boys to assist her when she was ill. She had home canned goods in the basement. She washed clothing the hard way on a scrub board and in the same tub in which we took our baths. Cleanliness was her watchword. She cautioned us to "scrape the feet." She would have no dirt in the basement, in the corners, or behind the ears. Her home was not always the easiest place in which to live, but it could be counted on to be clean.

I am certain that I know why poor people move frequently. They are exasperated with stale oldness. It seemed to me that landlords begrudgingly or never redecorate, or for that matter, care at all about the conditions in which poor people live. Poor people hunger for a change of scenery where they hope to extricate themselves from the awful drabness of poverty. Mama spoke longingly of a "new house someday, and a house of my own." Her dream was never realized.

Mama maintained a rigid discipline over her boys. She was acutely aware of what the neighbors might think—a feeling derived from our being Swedish. My brother Carl and I ran errands, helped with the baking and cooking, swept the floors and scrubbed them, and kept the yard clean. Infractions and indifferences were severely punished. Mama administered the required number of strokes to our bare behinds and when the matter was reported to Papa there would be a similar routine—not quite as severe. He would usher us to the basement and when the switch was lightly applied, would say, "Yell loud so Mama will think I am hitting hard."

I marveled at the ingenuity of her baking and cooking. She never used a recipe. She would mix the ingredients and taste the mixture with her finger. I would exclaim, "How do you do it?" Her reply was, "Edgar, if you put the right things in, they will come out all right. Remember that. Put the right things into your life. The wrong things will spoil what you want to come out all right." There was the Book that was never found. She would say, "Remember, your names are written down in a book, what you do—the gude things and the bad things. At times, I write it in the book. Do not forget." We hunted for the book, high and low, in the most unlikely places, but it never turned up. We would ask her where she kept it and told her that we wanted to see it. She would say, "Someday you will know where it is and some day you will see it. You will know that it is the Book of Life."

Mama taught her boys lessons in living in the manner available to her. I recall when she asked me to kneel at her knees as she fondly stroked my head. She said, "You are a gude boy. You must always be gude. You must not forget how your mama has scrubbed and cleaned the house and how she made you and Carl keep the corners clean." How often I had heard her explain, "A-ha, look, the corners are dirty. You cannot hide the dirt in the corner or under the rug. Now, you clean them up." She continued to tenderly stroke my head and face as she went on, "You may be a smart man and a big man. You learn in school what I don't know and never will. You may be a big man, a President or a minister, maybe. I don't know. But one thing I do know, to be somebody gude, you must keep the corners of your life clean inside your heart and inside your mind. I pray to God you know what I know."

As a family we did considerable entertaining. There were the relatives, most of them farmers, who came out once a year with much welcome produce from their labor. There were the immigrants, alone and unattached, trying to learn the ways of the new world. There were the sick, mostly consumptive, seeking health in the sunshine of the West. All were more or less poor, but for the time being didn't know it. They worried about their loved ones in Sweden. There were menial laborers, section hand workers, garment workers and tailors from various sweatshops, one or two bartenders, and a shoemaker, and the unemployed. The minister and his wife were welcome any time. There was the Ladies' Aid of the Swedish Baptist Church.

Christmas was a time of greatest hilarity when as many as possible slept on the floor awaiting the hour to attend Julatta, early Christmas morning service. Mama prepared Swedish food—sill (fish), patati Korv (Swedish potato sausage), sulta (pressed meat from a pig's head), ost (cheese), and Embergs dricka (a Swedish drink). The first course was gruel in which was placed a Swedish coin, a token of good luck and marriage. I am sure that Mama always placed the coin in the bowl of an eligible young woman. The lucky person would spoon it out with congratulatory shouts from all present.

Santa Claus came in person on Christmas Eve to exchange joyous phrases with all the guests, but seemed bent on scaring the children. He displayed more than a passing knowledge of their evil doings. The children promised to be "snalla pojkar nasta ar" (good boys next year). There was the noisy unwrapping of the gifts, mostly home made. The house was silent in the early hours of the morning as everyone snatched a few moments of rest before attending the 4:00 a.m. service at the church. I don't recall the nature of these services because I am sure that my brother and I were fast asleep.

Race relations were never a problem to me. We lived next door to blacks. (Not true when we moved into what some call a "better neighborhood.") I thank my parents and my next door neighbors. There seemed to be understanding between us because as "Swedes" we also suffered the barbs of bigotry. We had many happy and friendly experiences together. One black family lived next door and another down the street. In the first home, with three children, the husband was ill. When the father died and the family moved to live with relatives, our family followed them to help. Our other black neighbors were a Pullman porter and his white wife. They had the most beautiful garden on the block. My mama said, "They must love each other very much because their garden is so beautiful." We moved next door to the Rivers. Mr. Rivers was the editor of the black newspaper. My parents were impressed with this family because they were educated.

My mama never stood still. She always believed that the future had something special—a calling. She said, "You will see." She left Denver for California on her own and went to work as a housekeeper and then came back to Denver to pick up my younger brother Gordon, and returned to California. My papa didn't want to leave Denver, but sadly followed to reestablish his home in Long Beach, California. Mama was all for studying and took up Unity. Then came the Depression and Father Divine. She was attracted to the Father Divine Mission because from her own experience she knew that he was feeding hungry people—not just talking about the problem but doing something about it. She joined the Long Beach Mission and later severed all her family connections and moved to New York to help operate an Old People's Home for Father Divine. I tried to see her, but she didn't want to get upset or to upset me. I talked with Father Divine and received his promise to get in touch with me if ever I were needed. She died of arterial sclerosis and senile dementia in a hospital for the mentally disturbed. I visited her often and she pleaded to go back to 76 Washington Street in Denver ("just around the corner") to see her "three gude boys, Edgar, Carl, and Gordon."

I spent a whole day with Father Divine in Philadelphia some months after the death of my mother. I asked him, "What do you think about your people saying that you are God?" His answer was, "You claim to be a Methodist minister. Wouldn't it be kind of all right for your people to see a little of God in you? I don't say I am God. They say it."

Grade School

I started school in 1905, in the new Evans School named after the second territorial governor of Colorado, John Evans. His daughter-in-law, Mrs. W. G.

Evans, the mother of John Evans II, and part of the family continued to live in the neighborhood, just across from Grace Methodist Church and Evans Chapel, where I was to serve after 1930.

School was an alarming break from the cloistered pattern of a Swedish home and Swedish friends. My brother and I were frightened. We felt closed in and closed out. We were carefully groomed and dressed in the anxious concern of our immigrant parents. We were advised to be "good boys" and to listen "good to what the teacher says." This was easier said than done. Papa took the morning off from work and walked with us to see that we were properly enrolled. I entered the first grade and my brother was taken to the kindergarten. The rooms were filled to capacity so that the teachers had little time for each child. My brother and I walked hand-in-hand each day to a chamber of horrors. We knew few English words. We might have understood sufficiently if the teachers and pupils had talked slowly and distinctly. We heard only jumbled words which grew louder and faster as the teachers tried to penetrate our minds. At last it stopped. My mind shut out the jumbled sounds and it seemed we were ignored as hopeless "dumb Swedes."

My grades were low so I was held over in the first grade. This hurt my parents. I dreaded most the notes sent to my parents advising them that something had to be done. They had already stopped speaking Swedish in the home, which meant more silence than talk. As soon as I could write a few words, I answered these notes myself and signed my father's name to them. I recall one of these notes. The teacher kept me after school hours, gave me the usual jargon and handed me a note to take home to my parents. I was in despair. I didn't like to disturb my parents with another note or fool my teacher with another forgery. My guilt had caught up with me. I walked for a long time up and down the alley in the back of the school, not knowing what to do. I finally pushed the note under a porch and went home. I was severely spanked for not coming home on time. I could understand the justice of this. I feared that someone might find the note and that the last punishment would be greater than the first. I tried to retrieve the note but it could not be found. I was petrified with fear.

My brother enraged the kindergarten teacher a few weeks after our enrollment. He had missed the signal as to how to be excused to go to the bathroom. He did the only thing he could do. The odor was obvious. The teacher yanked poor "Cullie" into the hall and knocked hard on the first grade room door and my teacher called me out into the hall. I didn't know what she expected of me. My brother was crying, a heartbroken little boy. My feelings went out to him, not against him. He didn't know the signal, nor did I. The teachers talked so fast and furious that we could not understand a word. We were tongue-tied, rejected, and disgraced, and what was worse, every child in the two rooms knew it. One of my problems in those days was that when under stress, I stuttered. We were slapped. We were pushed out into the main corridor, forsaken, to go home and stay there until we had learned to live like civilized people. Fortunately for us, it was the day when Mama went to the Ladies' Aid. We sneaked home, pried open a window, washed my brother's clothing and climbed back out through the window and waited for Mama. I am amazed that we had the courage to return to school the next day. I have always had a certain inhibition in the presence of authorities.

Mama enjoyed her boys the most when they were the cleanest, most mannerly and best dressed in the presence of others. A constant threat to our happiness was the inevitable accident of falling and breaking our long stockings at the knees. My brother and I had an awful feeling when we wore Buster Brown suits, with bulged pants ending in the knees and starched wide collars with ribbon ties.

Friendships with other boys and their habits and interests came gradually. We learned to play baseball, to go to the library, to play marbles, kick-the-can, and other activities common to neighborhood boys. We owned one dog which a neighbor lady poisoned. I had made a successful marble skin game (chance). My papa discovered that I had an unusual number of marbles. He claimed that I must be cheating or stealing so insisted that I give them back. This was impossible, so I simply threw them away, watching the boys scramble for them. My avocation was to read every Horatio Alger book available in the city library. They represented a poor boy's American dream.

My progress in school was difficult and tedious until I reached fifth grade and we moved into the Sherman School District. The union had helped Papa so that he had better hours and a small increase in his pay checks. My first teacher there took a special interest in me and unearthed what was wrong with me. She found that my first years in school laid heavy in my life, especially the fact that I was behind due to spending two years in first grade. She helped me with my lessons and encouraged me to read the right kind of books. She inspired me to participate in an essay contest on Abraham Lincoln, who was my greatest childhood discovery. My contribution was carefully written in a tiny book in small print. I was the winner and affectionately presented the book to my teacher. I memorized several quotations from Lincoln, one of which she gave me, printed on a card with his picture, entitled "A Railsplitter's Philosophy." I have it in my study now, worn and faded. I repeat a quote from memory: "I do the very best I can, I do the very best I know how, and I mean to keep doing so until the end. If the end brings me out right, what is said against me won't amount to anything. If the end brings me out wrong, ten angels swearing I was right would make no difference." My teacher said one day, "Edgar, you are too smart to stay in this grade. You will skip a half grade next time. How would you like that?" I couldn't answer her. I threw myself into her arms and cried.

My progress was revealed in a bit of mischievousness in the seventh grade. The teacher was near-sighted and wore heavy lensed glasses. She had to hold a book within inches of her face to read. Some boys took pot shots at her, especially during study periods. For the most part she ignored such forays—sometimes smilingly saying, "That sure was a poor shot." One day I had a slingshot and a wet wad of paper and aimed at the book which covered her face. Unfortunately, just as I let go, she lowered the book and I hit her on the forehead. This she could not ignore if she was to maintain discipline. She inquired, "Who did that?" The hidden anxieties of my life threw me into terror. I stood up and confessed and was sent to the office of the principal. I was tongue tied, incoherent, and stuttered. The teacher was called to explain what had happened. She entered the office with her benign calm and beauty, and a knowing smile on her face. She explained to the principal and took my hand as she said, "I just wanted you to know that Edgar has really come alive. I think we are going to get along in great shape." We did. She encouraged me to go out for the school football team. I had an afternoon school job, as well as a morning job, but arranged with my boss to play. He seemed pleased to have me do it. I made the team as a tackle.

My teacher asked me to remain after school just before the end of the first semester of the seventh grade. Among the things that she said was, "I think you should skip the high seventh and go into the eighth grade. I think you can do it." Two teachers had been concerned about me, and the principal, and maybe the whole school. What could I say? I said softly for fear I would cry, "Thank you. Now, at last, I am an American."

I Leave Home

In 1911 I went to work with H.M. Chamberlain and Son, one of the better known landscape architectural firms in Denver which was located near my home. I had done odd jobs—taking care of furnaces, cleaning yards, cutting lawns and running errands for people in the neighborhood. The new job required that I take care of the yard, bed and groom and feed two horses, and keep a 1910 Cadillac bright. The hardest job was to eternally shovel the compost pile of horse, cow, and sheep manure with grass cuttings and certain powders added from time to time. The manure was pulverized and then sacked and sold to clients. This was an unrelenting chore because the pile would heat up and stink. I worked before and after school and Saturdays. The horses had to be fed on Sunday. I received three dollars a week.

W.O. Chamberlain, the son, acquired ten acres near Sullivan, southeast of Denver, and decided to operate part of the business from this site. He prevailed upon me to go with his family as "chore boy" and to live in their home. I had a room (an unheated back porch) and board, which was always good, provided usually by a hired cook. My pay was a dollar and a half a week. When it was cold I would heat two bricks, cover them with clean rags and put them into my bed before bedtime. I owned a second-hand bicycle and rode ten miles each way to high school. I trudged nearly three miles to the street car line when the weather was bad, except on days when Mr. Chamberlain left early for his office and would drop me off at school.

This job grew, so that I raised and took care of 1,200 chickens, four pigs, one cow, two horses, four hives of bees, raised each year an acre of mangle beets for chicken feed, cultivated the garden and nursery stock, harvested three and four cuttings of alfalfa, and hauled our drinking water from a nearby artesian well. An alarm clock roused me each morning at five. There were times when I fell asleep studying my lessons on the kitchen table. Sometimes the Chamberlains were away for a few days and I got my own meals. One morning I sliced off the end of one of my fingers. I wrapped it as best I could and rode off to school. The teacher in the first hour class noticed blood dripping from my hand and arranged for me to go to the Denver

General Hospital nearby where a doctor put three stitches in my finger.

My main problem was to find time to study. A partial solution was to use the lunch hour. I imbibed a hurried meal of three raw eggs in grape juice in an abandoned room away from the lunch room.

I had a misunderstanding with Mr. Chamberlain and quit my job. He called me "stupid" and I didn't like it. He apologized and asked me to stay. Instead, I acquired three newspaper routes for the *Denver Express,* two downtown and one near my parents' home. I had seven saloon keepers on my downtown routes. A saloon keeper threw a helpless drunk out onto the sidewalk who, no doubt, had made a nuisance of himself. The saloon keeper's last shout was, "Don't come back until you are sober. This place ain't no dump." I felt sorry for the drunk and helped him to his feet. I wasn't shy because I had helped my relatives in similar circumstances. The drunk wobbled to the corner and the street car line, where he was standing an hour later when I had finished my route. I stopped again and sought to help him. "Shay," he said, "do you know me? It's a damn good thing you don't. If you did, you'd be ashamed of me. Now, get me on one of those damn street cars." I asked, "Which one and which way?" He answered, "Any one, I don't give a damn where I'm going."

My former employer came to see me after some four months and urged me to come back to my job. My income from the papers had grown to about forty dollars a month with less effort on my part. Meanwhile problems at home had not lessened. Mama was deteriorating and with Papa's efforts to control the situation, irritation and arguments grew unendurable. Mr. Chamberlain and I agreed on four dollars a week and board and room, later raised to twenty cents an hour with a new bicycle thrown into the bargain. I liked and respected my employers. They did a great deal for me, teaching me social graces and helping me to appreciate music and good literature. They were college graduates and encouraged me to get a thorough education. We worked out a plan so I could finish high school and go on working while I attended the University of Denver. Mr. Chamberlain urged me to take special training in landscaping with the promise that upon graduation I would become a member of the firm. I was to break with this plan, but I have always been grateful for this part of my life, both the influences and the experiences. I loved the farm, the growing plants and trees and the farm animals. I was given more and more responsibilities at this end of the business and the dignity of being a manager. The experience was creative and exciting. The Chamberlains had confidence in me and we understood each other.

Life in High School

I enjoyed high school in spite of the fragmentations of my life. There was time for a few outside activities. My chum, Frank Blade, and I went to the Bungalow Shakespearean Theater. I took time to do a little skating with the Harvey sisters. I dated a far west-side girl, missed the last (Owl) car and walked about fifteen miles home. I bought my first present for a girl friend. I had hopes and fantasies about another girl who was good to me. I was happiest when she was around. I wanted most to go out for the football team, but time would not permit. The school made me "yell leader." I did not get a letter, but I did receive a large silk scarf in school colors with the letter "W."

I was vice president of the junior class and the next year president of the senior class and president of the student body. I was elected editor-in-chief of the high school annual. The big problem for me was that I could not dance. Moreover, I had never had a date. I settled the dilemma in my junior year by inviting a Swedish girl who didn't believe in dancing. My chum decided that I should take dancing lessons, so I bought a course of six lessons, but stopped in the middle of the first lesson. I was repelled by a woman I did not know. Frank was the beneficiary of the rest of the lessons and used them. The girl I wanted to invite to the prom was an accomplished dancer, but I lacked the courage to tell her I couldn't dance. Later I learned that she had expected to go with me.

I took four years of math and four years of Latin, largely because of Miss Wedgewood and Miss Sallie Graham. I was an "A" student in math, but just barely got through Latin. I wanted to quit, but Sallie Graham wouldn't let me. Miss Graham was the sponsor of the Castillian Society which competed annually with the Webster Debating Society for the debating and oratorical honors. Miss Graham asked me to enter the Oratorical Contest and I declined. She had me stay after school and upbraided me for being a coward. I rushed from the room and found a corner in which to cry. I had never been called a coward "with a yellow streak down my back." Another teacher found me and I sobbed out my story to her. She said, "If I were you I'd make Sallie eat those words."

I made arrangements with my employer so that I could spend four consecutive days in the city library, also skipping school. My topic was "National Honor." I was sold on the slogan of "The war to end all wars." I urged that we should once and for all get things straightened out so that we might have peace and prosperity for all time.

I presented my paper to Miss Graham for her appraisal. She was very pleased. But she said, "You have a poor ending and conclusion." I struggled with this problem and came up with a conclusion which she could not deny, from Abraham Lincoln: "With malice toward none, with charity for all . . . ." My paper was accepted as one of the three best and I became one of the contestants. I orated from my bicycle, to the pigs, horses, cow, and the chickens. The time of the contest came, the auditorium was crowded—imagine my surprise when the judges presented me with the medal! Sallie laughed out loud.

I was salutatorian of my graduating class which required a speech. The talk was prepared without any assistance or censorship. My English teacher told me following the meeting I had mispronounced "inevitable," using it without knowing its meaning. I was presented with a four-year scholarship to the University of Colorado, a vague something, which I didn't expect to use. I was committed to staying out of school for a year to save money.

Conversations Behind "Old Bill"

"Old Bill" was a dray horse used to haul men to their work and to haul heavy equipment as needed. His gait was measured and steady, usually a little faster when he was homeward bound. He liked to please and was well liked, but enjoyed teasing me as I was almost too small to harness him. He was a good horse to ride behind when you were involved in a discussion, a wise middle-aged horse who seemed to be interested in what he heard.

Walter Pesman and I usually rode in the driver's seat. Mr. Pesman had been reared and educated in Holland. He was an accomplished landscape architect, who achieved wide recognition in Denver and the West, the author of several books on flowers and plants, and a member of the Unitarian Church of Denver. I hadn't heard of this church. He had a sensitive concern for people and what was going on in the world, and was devoted to world peace. He was to become well known as he openly participated in controversial issues. He applied the teachings of Jesus in everyday life, believing that these teachings could reform the world to peace and goodwill. No doubt he was amused by my naive understanding of the Bible and Christianity, but he accepted my thoughts with respect and reviewed them with kindly evaluation. I was fascinated with our discussions of religion. I was in a "no man's land" with respect to religion—with little or no convictions. My transition from Swedish to English had blocked out all that I might have thought I knew and accepted. I knew that the attributes of God could not include wrath, anger, and punishment. I was skeptical of the virgin birth. I had monstrous thoughts about the beginning and end of the universe. It didn't seem to me that God was outside of an incomprehensible vastness, with a special authority to govern. God could not exist apart from the people.

Some of our conversations took us beyond my depth. We had lively arguments about the impending First World War. He was a Woodrow Wilson man. I wasn't sure which way to go. Nevertheless, I bet twenty-five cents on Hughes, the Republican, because Lincoln was a Republican. When it seemed that Hughes was elected, Mr. Pesman paid the bet, but I reluctantly had to give it back the next morning.

2. UNIVERSITY THROUGH SEMINARY, 1917-1924

University

It was in the late summer of 1917. I felt quite secure with the plan with Mr. Chamberlain—to drop out of school for a year and then attend the University of Denver. I visited a friend in Denver, who raised a disturbing question: "Will I see you in Boulder? I hope you are planning to go to college." I explained the arrangement and added that I didn't have enough money. He said, "Sounds like bunk to me. If you don't go, the chances are ten to one you will never go. It all depends on how much you want to go. It is too bad not to use your scholarship. Why don't you at least go to Boulder and see what you can do?" He gave me the names of several persons, among them a Walter Rose.

My timing was ill-advised as far as my boss was concerned. He was very disturbed and unhappy. He could have made me change my mind, but there were not the right words or understanding. He reinforced my resolve to go to Boulder.

This meeting took place on a Sunday morning. I packed my few belongings and was in Boulder that afternoon. I had nearly one hundred dollars, but my clothing and appearance concerned me. What was good enough on the farm and in high school wasn't good enough in college. I had one presentable suit and one white shirt and one white rubber collar, a Sunday dress outfit for the Swedes of that day.

Mr. and Mrs. Chamberlain made a trip to Boulder, a friendly visit to their prodigal son. This gave me a warm feeling, as if my own parents were there, like many parents with love and concern for their children in college. Mr. Chamberlain reiterated his promise to take me into the firm on condition I would prepare myself in business administration and landscaping. I thanked him and told him that at the moment I was thinking about law. I had had few such encounters with my own parents, not because they did not love me, but because as immigrants they could not cope with a culture so different from their own. Papa wanted me to be a tailor and had taught me some of the tricks of his trade.

I was in Boulder that same day with no place to stay. I was unsuccessful in a number of contacts. That evening I attended the youth meeting in the Baptist Church where I met Walter Rose.

Walter and his brother Clarence were popularly known as the Rose Brothers. They had their hands in a number of interests such as janitor services, house cleaning, window washing, as well as prohibition and anti-tobacco, the Baptist Church and young people. Walter explained that he had an opening in a co-operative eating club and a janitor job. I had no alternative but to accept. The students lived in the three back rooms on the second floor of the Sternberg Building. The building had three stories. Commercial businesses were on the street floor, a dance hall on the top floor and offices on the second floor with lawyers, salesmen, and a justice of the peace. Two of us students were selected to keep the second floor clean and to fire and keep the ancient furnace burning in the winter.

We took turns in the co-op with all the essential tasks. Things went well except for breakfast. "Skinny" invariably scorched the oatmeal and toast. I settled for a quart of milk each morning. We worked every other Sunday on the janitor job, which ended abruptly when my co-worker forgot to turn off the water that supplied the furnace. This raised havoc on the floors above. I took a cue from the Roses and organized a scrubbing floor business, a venture that became more profitable than I expected.

I lived in an unheated room. I decided that I wasn't eating as well as I should, so I accepted a job with the Quality Cafeteria where I was paid twenty cents an hour with a fifty percent discount on my meals. The employees were allowed to eat only what was determined by our lady employer. Nevertheless, the food was excellent.

Some of the "poor guys" who worked downtown gathered informally about twice a week in the back room of the Quality Cafeteria. I was the clean-up man and the only one in charge of the cafeteria. We lounged in the dirty linen and towels, and talked sometimes late and long. There were seven of us. Two claimed to be atheists, others had no special religious attachment. As I recall, one was a Baptist and another a Presbyterian. We called ourselves "The Damned Souls Club." There was much searching, many confrontations on controversial issues. We were revolutionary but not revolutionists. We believed in non-violence. We felt that we were underpaid and that there ought to be an easier way to get an education. Our group produced six ministers and one college professor, a Ph.D. in philosophy. We were sadly mindful that there had been only one black student and he could not find a place to live, so he dropped out of school.

The first year came to a close, whereupon I accepted a job as cook for the forest service. My friend Frank had graduated from high school and joined this gang of forestry workers. We worked in the mountains on the western slope of Colorado and participated in the first on-the-ground survey of lands that had come into the United States as a result of the Mexican War. We met up with lumberjacks, cowboys, and learned to catch trout.

I returned home with two hundred dollars, expecting to attend Cornell University in Ithaca, New York, where the girl whom I admired had enrolled and encouraged me to attend. However, my father was seriously ill with typhoid fever. I gave the money to my mother and returned to Boulder. My father remained in the hospital for many weeks and was confined at home for several months recovering from this dreaded sickness. His employer continued to pay his wages and kept in touch with my father's progress. Those were the days when there was no unemployment insurance, sick benefits or hospitalization coverage.

I returned to Boulder and volunteered for the Student Army Training Corps, popularly known as the Saturday Afternoon Tea Club. The campus had been turned into a military post. I lived in the barracks and went through the routine of army life. One difference was that we had four hours off each day to attend college classes. This arrangement took care of my pressing financial needs. We were paid thirty dollars a month less deductions.

I had a vicious altercation with a second lieutenant who seemed to despise college boys. His language was ultra profane. We were out on marching maneuvers and exercises. I was bawled out for three infractions, two of which I was not guilty. I was accustomed to profanity, but not when it was directed against a person. I stepped out of ranks and said, "I have never been the object of such cussing in civilian life and I don't think I have to accept such abuse in the army."

He called the company to a halt, sent me to my barracks with the admonition that he was going to take care of my future.

The major who was responsible for a decision said to me, "I am sorry this happened. You might have kept your head. Nevertheless, the officer has his faults and the manual clearly states that what he did was wrong."

The officer concerned was transferred and I got two weeks leisurely KP, which was a pleasant interlude in which I caught up with my reading. I was admonished, "Just stay out of sight. You don't have to do a damn thing. Better hang around the mess hall."

War

The influenza epidemic hit Boulder very hard. Hundreds became ill and many died. I was taken ill and reported daily for sick call. An attendant swabbed my throat with iodine. Emergency hospitals were set up everywhere. Fortunately I had a weekend pass, suffered on my bunk for two days and then two of my buddies dragged me to the interurban for Denver. I stumbled into my parents' home. Dr. Von Der Smith was called and struggled for three days to control my temperature. I was semi-delirious for two weeks and returned to my barracks very weak.

Army training included lectures and briefings to get the soldiers into a proper attitude towards the Germans. Emphasis was directed toward the depravity of the enemy. Among the remarks addressed us was: "War is war. There is no place for sympathy in it. It is your life against his. It is your patriotic duty to hate and to kill him. You cannot be a good soldier unless you hate your enemies. I don't give a damn what the Good Book says. You are primarily, first, last, and always, killers of Germans. It is your commission to kill off these filthy vermin. Let there be no nonsense about this. Prepare yourselves to kill every one of them—yes, exterminate them. Your nation's safety is at stake as long as one is alive. This must be your religion. Pray each night that they may die. Your business is to kill by whatever means is best, by gas, rifle, grenades and bayonet. When you get the feel of it, you will like it."

It was disturbing to me that I should have gone to college to learn to kill my fellow men. The grenade called for three movements and the bayonet for four. I cannot forget the harsh words of the sergeant about the third bayonet movement. "Get 'em in the pit of the stomach where it's soft. It's as good as the heart and you won't get your bayonet stuck in the ribs." The fourth movement was livid as we were taught to kick the enemy off the bayonet. "Don't forget he ain't dead yet. Look out for the death struggle. Be sure to stick him again to be sure he is dead. It may be your life or his. And it's more human—but humanity ain't got nothing to do with it."

It was in this context that the YMCA gave each soldier a free copy of Moffat's translation of the New Testament. Somebody had to be crazy. I was distressed by the futility and sinfulness of war. I predicted an age of growing violence. I knew I would never kill a man. I wished that Eugene V. Debs could move over in his cell and make me his cell comrade.

We were mustered out in December, but I knew that we had not fought a war to end war. Violence begets violence. Peace, love, and cooperation beget peace, love, and cooperation.

Once more I was confronted with the problem of self-support. Clarence Rose was in military service and Walter had contracted tuberculosis and was faced with a long convalescence. He suggested that I take over the window-washing business. Frank and I became partners. We moved to the YMCA and as a courtesy of Secretary Scatterday received our calls over the YMCA phones.

The flu had weakened me and I had a relapse. Frank was doing well with the window business, but he could not care for both of us. I sold most of my belongings, including a Kodak and a violin. A Jewish friend learned that I was ill and came to see me. He had a waiter's job in a sorority house and I had helped him out on several weekends. He handed me a check for fifty dollars and chided me for not turning to him for help. I protested and said, "It might be impossible for me to pay you back." "Stupid," he said, "what in the hell are friends for? Pay me back if you can and when you can. If not, I've made an investment."

Out of School

Mr. Leland F. Scatterday went to the YMCA in Council Bluffs, Iowa, in the fall of 1920 and prevailed upon me to go with him as Boys' Secretary. My affection for "Scatt" had a lot to do with this decision. My expenses in Boulder had grown beyond my anticipated income. I no longer wore rubber collars. I had joined a fraternity and enjoyed some of the social functions. I found time for dating. I was engaged to a sorority girl. All this took money, so with what was then an offer of the generous salary of $1,800, I could hardly refuse to go to Iowa.

My heart was inclined to the poorer boys, newspaper carriers, factory workers, boys with menial jobs. Most were employed. Few had any prospects of going to school. There were no laws restricting the age of working boys and girls. This interest in their welfare led me first to the congregating centers of the Omaha and Council Bluff newspapers. The boys were organized into bean and prune supper clubs, around which we developed a program. Most of the boys had never been in the YMCA. The HI-Y clubs found the "bean supper" idea stimulating and met two times a month to get involved in service projects which included the "Employed Boys Clubs." A high occasion of the year was the Community Bean Supper to which everyone was invited.

Board members and other community leaders came to the Community Bean Supper. One board member of considerable means was shocked to find black boys present. He ordered one of these boys from the building, but the boy refused to go. I got into the scene when the board member was beside himself with anger. He claimed that the black boy had insulted him and if I didn't get him out, he would call the police, which he did. I was certain that this boy had never insulted anyone. He was an excellent member of the HI-Y and the high school football team. The team used the YMCA for showers and dressing. Up until this year the high school had had trouble finding a place where whites and blacks could shower and dress together. I told Mr. Kern the principal that the "Y" was a place for all people and that I believed in the one human race. The black boy and I went to my office where he poured out a story of frustration and humiliation. He went back to the festivities while I waited for the policeman, who was not long in coming. My "great white brother" met him first. I suggested that we talk things over in my office. I refused to include the boy unless he had committed a crime. The officer agreed. Mr. D. shouted his rage and bigotry. The officer adjourned the meeting. He said to me the next day, "How dumb can some guys get?"

"Scatt" complimented me on a job well done. The board member was at least consistent. He was never seen at the "Y" again and withdrew his support.

Then there was Dempsy, an employed boy accused of stealing a bicycle. He was discouraged and said, "What's the use? I try and it's no good. I know that I had a reputation for stealing, but ever since I met you and came to the 'Y,' I've been straight." We proved he was innocent of the theft.

I had a yearning to wear good clothes such as I had never had. For the first time my income made this possible. I splurged. I bought a complete outfit to the tune of $300. I enjoyed gloating over my clothes for a few days and then they disappeared—stolen. It was an unhappy Boys' Secretary who joined the morning devotions. Scatterday prayed, "We thank thee, dear Lord, for the blessings that have come to us during the night...."

I interrupted his prayer to say, "That prayer doesn't fit," and I explained what had happened to my wardrobe. He prayed again using the same words.

Later he said to me, "You may find that you learned a lesson in humility. It is not what you put on that counts—and I don't mean it was wrong to have the clothes."

Back to School

My chum Frank and I became partners in a hole-in-the-wall restaurant specializing in chili, hamburgers, pie, and coffee.

The idea of going into the ministry goaded me from time to time. There were a number of great liberals in the church. It seemed to me that the shortest way to the Kingdom of God on earth was through the radical pronouncements of Jesus. I had never severed my membership with the Swedish Baptist Church and, curiously, I never formally accepted membership in any other church. I discovered that my name was in the Methodist Church bulletin of Boulder, Colorado, along with Donald H. Tippett, as a local preacher.

I received a telegram from Dr. Orrin W. Auman, district superintendent in Denver, offering me the position of director of religious education in the Fifth Avenue Methodist Church with the understanding that I would attend the Illiff School of Theology. I accepted without having the slightest knowledge of what such a job required. I was to be paid $100 a month from mission funds. The church was located not far from where I was born.

I had an interview with the minister of the church, who was chewing tobacco and spitting through an open window. He didn't know anything about my duties except that I was to make myself useful. He said that he didn't ask for me but was willing to accept anybody who was "free." He was a wiry, hard-fisted character. I suggested that we have a children's church and perhaps I could work with young people. I soon ran into trouble. A few adults preferred to attend the children's church. I was given strict orders to refuse to admit adults—not even a pianist.

In this church I met my wife. She was in the choir on that first Sunday. I sat on the platform and gazed at her beauty, especially her long red hair. I met her after church with some of the young people; we had a picnic that afternoon. She and I soon became engaged and we were married in November 1921. I had asked her, "What would you say if I asked you to marry me?" She replied, "Ask me and find out." I found out. She wanted to be a minister's wife.

The minister was displeased with my courting Eunice, who was a close friend of his wife. He was concerned that the children's church was doing so well. The congregation was divided about a number of things. I was totally naive about what was going on. I resolved to get out of the job and give up any thoughts of becoming a minister. I went to the district superintendent and related my feelings. He sent me back with the admonition, "Stay with it. It will be good discipline."

The storm broke in the next quarterly meeting. I was amazed and silent as I listened to the garbled harrangue and attack on me. According to the minister, I was to be blamed for everything.

Dr. Auman had been unaware of the situation and apologized. He offered me another position which I refused to accept. He advised me to think it over.

Stockyards

Dr. Auman sent us to the stockyards—Globeville. The work there had been abandoned for a number of years. The people were poor, but didn't say much about it. They were mostly immigrants raising new families in a new America.

There was no porch or steps leading into a one-room ghost of a building called a church. Walter McGlenegan, a fellow student living on a disability pension from the Army, furnished the money and the two of us built the cement steps which have survived the old church. We cleaned the church and dusted off the furniture. The piano was woefully out of tune, but that had to wait. There were 40 chairs, and 67 people crowded in for the first service.

My wife and I rented an unattractive, unmodern, and unfurnished five-room house for fifteen dollars a month and moved to Globeville to breathe the stinking and polluted air along with our parishioners. The packing plants nearby sent up a constant stench. Globeville was the farthest settlement north of town, and the school we both attended was the farthest south of Denver. The streets were unpaved, dirty, dusty, and fearfully muddy when it rained.

The people were delighted to have a minister and did everything to make us feel at home. They painted and papered walls, varnished the old floors and brought in all kinds of food and some furniture, all this from meager earnings.

The saddest men were those who had been blacklisted as a result of a recent strike. The northern part of Globeville was covered with thousands of tons of hardened sludge from the smelters, which had stopped operating. The poorest of all people were those who lived in Retreat Park, some of them very sick from industrial diseases. Idle machinery and buildings and long piles of slag attested to the days when hundreds of workers labored in a thriving industry. Many who remained were in one way or another casualties of a way of life that isn't too concerned about people.

We had a number of repercussions as we tried to improve conditions. The Ku Klux Klan was harrassing the immigrants. I preached an evening sermon entitled, "The KKK and the Dagger Societies of Europe." I announced that anything to which my father and my congregation could not belong was un-American and un-Christian. The church had been packed and over two hundred people surrounded it outside. My parishioners surrounded us and saw to it that we got home safely.

Retreat Park gave me insight into the nature of our society in which there are growing pockets of poverty—hidden from public view. The settlement of Retreat Park was about two miles from Globeville with no means of transportation except walking. We found a few junk cars there, long since in disuse because the owners had no money to buy parts. Shacks and old houses surrounded a small schoolhouse with one teacher for some 60 children of all ages. The schoolhouse itself was a symbol of poverty and the wretchedness of the human beings who were the cast-outs of an industry that had died.

Nevertheless, these people warmly welcomed the young preacher and his wife. It was the custom in those days to invite the minister to eat with the family. I shall never forget one such experience. The room in which we ate was furnished with a rickety homemade table and wooden boxes for chairs. Grace before meals was a must so the minister was asked to perform this rite, after which we had cornbread and navy beans, prunes and water. Our hosts offered no apology for the scant food for which I was pleased. These people were poor and physically ill. They were uncomplaining and grateful. For what? A minister and his wife had called on them.

We organized a Sunday school in the schoolhouse and had a church service. The response was electric as everybody who was able came to the church services. I never once asked about their church affiliations or preferences. Humanity had become more important to me than any Christian sect.

I wanted more than anything else to provide a wonderful Christmas for this small community, so I went to the *Rocky Mountain News,* which was supporting the Good Fellows, and my dream came true. It was to be Christmas 1922 and we were determined that Santa Claus would know about this proud and neglected community.

The *Rocky Mountain News* and the Good Fellows appointed a committee who in their turn discovered Retreat Park. They could not believe that people could be hidden from the sight of society—so poor and yet so proud. They could not believe that this is the way it is in our society. There never was such a party, which lasted not for a day, but for a long time.

The huge piles of smelter sludge and Retreat Park are now long gone. But the story about the poor in our world continues to repeat itself—shut out and hidden from the concern of the civilized world.

Globeville was a community of about 1,200 people living in clusters of small homes related to five ethnic backgrounds—Russian, Polish, and three German groupings with a scattering of Irish, English, Swedish and Latvian. A great number had lived in the community for three generations, serving the smelters and after the smelters ceased, the stockyards, railroads, and in many menial and low-paying jobs. There were a number who were unemployed because of age and the anti-union blacklists.

There were four small German churches of different persuasions, and one large Russian Orthodox church and one large Roman Catholic church across the street from our small one-room mission church. There was constant turmoil within the Russian church between those who wanted to be loyal to an American authority and those who wanted to maintain their origins. It seemed that the German churches had a number of things about which to quarrel as each sought to survive.

Greener Pastures

Dr. George Nuckels offered us a position in the Washington Park Community Church in a suburb near the University of Denver, where my wife and I were attending the Iliff School of Theology. It was one of the most prestigious churches in Denver. We lived in a furnished apartment rented to us by a teacher who had taken a sabbatical year to study in Europe.

One of my responsibilities was to conduct a junior church completely organized like the adult congregation—official board, ushers, treasurer, committees and activities. We had the children's church in the gymnasium next to the church sanctuary, but on the floor below. We had a variety of programs that disturbed the peace and quiet upstairs.

One Sunday we had the Grand Army Fife and Drum Corps. An usher handed me a note from Dr. Nuckols which read, "Please settle down and make less noise, we can't hear ourselves think."

I hurriedly scribbled a note in return. "If you don't like it up there—come down here if you can find room!"

Graduation

Graduation time had come at last. I had completed the right number of courses at night and on Saturdays. I sat in the auditorium of the University of Denver with my thoughts as the services developed and each graduate received a diploma. I wondered what it was all about. Just what importance does a piece of paper have? I thought of the long hours and punishment I had endured. I was tired and lost in my meditation. There had to be a better way for all.

What is it that really counts? What is success? The speaker had talked about success and achievement. But how could he know? A bishop once asked me, "Do you say your prayers every morning?" I replied, "No, not every morning. I have been where I have had to pray. From what I know, you haven't been there."

I thought about that. Where is the place? I fought to get into the channel. Is that what life is? Now am I to fight to get into another channel? Which one will it be? What is at the other end? Western civilization would seem to have passed its zenith. What does one do when the destiny of all is downward? What was I doing in this educational dramatization?

My wife nudged me and said, "Where are you? They have called your name three times."

We graduated from the Iliff School of Theology the next year. All I can remember is that we were late and had held up the show for some twenty minutes.

3. MINING CAMP, 1924-1926

Hiawatha, Utah

The time had come for a full-time pastorate. My friend Dr. Auman was in California, recovering from a serious illness. He wired us and promised to look out for us if we could just wait a few weeks. He knew that Dr. John J. Lace, superintendent of the Utah Mission, was badgering us to go to Utah. He wanted us to go to Hiawatha, a coal mining town. There was no church there, just a small church school meeting over the pool hall. He offered us $1,500 and a house. We wanted a few days to think it over. He thought we were bargaining for money so in a few days he raised the ante to $2,000. We decided to go to Hiawatha, some 500 miles west of Denver, over a desert road that changed with the shifting sands. My wife was pregnant. Dr. Auman wired us: "It's too early in your career to isolate yourselves in Utah, if you want to get ahead in the Methodist church."

The hazardous trip from Grand Junction, Colorado, to Hiawatha, Utah was taken in our old Model T Ford. My brother had cut down the back seat so that we could have a bed, which proved quite essential for an expectant mother. We packed all our worldly goods and headed out.

Preachers in those days were responsible for their own moving expenses. We rode to Colorado Springs, 75 miles distant, over the only paved road in Colorado. The roads were rough and sometimes dangerous. We traveled over the continental divide through Carlton Tunnel, now abandoned. It took us four days to get to Grand Junction. We had three flat tires each day.

For miles the roads were only trails and shifting sands. Rains filled the dry gulches and arroyos that became raging rivers. The trail road would then be completely obliterated. The few people who traveled that way would have to wait so that they could help each other. Every car carried a shovel. We were always outdistanced so we were the last to arrive and once we were left to shift for ourselves. The sun and heat beat down upon us.

A lone hitchhiker who had failed to get a job as a sheepherder and was bedraggled, hungry, and tired hailed us. He begged us to take him and his dog into Green River. He said that it was a matter of only a few miles so we took him on, only to discover that he too was headed for Hiawatha, a distance of 150 miles over the same kinds of roads.

Green River was a welcome oasis where we stopped at the village inn to clean up and let my wife rest. There was no other way but to take our homesick traveler all the way home. We learned from him certain facts about Hiawatha that I wished the church superintendent had shared with us. There had been a prolonged strike in this company town and the people were unhappy and impoverished. The mines were worked only one and two days a week. The miners owed the company stores so much that they couldn't leave. The area was policed by armed guards. Our hitchhiker wondered if we would be allowed to enter. He said, "Strangers are not welcomed there." The boy was a Mormon and he gave us our first comprehension of the Mormon Church.

We arrived in Price, Utah, late in the day, 18 miles from our destination. It was Saturday and I was expected to preach the next morning. Our money was gone but we had a few groceries and pondered the idea of staying in Price that night. I wasn't sure that I wanted to preach in a company town with the surveillance of its inhabitants. I contacted the people in Hiawatha who had been waiting for us all day and they urged us to come the rest of the way.

Most of the distance was uphill over a curving, bumpy road. I couldn't understand what was wrong with the car as it continued to sputter with heat. We would travel a mile and let the motor cool and then push ahead another mile.

We arrived shortly before midnight. Folks warmly welcomed us and wondered why we had taken so long. We had been stopped by two armed guards who made certain of our identity and then pointed out the house in which we were to live for two and a half years.

I was disturbed about the guards and was told, "You will learn soon enough. Union organizers, agitators, and 'Reds' are not welcome here." I was dismayed but too tired to discuss the matter.

These people were sensitive to our needs so they left after a gracious welcome, leaving a pork roast in the oven and everything to go with it on the stove and the table. We ate very little. After examining the four-room parsonage and taking baths, we went to bed exhausted.

Sunday was a busy day. The company doctor and his wife were our guides. We went to the room above the pool hall and met about 50 children and 20 adults. The doctor insisted that we go to the ballgame in the afternoon. Our appearance at this public event had a salutary effect; it seemed that everyone was curious about the new minister.

Hiawatha had been prosperous during the war years. The mine superintendent had great plans for Hiawatha—a recreation park and lake, playgrounds and a medical center. They never materialized. The area was in a depression because sales were down. The after-effects of a prolonged strike, the coercion and animosities had splintered the people and nullified the paternalism of the general superintendent. There had recently been a coal mine explosion in a nearby community in which 300 men had been killed.

The grimness and sorrow of the people was appalling. Men were often injured or killed. I had my first funeral in the first week of my pastorate. The miner had been killed by falling coal deep in the Hiawatha mine.

I agonized over being caught up in a part of corporate imperialism. The congregation was made up almost entirely of company officials who hoped that the church would build morale. These were good men who faithfully performed their duties as churchmen. The mine superintendent was kindly and concerned about people who would cause no trouble. He was bitterly opposed to unions. Nevertheless, he blamed the sales force for his troubles. He never went to church although his family was devoted to the church. The superintendent had brought in the YMCA and the company paid the salaries of the staff. He was building a Gentile church for the community and a Mormon church. The church to him was a way to keep people happy. I consoled myself with the fact that the company was not paying my salary.

The town was divided into a number of sections located between the hills and the mountains. There were a number of nationalities—Austrians, Italians, Welsh, Chinese, Japanese, and the general mixture of people from various states in the union. Mormons were preferred as workers because they came up from their farms and worked in the mines during the colder seasons. Each nationality had its own clubhouse where the men went for relaxation, card playing, drinking and festivities. Nothing was done for boys and girls and young people. The town had only one elementary school. They needed a high school.

Our church became the center of youth activities including a Scout troop to which both Mormons and "Gentiles" belonged. This was unique in Carbon County, where the Mormons carried on programs for all ages in their stakes. We planned a summer camp and almost every youngster in town came. The hills around the town were full of Indian lore and history. We had hikes to uncover pieces of pottery and arrowheads. I umpired most of the Sunday baseball games. We built a cabin on top of a hill for a number of rendezvous.

A church dance was successful and brought in several thousand dollars. The city council appointed my wife and me chaperones for all dances. Our dance was the first in which the jail was not used to house a few drunks and unruly persons. Dancing, in those days, was considered a sin in the Methodist Church.

Sorrow

Hiawatha was the scene of our first sorrow. The doctor who had welcomed us left for California and a company doctor had taken his place. We were not happy with his lack of skill and his indifference towards his patients. Moreover, he was an alcoholic. I had looked him up on a number of occasions on behalf of sick children and adults, only to find him in a stupor. One case was an emergency, a sick little boy. The nearest doctor was 18 miles away. I was in despair. I jerked the doctor to his feet and walked him around the clinic until he came to his senses. Then I took him to the child.

Our first baby was a boy. He was born in January in mid-winter. The doctor neglected to pull the phlegm from his throat and the baby choked to death. After consoling my wife Jimmie, I took our baby boy into my arms and prayerfully sat in a rocking chair until early morning, not knowing what else to do. Finally, a motherly member of the church took the infant body from my arms and carefully dressed him with the clothes that Jimmie had made in the days of preparation. A wonderful thing happened. Mormon women and men made a beautiful casket as they had done for their own dear ones. They brought the casket to our home in a tender and knowing silence that broke the spell of tragedy. I knew then what I have always known, that sorrow is love so deep that it hurts.

Our baby was laid away in a desert cemetery on a cold winter day. The Methodist minister of Price church went with us. The men of the church stood beside me as I tried hard to speak a few words. My wife was home in bed, unable to be with us.

It was a bleak place for a little baby who had been warm and protected in his mother. No matter how friendly and intimate we may be with others, sorrow must heal in the loneliness of a single soul. Friends remained by my wife's side. Later, when Jimmie was sufficiently recovered, we went to the grave together. Her hurt was greater than mine. I would awake at night and hear her sobbing, "My baby, my baby." We had named him Edgar Malcolm Wahlberg, Jr.

Then came Decoration Day. Jimmie had gathered wildflowers from the hillsides to decorate the grave. An incident prevented us from going until the next day and we felt sad about this. All the graves around seemed to be covered with paper flowers marvelously wrought by humble women. We looked for an empty spot, but our child's grave was prettier than all the others. The wives of the coal miners had done their best for us. Across the grave were the words in paper flowers, "OUR BABY."

Father Giavannoni

The Catholic priest stationed in Price, the county seat of Carbon County, became one of my best friends. He served the whole county. Hiawatha was 18 miles away. Consequently, I would call on him whenever Catholics needed his services.

Everything went along fine until the Ku Klux Klan raised its ugly head to attack Catholics and people of foreign birth. The KKK burned crosses on the church lawn and in the foreign sections of Hiawatha. Father "Jo" sent his assistant to Hiawatha to call on Catholic families frightened by the KKK. This assistant bore no grudge but was less than kindly toward Protestants in general. The KKK claimed to be true Protestants.

Catholic children dropped out of the Scout troop and other youth activities. They dropped out of the Sunday school. Catholic families seemed to lose some of their friendliness toward us. It may have been fear because KKK burned crosses in front of my community church. I determined to see my Catholic priest friend and had the encouragement of other Catholic friends, one of whom ran a non-company store off company property. Father Giavannoni received me cordially. He greeted me, as he always did, "Would you like a bit of communion?" meaning, "Would you like a drink?" I made it clear that I would not proselytize—that I didn't like what was taking place. I was concerned with keeping faith with our experience in friendship and goodwill—I wanted to be of service to anyone in need and far removed from his church. He understood and smiled as he said, "I'll call off my dog. I like you very much, but do you know that if you would join the Klan, I'd get a lot of members without even trying? It would pay me to give you a thousand dollars if you would join the Klan, but you won't, thank God."

The Fassios

The church door faced the sidewalk which extended to the end of the street. I carefully watched the Sunday promenade and tried to have a word for each one. One morning there were nine new children, walking as if they belonged to the same family—all sizes and ages. They could be seen as they turned the corner two blocks away—no doubt coming from one of the ethnic sections.

A little girl perhaps four years old replied to my greeting rather faintly, "My name is Annie Fassio." I said, "Glad you are here." I turned to a small boy and asked his name. He said, "My name is Jack Fassio." I spoke to the next child, reaching a little higher as I extended my handshake to meet more and more hands—each one greeted in the same way. They were beautiful, clean, and sweet. They were Margaret and Fran Fassio, Julia Fassio, and Ruth Fassio, and Antonio Fassio, and Judith Fassio, and Albert Fassio—all nine from the same family.

My wife and I called on the Fassios the next day. I knocked on the paintless door of a typical weatherbeaten and cheaply constructed miner's house. It was a hot day. The summer heat beat down unmercifully over the rock-strewn unprotected hillside. There was first a silence and then a commotion inside as someone hurried toward the door.

The door opened and there stood a large woman with proportionately large features. She looked inquiringly down on the stranger at her door. I was taken aback as I observed the lady. Her dark hair was tightly drawn back over her head. Beads of perspiration drifted down her forehead. The middle of her body was bound tightly by apron strings. Her arms were folded over her bosom—raised slightly to keep the fresh dough from smearing her dress. She had been kneading bread when she was disturbed by the knock on her door. Her dress was high in front and reached the floor in back—revealing two stout underpinnings covered with cotton stockings.

I gasped and forgot my mission. I just stood there. She broke the spell with, "Vot you vant?" I replied, "Hello, what did you say?" She said, "Vot you vant?" She was in a hurry to get back to the baking. I regained my composure and explained that I was the minister of the Community Church. She hustled us into the house saying, "De Community priest, cum in, cum in. Sit don—sit don." I sat on an empty apple box. She went over to the table to scrape off the dough on her arms. She then sat on a box and beamed on the minister. The flies buzzed busily around the room and the occupants. There was no screen door but the flies did not bother Mrs. Fassio.

"You sent your children to the Community Sunday School," I said. She emphasized, "Sure, I send my kids dere. You know why?" She answered her own question. "I go to de Alexander funeral in de church. I see de flowers, de purty flowers—all de flowers—I see in de meedle de real flowers—de card, it say, 'From de Community Church.'" She stood up and gestured with her right arm. "My Gott," I say, "I send my keeds to de Community Church all de time."

We talked mostly about her boys and girls. She knew each one perfectly and for each one there was a beautiful and delicate dream. She pictured for her children opportunities that had never been hers. They were good children and America would be proud of them. It made her happy to reveal her soul's desire—the purpose of her unending labors. Her children were to become a part of a rock-ribbed citizenry of the greatest nation in the world.

I had misgivings as we went back down the hill. Would America fulfill its obligations? Its full measure of devotion to growing childhood?

Work for Boys

We developed a fairly adequate recreation program for young people. Nevertheless, the older boys wanted meaningful labor which seemed impossible when their parents were working only part time. The so-called security police had been given the jobs caring for the streets and lawns around the company buildings. One of these guards showed me the company arsenal. This was a fairly large room lined with various caliber rifles, machine guns, and hand grenades. There was also a small cannon. I couldn't believe my eyes. This guard was fed up with the charade of safety and security. He didn't like the make-work to give the guards a different image. This gave me the idea of turning all the street and lawn work over to the boys. I talked about it with my church members, officials and union sympathizers. Some criticized me, saying that any such plan would make me a company man.

I had the confidence of the workers. The company had taken away my privilege to visit the miners at work in the mines. They said that it was for my safety. The company was pleased with the plan, and told me that I could have as much money as needed. "Jack" Smody was my foreman. The library became the office. The payroll was to be handled by the paymaster in the same manner as it was for the men. The guards disappeared except for two, who became the town police.

We blueprinted our plans and responsibilities down to the last boy. Over 40 boys benefitted from the plan. The whole town was pleased and the boys took to the program readily. The town had never been cleaner. Delinquency went down. The boys lined up with their dads to get their paychecks. The boys were told that they would have their own meetings to talk things over and give us their recommendations. We didn't call this a union. Nevertheless, union sympathizers were pleased. We responded to several suggestions for higher pay and for the boys to elect their own bosses.

Jack Smody

Jack Smody was my right-hand man in the boys' work project and helped select the best boys for the jobs available. It was his idea to develop a rotation system for the growing number of boys who wanted work. He also kept his mind on the boys who for one reason or another most needed to work.

He was tall, strong, sensible and popular with his peers. He had completed the elementary school and wanted to get an education, but his family could not afford to send him somewhere for more education. He was patiently waiting to be old enough to go into the mines. He made good use of our community library.

I was hoping that I could get Jack to attend the church school. I felt he might set a precedent for the older boys. Jack would say without commitment, "Okay, I come sometime, I come sometime." Then he said, "Okay, I come sometime but I don't like to go with them little guys."

I replied, "Okay, why not get some of the big guys to attend?"

Whereupon, as if he had been thinking about it, he said, "Okay, you come to my house at nine o'clock next Sunday morning and we collect big guys."

When I arrived at 9 a.m. the job was nearly complete. There were 23 "big guys" ready to make the walk to the church. I knew that some of the young men were Catholic. There were no Mormons. I asked if it was all right with the Catholic boys. He said, "I don't know. You said, "Collect big guys.' So I collect."

We marched toward the church but stopped to pick up Alec. Jack went into the house, rooted Alec out of bed, and hardly gave him time to dress.

Then Jack was taken critically ill with pneumonia. He lay in bed day after day in the hushed silence of his loved ones and the big and little guys of the community. We called on him when he hardly knew we were present. It took a few days to get some real flowers from Price. We took them up the hill to give to Jack. I knew that he had passed the crisis. I unwrapped the flowers and his tall, thin mother began to jump up and down, shouting, "How purty! How purty!" I asked for something to hold the flowers and a sister brought me a cracked pitcher after filling it with water.

I took the flowers into the bedroom and placed them on a chair beside his bed. His eyes dimly caught sight of the flowers and focused on them. He picked up one hand with his other hand as he reached for the flowers. One finger touched a petal and then he slowly pulled his hands before his face as he thoughtfully looked up toward me. He repeated this movement several times as if his thoughts were unclear but was reaching for words. He pulled out a flower from the pitcher and held it before his eyes and then turned his face toward me. His eyes filled with tears as he asked, "Wallie, are they real? Are they real?"

I assured him that they were real.

Tony

One of my indelible friendships was with a small Italian man who could sing "O Solo Mio" as well as Enrico Caruso. Mine tunnels and rooms sunk deep in the mountains vibrated with his soft and dreamy voice as he sang while he worked. He was unhappy when he could not sing. Tony yelled at me from across the street. "Father Walgub, Father Walgub, I want to talk on you, I want to talk all over you. I mad. I mad. I mad as hell."

I wondered at his anger, which he soon explained. "Dey no ask me for no subscrip." I knew at once. The finance committee of the church had made a canvas for the annual church budget and had passed up Tony. He gave me five dollars and said that there would be more. He explained that he was temporarily hard up but times would be better. Times were destined to get worse. I thanked him for his contribution and urged him to come to church. He encouraged me and said, "All right. I come all right."

I said, "Do come and bring your wife."

He responded emphatically, "No, not my wife. I no bring my wife."

I asked, "Why not, don't you love your wife?"

He was astounded at my lack of understanding. He said, "Love my wife— sure I love my wife. But she no speak English. She no understand English. But I love her." His mood changed into fondness and he said, "I go to your church to de funeral. I see de cross in front of de church." He took my hand and held it to his heart as he continued, "Your cross, my cross. Your God, my God!"

A Puppet Government

The town had a puppet city council, presumably elected by the people, but the candidates were nominated by company officials. I was an election judge one year when only 16 votes were cast. Three of the votes for mayor were written in for a known "half wit"—cast by three persons who expressed their silent and sullen anger.

Miners were expected to trade at the company store where prices were high. Secret witnesses reported those who did not trade at the store. There were two stores just off company property where quite a number of protesting families made their purchase.

Renters signed rental agreements under which they could be moved out immediately. Company officials openly traded in Price or Salt Lake City where prices were lower and where there was a larger variety of goods. It was a strange environment, where everything that one did or did not do was observed—to whom you talked or did not talk. I visited the mines and talked to the men at work. This privilege was soon cut off. I never knew the reason, but it wasn't hard to guess.

I visited, house to house, the various ethnic neighborhoods to learn what I could and how to be helpful. The Chinese wanted a class in English which I tried to provide. Most people were concerned about their children. I observed a mine closed without notice to the workers who turned out to work. I saw a procession of people carrying their worldly goods on their backs and in carts drawn by women and children.

Our older daughter was born a few months before we left Hiawatha. We took great care this time. We sent Jimmie to Salt Lake City for the delivery. I grew impatient and took the train to Salt Lake City to find a surprised wife. She was supposed to call me when she went to the hospital. My hunch was good. Lois was born that night. I shall never forget the tiny, cute little pink foot that appeared above the basket into which Lois was placed.

Leaving Hiawatha

We were disturbed about leaving Hiawatha. We knew that a storm was brewing and we didn't want the church to be caught in it. There was much which we could not accept, but the people we could accept from all levels of life.

We visited Hiawatha a few years ago and the church had burned down. It gave me a strange feeling. No one has attempted to rebuild it. The mine is still open but down to the bare necessities.

I had given the district superintendent a plan and if initiated we intended to stay. We felt that the church should be built on its own property and serve the people of all the camps in Carbon County. We waited for a reply but it never came.

4. GOODWILL RURAL PARISH, 1926-1930

Transition

We cut our ties with Hiawatha. I had come to the end of my endurance and ability to compromise with the theocracy of a coal mine corporation and community. It was anything but an industrial democracy to which I was by conviction committed. My thoughts lingered on the forgotten human beings whose dignity and well-being were crushed. Some of these people were officials, but most were poor and wretched.

We were headed for Denver where the annual conference was held and where our next move would be determined. We travelled back on the same road, still unimproved, which took us to Hiawatha. It had rained and the waters rushed down the usually dry creek beds, obliterating any path other cars may have traveled. We were in a hurry, but we should have waited. The wheels of our car became embedded in quicksand which held like cement. two other cars came up behind us. We went to work when the water subsided; digging the sand away was like building a new road.

We drove through western Colorado—through Mack, Loma, Fruita, Bethel, Grand Junction, and Clifton on our way to Denver. The Bethel church was in a good location, situated at a turn in the road. The building was dilapidated, and reflected what had happened to the farmers and their farms which had been apple orchards yielding handsome profits to the owners. The land had gone sour as a result of irrigation which brought alkaline salts to the surface, killing the vegetation.

Most of the farmers were poor and could not pay their taxes. Ditches had been dug in the direction of the Colorado River in an attempt to reclaim the land. We slowed down to take a look at the Bethel church, appalled that a church should be in such a prominent location and look so terrible. I said to my wife, "Isn't that about the worst Methodist church you ever saw?" Little did we know that we were destined to go to this church and serve it as part of the "larger parish."

Dr. David D. Forsythe was the executive secretary of the Board of Home

Missions of the Methodist Church, a man ahead of his times, one who had influenced me to be a minister. He was physically large with a leonine shaggy head. He was great as well as big and had a heart and mind for expanding Christianity into the frontiers of America, with an eager concern for minorities, the deprived and the unjustly treated. He explained that he wanted to discover what to do with country and rural churches that had "one foot in the grave and the other on a banana peel." He said that there was a chance to develop a "larger parish." He knew about my plan for Carbon County, Utah, and wondered if it could not be applied in a poverty area in the country. He also restated his plan to make me national secretary of frontier missions. The job never came because Dr. Forsythe died suddenly after we had moved to our parsonage in Clifton.

Ominous Words

The district superintendent was not happy about the board of home missions more or less taking over his prerogatives. The mistake, according to him, was that Dr. Forsythe had had direct conversations with me instead of going first to the superintendent. The superintendent made no bones about how he felt. He said, "How do I know whether I want you for one of my ministers? I don't know you, you are labeled a liberal. One thing is clear, you are responsible to me and your promotions will depend upon my recommendations. I have one criterion and that is evangelism and the winning of souls. Your reputation will depend upon how many members you take into the churches which you will serve. I don't go for modern ideas about rural parishes and all that goes with it."

I wondered what he thought about the Bethel church which he no doubt had entered from time to time. He had no comprehension of the conditions of the valley and the poor farmers. Perhaps he held to the idea that "saved souls" could eat "pie in the sky when they die."

The Churches

The Clifton church was the largest church in the parish, a framed build-in painted white and well kept. It had a mortgage, but payments were up to date. The one drawback was that when it rained access to church was nearly impossible. The roads around the church would be so deep in mud that even parishioners living nearby could hardly make it. This was rectified some months later when we organized a boys' club and instituted a gravel and clean up day.

The town was in a mess, covered with debris and cast-offs. The bank had gone broke. There was an Odd Fellows Hall, a pool room, and a small restaurant. There was a lone elderly doctor who was one of the best I have known, who had been the head of a hospital in Washington but had resigned in favor of Clifton, when Clifton was prosperous fruit country. He went to Clifton to help his wife's asthma. Both were fine people from England. He was a liberal and at one time had been elected county coroner on the Socialist ticket. I called on him, even though he and his wife did not go to church. People believed he was an atheist. He made me a promise: "I'll do my best to keep you out of heaven if you will do your best to keep me out of hell." He would sit in his car on warm days when the windows of the church were open and listen to my sermons.

Gravel and clean up day was a memorable event. Farmers came with their trucks and wagons, hauled away the rubbish, and graveled the streets from the main highways to the church. It became an annual event. After that the Clifton church was full.

The parsonage was next to the church and was an unmodern two-story house. We hauled our drinking water from Grand Junction and poured it into a cistern over which was a pump to draw water when needed. The doctor had said the irrigation water was polluted and not safe for human consumption. We had a two-holer outhouse. My study was a small room next to the kitchen.

The Bethel church was as run down inside as it was outside—and yet when it was cleaned up was inspiring.

The Loma church was a drab one-room church with a basement. A few people were devoted to its welfare but most people stayed away. The "greater parish plan" inspired some to give it a try and before long the church was more often full than empty.

The Mack appointment was a misnomer. It was a railroad shop and a company-directed community. The superintendent was pleased with my visit and assured me that I would be called if needed. I preached in the company hall a few times and took care of a number of funerals.

The Goodwill Industries store was run by a very influential widow who welcomed me graciously. She was a friend of Dr. Forsythe and he had written to her. With the help of some friends, she had purchased a small two-story house and a vacant property across the street for future development. She was devoted to the poor Mexicans, Italians, and so-called marginal farmers who were mostly migrant laborers with no place to go except the dry lands in the bluffs south of town. It wasn't long before I met most of the leaders of Grand Junction who were enthusiastic about doing something for the people in the south end, across the tracks.

We built a fairly adequate store, recreation center and workshop. We collected used clothing, furniture, and many other materials from the residents of Grand Junction and other communities. Soon we were able to hire about 20 impoverished people and sold (sometimes gave away) thousands of dollars worth of serviceable goods to hundreds of marginal farmers and underpaid and part-time workers.

My Sunday schedule began in Clifton at nine a.m. and then to Bethel at 11 a.m.—a distance of 16 miles. One of the Bethel parishioners would provide our Sunday dinner—which I am sure became quite a chore. My wife usually went along. The next stop was at the Goodwill Industries in Grand Junction at 3:30 p.m., and then to Loma-Mack at 7:30 p.m., which was nearly 30 miles from home. Sometimes I would stay overnight in Loma in order to make pastoral visits on Monday. I was rather systematic about visiting, giving each church a minimum of one day every two weeks in addition to Sundays. Illness, death, and weddings required extra visitations.

I didn't think that it was my job to be on hand for every meeting, except for monthly official board meetings. We developed an overall parish committee to plan for parish responsibilities and programs. It was difficult to get these gnarled, good-hearted poor farmers to think beyond their usual premises. It wasn't until we had our annual elections and elected younger members to church boards that things began to happen in cooperating and planning together. Among other things, we worked out an inter-parish baseball team for the boys.

The Goodwill boys' baseball team were too good for this inter-parish league. We entered a team with the Western Slope semi-pro league and to our amazement we won the championship one season. We took it away from the much-lauded team of the Denver and Rio Grande Railroad.

People

Many people of some means had settled in this valley thinking they had found a good place for the rest of their lives and prospered for awhile. The whole valley was covered with fruit trees. There were apples, pears, peaches and other varieties of fruit and berries. Some settlers belonged to combines, and hired managers and other employees to do the work.

The first calamity came when the soil turned sour from alkali. The upper part of the valley seemed to be most suitable for peaches and to some degree continued to prosper. Then, for the rest of the valley the growers fought a desperate struggle to save the land. Trees began to die and continued to do so until hundreds of acres were cleared. Another calamity struck the apple trees—an insect that wholly spoiled the apples. The only successful remedy to fight the insects was a lead spray which had to be applied nine times each growing season. Apples then had to be washed before they could be marketed. The growers formed co-operatives for purchasing the necessary supplies and equipment and for marketing the fruit. The combines and many growers gave up. Competition with other parts of the nation also inhibited the growers. They could make money only if crops elsewhere were poor.

Hundreds of families had to give up. Many tried to eke out a living by raising potatoes, onions, strawberries and other plants. Most people were impoverished and aghast at what was happening. Some held on tenaciously at a much lower standard of living.

I announced from the pulpit that if anyone needed a helping hand, the preacher was available. I was surprised at the response. I was asked to wash apples, pitch hay, etc. I recall one man who harvested his last crop of alfalfa. He was too feeble to do anything and was amazed at a preacher who could harvest his crop for him.

An old lady needed me to harvest her potatoes and a few pears—which I did. Old and nearly infirm, she was mostly confined to her little home. I learned that she had been the wife of a soldier in the Revolutionary War for Independence, a boy soldier. She had married him when she was 16 and he was quite old. She was chipper and full of surprises, living on a small widow's pension provided for the widows of Revolutionary War soldiers. She said, "I don't have a penny to give you for your work, but I got something much better." She asked me to give her my hand and went on, "Now, you are two hands away from General George Washington. My husband shook hands with George Washington when he was a boy soldier in the Army of the Revolution. My husband shook hands with me. Now I have shaken hands with you. Aren't you lucky?"

Hundreds of marginal farmers, "squatters," lived around the edges of the valley and on the bluffs, above the availability of water. They scrounged to live, eating rabbits, squirrels, birds, dandelions and any available living creature or plant. They farmed a little, hoping for rain which didn't come often, working when a day's work or job was available. They lived in the silence of the world in which they found themselves.

Then there were the people who worked for the sugar company and other plants and lived in the dirt-floor hovels provided for them. The area in which they lived smelled of human excretion and refuse. There were no conveniences.

There was a fourth group—the migrant workers, who camped on the banks of the polluted Colorado River. They had arrived by foot and in jalopies. There was also a man who was paid by the growers to haul them in—"as many as possible." There were no water facilities except the river, no outhouses. They burned shale rock, which could be gathered in abundance along the river. They had no way of knowing whether they would get work. Some growers brought back the same families each year.

The Colorado River was dangerous at times. Several children were drowned. I talked about these conditions quite often but most people shied away from the problems. They had enough of their own. My friend Melville L. Dilley came to me and said, "What you are saying is that we have no right to exploit people for our own purposes without looking out for their welfare. I have an abandoned house on my farm. I'm going to fix it up and have one of these families the year round."

The Ku Klux Klan

The KKK was going strong in Mesa County and harrassed me on several occasions. A committee came to me and made note of the fact that I did not accept the purely Protestant tenets of the order. They reminded me that many of their members belonged to my church. These members wouldn't talk to me because they did not want to bring undue pressure upon me, although they were unhappy about my beliefs. They wanted me to know that I would make a great many people happy if I were to join the Klan and allow my church to be used for Klan meetings. Furthermore, they would make me a chaplain in the Klan which would be a feather in my cap. In return, the Klan would make a generous contribution to the church mortgage. I turned them away. Evidently the other minister in the community had accepted some such offer. His church prospered for awhile as it basked in the favor of this hooded order.

Walter Walker, the editor of the *Daily Sentinel,* fought the Klan to a standstill. We worked together on this and other worthwhile endeavors. He was a tremendous asset in building the new Goodwill Industries.

I was asked to officiate at the funeral service of a man in my church. Nothing was said about the Klan in the arrangements. I looked out through the front door of the mortuary and saw a hooded Klansman on a white horse. I went back to the sorrowing family and asked if anything had been worked out with the KKK. The widow tearfully told me that nothing had been done and they didn't want the Klan to be present. I went out to the Klansmen and said that I would not tolerate their intrusion in the service. However, while my eyes were closed in prayer someone placed a Klan cross in front of the casket. I paid no attention, but it occurred to me that I should henceforth keep my eyes open while I prayed.

Two Babies

It was in the Bethel church that I was confronted with whether or not I would christen two babies born out of wedlock. Two sisters became pregnant about the same time. Their mother had died and they lived with their father and grandfather in an old ramshackle farmhouse. The older man was unable to do more than a few light chores. The father was depressed and didn't take much responsibility for operating the farm. The grandfather was a member of the school board in spite of the fact that he was illiterate and believed in only the rudiments of "readin' and writin' and figures." The girls were unhappy about the house in which they lived and the strict discipline of the two men. They became acquainted with two boys living in Grand Junction and found ways to be together. The father went out nights and the old man went to bed early. One of the girls was a Sunday School teacher in the church school.

I counseled with the girls and one of them married her boyfriend. Marriage was not possible in the other situation. We planned to christen all babies on Easter Sunday morning. There were 20 babies and small children to christen in this class because church services had not been held for some time. The word got around that I was to include these two babies.

Some people were outraged that these two babies would be included in the Easter service. I received a number of anonymous letters and some members threatened to withdraw from the church. I felt that this antagonism was inspired by the Klan and called on a number of people, but to no avail. The service was held and included these two children. The church was crowded that day.

The Blacksmith

One of the chief centers of communication in the horse-and-buggy days were the blacksmith shops. This was true in Clifton. It was fascinating to watch the blacksmith at his work, pumping air into the forge to make the coals red hot and with long prongs hold the horseshoe or iron in the forge until it was almost molten red with heat and then pound the iron into shape, and when ready, dip it in cold water. Idle men would sit around the shop and discuss almost anything. In Clifton, the blacksmith did much of the talking. He was an ardent Klansman and had perennially been the treasurer of the church. Moreover, he didn't like the young minister, and had stopped attending church. He continued to come to the Sunday evening youth group where he wasn't needed or wanted. He felt that it should be a witness meeting and he took up much of the time testifying to his early sins and omissions and emphasizing his conversion to Christ.

The young people had nothing to say while he was present. He explained to all who would listen that he had stopped attending church because the minister never preached on "sinners and sin," that the minister didn't believe in "hell, fire, and brimstone," nor a "personal devil." The smithy felt that the church was going to hell, and expounded his views daily to those who congregated in his shop. He was a nuisance but I tried to ignore what he said. Folks reported these things to me and felt that it was "shameful, the way the blacksmith talked about the preacher."

I picked a cold day to see the blacksmith, when I knew that we would have a number of listeners. After the usual courtesies, I addressed the smithy. "S—, I understand that you stopped attending church because the minister doesn't preach on hell and a personal devil."

He hedged until a member of the group said, "Now S—, ain't that what you have been telling us almost every day?"

I spoke up. "I have come to tell you that I do believe in hell and I do believe in a devil because it takes a devil to raise hell, and you are raising plenty of it."

This brought a laugh from the crowd. One droll farmer was heard to say, "I allow that the parson thinks we-uns got enough hell as it is, ground goin' sour and no prices for what we raise."

S— dropped out for good, the congregation grew, and we elected Mr. Smith, a Democrat, treasurer.

Doctors

We built a new facility at the Goodwill which included a wing for sales and another wing for a workshop with a larger room extending to the back for recreation, dances, boxing, and church services and classes. We were able to provide employment for a number of persons. There was a school children's luncheon, which an unkind person labeled "The Soup Eaters." I did not receive a salary from the Goodwill although I spent a lot of time directing the program.

I tried to get a doctor to examine the luncheon children but almost to no avail. When finally these children were examined, we found that they were all undernourished—four had tuberculosis and others needed medical help. A little boy broke his arm while playing in front of the building. The break was halfway between his wrist and elbow and his arm was bent in an angle. I picked up a few rulers, gently straightened out his arm, and with rulers for support wrapped his arm. He needed medical help so I began to call doctors who seemed to have reasons not to respond. I felt that I was getting a run-around. I called a fifth doctor and insisted that he do one of three things: either come to the Center, go to his office, or go to the hospital. He grumbled about being made the goat, that it was a charity case and he would never get paid, but he would see the boy in the hospital. The hospital was administered by Sister Superior Mary Linus, an admirable woman. (Later we went together to the Medical Association to work out a plan to provide medical assistance to the poor.) The doctor reset the arm and complimented me on my emergency effort; he was finally paid by a grateful father who over a period of months paid off the bill. The doctor was impressed as he told me the story and urged me to call on him any time.

There was a transient family in the neighborhood. The father had the reputation of being lazy, refusing to work—allowing his family to be destitute. I called on the father and mother and four little children. They lived in the shell of a one-room house—hungry for food, understanding, and love. I recall the eyes of the man—filled with pain, distrust, and helplessness. I didn't have to ask about their needs. He no doubt felt my thoughts and incredulity about how little good people were helped in their times of greatest need. I listened to him out of my own hidden agony. He said, "I guess you folks who know what's good for people can't believe that a man can have an awful sickness."

I asked why he didn't go to a doctor. He said, "I have and it didn't do much good. They know that I can't pay, so they don't have time for folks like me."

I asked a doctor to make a house call. The father died two weeks later from cancer. The doctor commented, "It was a damn shame. He must have suffered a long time."

Those suffering half-blind eyes haunt me to this day, partly because I have seen so many of them. Those were pioneer days in social work. Everybody knew where the "poor house" was—something to be shunned. Few people in need knew where to go for help.

Valentine

The boys around the Goodwill Center repeatedly told me about "a mean old man with a mean dog living under the nearby bridge over the Colorado River." They said that he was dressed in rags and that he picked up food from garbage cans behind the restaurants and cooked the garbage in cans over an open fire. The boys said, "He stinks and won't let the kids play under the bridge anymore." The weather was getting cold, so I investigated.

There he was, trying to keep warm over a shale rock fire. The dog snarled and warned him of my approach. The old man looked steadily at me, wondering who I was. He said, "You needn't come any closer. You are one of those do-gooders. Please leave me alone. I am not going to the 'poor house.'" I continued to approach him and he threw a stone at me, missing the mark. I crouched beside him. I explained who I was and suggested that if he wanted a place to stay and clean up, we had a room at the Goodwill Industries. Winter was on the way and he couldn't exist where he was. I added that if he wanted a job, I could take care of it and pay him a few dollars. He seemed interested and then in a gesture of hospitality offered me some stew which he was preparing for himself. A few days later, he returned my call preceded by some of the boys shouting, "That's the guy we told you about." The old man was embarrassed and seemed ready to turn away. I gave him an upper room in the old house and outfitted him with some of our used clothing and gave him a job as a shoe repair man. He knew nothing about the business but after a few weeks of practice did an acceptable job. I was certain that he had seen better days.

I asked the Methodist minister to make him a visit, which he did. Mr. Valentine was pleased. He became very secretive about his room after he had been with us about six months and would allow no one to enter. He put up a sign that said, "Please Keep Out." We restrained our curiosity as we heard him talk to his dog and busy himself with something that sounded like scratching—all this following his working hours. Then one day he proudly presented me with a willow stand about four feet high filled with paper flowers. He remarked that he had hoped to give them sooner but it took a long time to learn how to do it. He had gathered the willows from the river bank. He asked, "Do you think that the preacher downtown would like one?" I agreed that it would be a wonderful gift.

The Methodist minister called me some weeks later and wanted to tell me about "the old man." He and his dog had gone to church the previous Sunday and sat uneasily in a rear pew. He had a willow stand, table high, filled with paper flowers. He encouraged his dog to sit under the pew. Actually, he was figuring out the most appropriate time to walk down the middle aisle with his now friendly dog and present his gift of love. He picked the moment of silent prayer when the parishioners bowed their heads. He was ill at ease as he approached the minister. He awkwardly and lovingly presented his gift. He explained, "I should have gone to your home, but I didn't know where you lived." He turned around and humbly walked out of the church.

Mr. Valentine became quite a personage as he continued to repair shoes and make baskets of paper flowers for his friends and some to sell. However, after over two years, he became restless and guessed that he ought to move on. He didn't say where he was going. He never talked about his family or anything in his past life. We never prodded him. He bade us an affectionate farewell, saying that no one in his whole life had done as much for him. I met my banker friend, Mr. Weiser, on the street a few days later and he said, "I see we have lost a good customer." I wondered who he meant. He went on, "You know, your old man, down at the Goodwill. He came in every week with two or three dollars for his savings account. He drew it out the other day and said he was moving on. He was a great guy. Now I know his name, Valentine." I didn't know about his saving money out of his small earnings and asked Mr. Weiser how much he had saved. He said, "Over three hundred dollars."

His daughter came to see me about a year after he left. She said that her father's last request was for her to see me. She said, "Father was the meanest man in town. He was a barber in a village in Utah. It got so that no one had any use for him, so he left and no one knew where he was. I know now that he was unhappy, with Mother gone, and nothing for which to live. He came home a year ago—a changed man. He was well dressed and had presents for all of us—including willow stands with paper flowers. It was wonderful to have him around. He died a few weeks ago. He had asked me to see you. He wanted me to say, 'Thanks, Wallie, for what love can do.'"

A Sick World

Mesa County had its own troubles through the nineteen twenties. Then there came a false glimmer of hope which many people thought genuine. The stock market went way up. Many people put every cent they could get into City Service stocks, which climbed to 66 and over. I was apprehensive and urged a number of people to sell before it was too late, but they held on, feeling they had at last made it and had some security for the future.

I read how banks and International Harvester and others had helped farmers overextend themselves and then suddenly things broke loose in Iowa and the farmers lost everything they had—but the truth is that everyone was in the same boat, and our whole society was riding on a false prosperity. City Service went down like a flash and people were ruined. The papers wrote about people killing themselves on Wall Street and in New York City. The same thing happened all over the country. I had services for seven suicides in a row. Three were farmers who just called it quits. One was a widow who still lived on a farm but didn't work it—she was counting on her stocks. Three were young people whose worlds seemingly went down with the crash. I knew one of these young people very well, but not well enough to save him. His family had broken up and he lived alone, working for a farmer for his board and room and a few dollars. A senior in high school and the ace player on the basketball team, he had led his team to the top of the league. He had a girl friend whose parents did not take kindly to him. One night he went into a cold depression—he played his last basketball game on Saturday night—he saw his girlfriend and went to his room to think things out. He learned that his farmer friend for whom he worked was in financial trouble. That was the last straw. His world had been hard all the way. He had a phonograph and put the record on "Repeat." They found him after he had shot himself and the record repeated over and over:

> "I'm forever blowing bubbles,
> Pretty bubbles in the air.
> They fly so high; nearly reach the sky,
> Then like my dreams they fade and die.
> Fortune is always hiding,
> I've searched everywhere
> I'm forever blowing bubbles, pretty bubbles, in the air."

Grand Junction, 1927. The author (sixth from right) is shown here with a group of boys prior to an outing in Mesa County.

"Old Man Valentine," a transient I had found beneath a bridge in Grand Junction. He had been eking out a marginal existence by searching garbage cans for food and burning shale rock for fuel. We gave him a job repairing shoes and eventually he was able to save enough money to return home to his family.

Grace Church Denver sometime during the 1930s.

5. DENVER, COLORADO, 1930-1944

Grace Church

A number of my friends felt that I was making the wrong decisions as far as my future in the church was concerned. First, it had been a mistake to isolate myself in Utah. Then I should not have accepted the greater parish with its languishing churches in western Colorado. My friends felt that I was identifying myself with a so-called leftist trend. I had a number of invitations to pretigious churches and positions that could have brought me recognition in the church. I heard clear and loud: Stay away from controversy—don't deal too sharply with issues—identify yourself with respectable good middle class churches and if you are fortunate, with some rich people thrown in—we don't expect you to give up your convictions or ideals, but be sure when and how you express them—don't upset the apple cart.

Such approaches gave me cold chills about religious institutions. The truth is that for all intents and purposes the Protestant church is middle-class and cannot go all-out in the teachings of Jesus. I have a friend who made a blueprint for his success—the right churches, the right things to say—and he was in his own eyes a great success. He became a bishop, but it took a lot of politicking.

Preachers often move on the basis of the salary scale. Few take less money to move to areas where they are most needed. I believe in a system of equalized salaries and certainly in a minimum salary. We had no such prerequisites in the old days. My wife and I had reached a respectable salary of $4,000 and a house. We went to Grace Church as associate for $100 per month and paid our own rent and other expenses.

A friend of mine high in the councils of the church wrote: "Don't go to Grace Church. It will ruin you and cut you off from the recognition you rightly deserve. You have given of yourself sufficiently to test your genuineness. Grace Church is stamped as "RED" and leftist and nothing you can do will change it. Let Grace Church die a natural death. Stop fooling around with lost causes. Grace Church is not the place for anyone in his right mind. You have to start thinking about yourself. . . ."

This letter helped me to make the decision to go to Grace Church, Denver, Colorado.

Grace Church was one of the historic churches of Denver—a mission concern of the Lawrence Street Methodist Church—now the Trinity United Methodist Church. In 1873, a small mission Sunday School was organized in an ice-house back of the property on which was built the complex of buildings known as Grace Methodist Church (later called Grace Community Church). In 1878, Governor John Evans donated the brownstone chapel in memory of his daughter, Josephine Elbert, and land for further development. John Evans was a remarkable character. He had three careers—one in Indiana, where he was a medical doctor, and pioneered in the field of the mentally disturbed; then he moved to Chicago where he made a fortune in real estate and railroading, helping to establish Northwestern University and selecting the site for this great school. The city of Evanston, where he and his family lived, was named after him. He was a delegate to the Republican Convention where he helped to nominate Abraham Lincoln. The new president appointed John Evans second territorial governor of Colorado. He was successful in his business in Colorado and was admired for his life as a pioneer statesman and his influence as a citizen. He helped found Colorado Seminary, now the University of Denver. Evans Memorial Chapel was dedicated by Bishop Simpson of the Methodist Church, a close friend of Governor Evans and a friend of President Lincoln. The chapel became a regular Methodist appointment in 1879.

The minister's salary from 1891 to 1895 was $5,200, perhaps the highest in Denver, and the church paid as much as $4,000 a year for music. By 1900 the salary had dropped to $1,200. The site of the State Capitol building had been decided upon and those who could afford it built guest homes east of the Capitol building. Anyone living in this area had to be somebody. The influential moved to other churches. A few of the affluent remained to pick up the deficits when necessary. The population of the neighborhood increased and took over the homes and stables of those who departed and converted them to rooming houses and apartments.

Dr. Christian F. Reisner came to Grace Church in 1903. He had a great love for people and delighted in large audiences and would do anything to get them. He contrived to get the Denver Symphonic Orchestra to play every Sunday night and he threw in a popular sermonette for good measure. He would preach on "The Bread of Life" with stacks of bread (all donated by the baking companies) on the platform. One topic on a hot Sunday was "Keep Cool" while he stood between two pillars of ice. The florists furnished him with thousands of roses on Rose Sunday. He had the first electric sign ever in front of a church. He had a unique genius for getting money out of anyone. He left in 1910 to build a church high enough to be seen on the skyline of New York City, but he died before his dream was realized.

The crowds melted away. The church fell back to a more conventional program—but who could follow Reisner? A high level committee, including Bishop Francis J. McConnell and Dr. Orrin W. Auman, met to discuss the future of the ailing institution. Dr. George S. Lackland, a young man, was called into the deliberations. They knew that the church could not survive if it continued a conventional program. They decided to adopt a community program and build a Community Center building. They sought national support for what was then new and unusual. Dr. Lackland had remarkable success. The neighborhood was going down, but there were more people because there were more rooming houses. The new City Hall was to be erected one block north of the church.

Grace Church became a popular center for recreational and community activity. Dr. Charles C. Weber of the Italian Mission had organized a labor college in cooperation with the Denver Trades and Labor Assembly, but soon discovered that his facilities were too limited. He conferred with Lackland who was delighted with the prospect of the labor college and offered his cooperation. Many members of organized labor were eager to set up educational courses and to develop intelligent leadership. This program was extended to include the Denver Open Forum which flourished from the beginning. Speakers of note were brought into Denver. Dr. Lackland soon advertised widely, "The Church with 78,000 people." Dr. Lackland left in 1926 after eight years. He was a friendly person who loved people and who sought to get people to think. He became involved in a number of controversies, but few people could hold him a grudge.

Dr. Allen A. Heist followed Lackland in 1926. He came from the Methodist Federation for Social Action with national recognition and wide acquaintance and experience in labor and social problems. He defined the Christian religion within the framework of the Sermon on the Mount. He took an active part in labor struggles. He could be subtle and sarcastic at the same time. There was a dividing line between those who loved him and followed him and those who disagreed with him. Sure of his facts and undismayed by his critics, he was intelligent and intellectually speaking it was hard to disagree with him. He was outstanding in premarital counseling and devoted to civil rights and liberties. He believed that a revolution was essential and was opposed to palliatives that might dissuade men from the truth. He was a man of peace and believed that change could take place without violence. I had worked with him on several conference committees and admired him.

It was Dr. Heist who approached me about my filling in as associate minister for six months when he would become the educational director of the Columbia Conserve Company. I had walked by the church many times when I was a boy, but I had not been inside since the time of Lackland. We didn't mention the condition of the church in our correspondence or its financial status. I was naive about these matters.

My wife and I found a little place on Inca Street which we rented for $25 per month. She was pregnant. We had become parents of a red-headed boy while in Grand Junction. He arrived on Mother's Day and I preached three times that day. I was told later that all I talked about was Bill. So we had a girl and a boy and another child on the way on a very small allowance.

My first step was to get in touch with Dr. Heist and become acquainted with my interim job. I was totally unaware of what was ahead of me. Dr.

Heist was busy, so I had time to look around. I was appalled. The buildings had not been decorated since the erection of the Community Center. The lobby was in fair condition, but parts of the buildings had not been used so they seemed neglected. There were broken windows covered with cardboard and leaks in the roof. The gymnasium floor was rough and splintered, bulged from dampness. The chapel and church doors were shabby and weatherbeaten. Worst of all were the men's and boys' toilets with leaky plumbing, unpainted, and with the worst kinds of obscenity on the walls. I was chilled. There was little evidence of pride in the once proud structure.

Dr. Heist, seated in a decent office, said, "Welcome, I see you got here." I began asking about the program and financial status of the church. He said, "If you are a Christian, you can't have it all, you know." It was evident that income had long since stopped keeping pace with the expense—although most of his loyal friends were giving far beyond their means. Moreover, the church had sold interest-bearing certificates to people who were sacrificing their savings. There was a $30,000 mortgage held by the banks on which interest had not been paid for several years. Some firms had put the church on a cash basis so that necessary items like coal were not delivered without money on the line. The church owed Public Service over $2,000. (My small salary of $1,200 came from the mission board.)

Dr. Heist was unperturbed by this financial situation. He was an idealist. I must say that he was unbridled and was the same way in his personal life. He was getting by somehow. He said, "Don't worry about it. This church won't last another six months, and when the ship goes down, we will do it with honor—I hope we go down together."

I suggested that we had had enough for one day and that we might pursue the subject later. I was very depressed and wondered if this was the price one had to pay to be Christian in our kind of world. I know that Dr. Heist was sincere. I knew that he felt crucified and a martyr. I didn't want to be a martyr. I felt trapped. I didn't want to tell my wife about it, but she wormed my feelings out of me. She said, "Don't worry about it. Maybe there is a way." Perhaps, but I had a family I loved, as well as my faith to do the will of God.

Those six months were mighty chilly, at least inwardly. Outwardly we kept up appearances—triumphant in the last battle and ultimate defeat. I asked hundreds of questions and made as many suggestions. I asked for the names of people who were most likely to contribute. I felt that we should do it together because he was senior minister, but I soon realized that I would have to do it alone. I shall never forget one man who said, "I planned to give you five dollars, but now not a damn cent. I allow that my faith is as sound as yours." Heist responded, "That's okay with us, we don't like your kind of money."

I suggested that we invite Dr. Reisner and Dr. Lackland to spend several weeks with us to stir up old loyalties. The answer was, "They can't do us any good. We would wholly misrepresent our image." There was a good side to this apprenticeship. I wrote down many ideas which I pursued when I became minister. The unemployed were in the streets and I suggested we give them a meeting place and see what could be done. The answer was, "That isn't worth trying. All you can do is to provide palliatives which in the long run will do more harm than good." Then came the farewell message in which he repeated, "Let us be thankful for the last victorious five years."

I was anything but idle during my months as a beginner in Grace Church. I was overpowered by the strength of Dr. Heist, and felt helpless and subordinate—as if I were living in a vacuum with Doomsday just ahead. I thought about getting out—to ask a change of jobs. I had a feeling that Dr. Heist was suffering and was not at his best. He was negative and evasive. Our minds were far apart. I fantasized that there might be a way to save the church, to include Heist and myself. I studied lists of old membership rolls for names of people who were former members. I searched for organizations and persons who at some time or other had had reason to contribute. I talked to members of the church who for the most part felt that the membership had gone as far as it could to give more. I made a list of labor unions, liberals and radicals—all of whom had been befriended either by Dr. Heist or the church. I searched for ways to get publicity and dramatize the church as Dr. Heist saw it. We didn't come up with anything.

I then went out to visit possible contributors. The Great Depression had begun and many complained about their fears and could not give at the time, however worthy the cause. Most of my contacts had good things to say about Dr. Heist. Quite a few inquired about the whereabouts of Dr. Lackland. Some responded and I came up with several hundred dollars, which was too little and too late. However, I appreciated the fact that there was a great potential if the church could really come alive with a program for all the people. The church membership responded with increased giving. Financially, conditions seemed to be looking up. I am sure that the thought came to Dr. Heist that he could stay on at Grace Church, but he was too deeply committed to leaving.

I became minister in charge of Grace Church on April 1, 1931. The small congregation was divided and confused. Some believed that I had nefariously forced Dr. Heist out of his position, an idea which crept into a newspaper article. A few believed that the new minister was too young. Others were sure that I would be a rank conservative.

A baby girl had come into our lives in November. We now numbered five, living in a tiny terrace. We moved into the parsonage in April 1931, which was to be our home for fifteen years. It was ample and comfortable. Our salary was $1,200 as before because a raise was impossible. We gained in rent and heat because the parsonage was part of the church's heating system.

I stopped in the office and the things that had to be done went sifting through my mind. Where to begin? I was alone in the vastness of the situation. I was exhausted from six months of frustration and was now confronted with a conspiracy of silence and felt extremely alone. I had to prepare my first sermon. Why didn't I sit down and write it? Somehow, I felt that it didn't matter; no one would listen to me anyway. I was conscious of cold, staring eyes—and yet there were those who seemed interested and willing to do something. Then there was that dilapidated and stinking men's room downstairs. I reached into my pocket and counted my change. I figured there was enough money to buy a can of paint, a brush and a putty knife. That was my first job in Grace Church—to clean up the "john room." My wife would seem to have been the only one who knew, but it is curious how the word gets around. There was very little smut on the toilet walls after that.

People phoned and came in to see me and wish me well. I had made up my mind to confront honestly the congregation with the facts about my coming to Grace Church. Here are a few quotes from that sermon. It would have helped if Heist had advised the people about the facts, but for some reason he didn't.

"I think in all fairness to all concerned a word must be said about the circumstances which brought your present pastor to Grace Church. . . . I was invited without solicitation on my part to the consideration of succeeding Dr. A. A. Heist, should he leave his pastorate. . . .

"Under correspondence from Dr. Heist of July 11, 1930, Dr. Heist wrote, 'Things are developing which make me want to get in touch with you. I have decided that I shall have to move both for my sake and for the sake of my family; probably I ought to add, for the sake of the church too. I don't know whether anyone ever succeeds in doing two things in a church—deflating and rebuilding. The former takes too much of one's nerve, so I think a new voice is needed here. . . .'"

I pointed out that the first job was to develop confidence in each other. I said that we would democratically discuss matters of change and that I was ready to present some ideas in the next board meeting. I won over most of the congregation that first Sunday.

We had our first board meeting, which was quite somber and skeptical as we were confronted with the financial problems. It was not a crisis—it was a disaster. The banks had sent a statement in which it seemed foreclosure was inevitable so that we were involved in an excercise in futility. We had no credit rating because of outstanding bills. However, these good people had supported the church for many years and hoped that there might be a way out of this dilemma. There were a few dissenters who would rather have given up the ship. I requested that we hold on and perhaps discover a way out. A motion was passed to the effect that the preacher be given an opportunity to go ahead. Perhaps it was a vote of sympathy. As some said after the meeting, "What else could we have done? But don't feel badly if it is more than we can chew."

One thing was certain, there was no money to spend. I wrote to my friends Dr. Christian F. Reisner and Dr. George Lackland and asked them for at least a week of service. I then went to the bank and was presented to the president who greeted me cordially and invited me to sit down, as he reminisced about the old days of Grace Church and the people he knew. I had been frightened about going into the bank and had walked around the block in apprehension. This man made me feel at ease. I brought up the subject of the mortgage and the letter of foreclosure. He said, "Yes, I know about that—I hope you can begin to pay something on the interest." I told him all the details of our financial structure and that it might be some time before we could pay a dime. I added, "You may think that you have to foreclose. Just remember this—if you do foreclose you will have a church on your hands. I'm willing to give it a try and trust that you will help me." He agreed and asked me if I knew Mr. Dines, president of the United States National Bank, and John Evans of the First National Bank. We settled that mortgage some years later with a discount and a $5,000 gift from the Associated Bankers.

Lackland and Reisner

Dr. George Lackland and Dr. Christian F. Reisner accepted my invitations and each gave us eight days out of their busy lives to come to Denver. These men were extremely different. Both did Grace Church a lot of good, which I had anticipated. We were obligated to pay their expenses, but they refused honorariums for their time spent on the job. The money was rather easy to accumulate. We made up lists of their friends and simply told each one that Lackland and Reisner were coming to town. It wasn't long before we had the expenses and a little more to bring Lackland from Pennsylvania and Reisner from New York—first class.

Each one wanted to look over the premises. Lackland stopped in front of one of the large church doors and said, "Look at those doors. They say to me, 'You are unwelcome.' Varnish those doors even if you have to do it yourself. If you are broke, I'll pay for it. People see the doors first and if they say 'welcome,' they might come in. The first impression is the best. Secondly, they will look at the minister and I can't help you about that!" The doors were varnished.

We visited with old friends during the day and had meetings every evening. Lackland called mostly on labor union members, labor union meeting places and headquarters, and on university teachers and staff. Everyone seemed eager to shake his hand and talk "shop" for awhile. This was a great adventure to me. Lackland said that when he was in Denver he called on each union at least once a year. They always asked him to make a talk. He recommended that I be appointed a ministerial delegate to the Denver Trades and Labor Assembly. All were invited to attend the evening meetings and many did.

Dr. Reisner was something else. He noticed the newly varnished doors of the church and remarked, "That's a good thing for now. The next step is to refurbish the inside." I wondered when and how that could be done. Our first visit was to a printer friend. Reisner ordered up a great quantity of publicity, fliers and signs about our meetings and said, "Have them ready tomorrow." He suggested this be a donation, inasmuch as the printer hadn't made a donation since 1910. The printer seemed slightly aghast but the publicity was ready the next day.

Our next visits were to the newspaper offices. F. G. Bonfils was the owner of the *Denver Post*. Reisner invited him to the meetings and talked about his salvation. He told Mr. Bonfils that he needed salvation and he had better get it soon because he probably didn't have long for this world. Mr. Bonfils retorted that in his mind he was as saved as Reisner—that they really were not too different, that they were both sinners. They seemed to be on the best of terms. Reisner had for a short time before 1910 edited the *Kansas City Post* for Bonfils. The *Denver Post* carried splendid articles about the meetings. We went to see the presidents of all the banks. We went up and down elevators, to and from important businessmen—and wherever we were he would reach out his hand and say, "I am Dr. Reisner from New York City. I'm preaching at Grace Church. Come out and hear me." He must have approached a thousand strangers in this manner during his stay. We went to Gano-Downs, a men's clothing store, where he asked the proprietor to fit me out with an excellent suit. He wanted me to look my best. The suit, like the publicity, was a contribution to the church. He took me to the Kraft Cheese offices and we came out with a year's supply of cheese. He would say, "I do all this for the good of souls. Keep it up and you will get one once in a while." He even talked a policeman out of giving us a ticket for over-parking. He explained that we were trying to get some money from a businessman and it took longer than we knew because we also wanted to save his soul.

This was a remarkable experience. Lackland and Reisner were good speakers and human. Together, they would have been incompatible. Separately, they were superb. They loved people for what they were. They demonstrated a warmth which spread throughout the constituency. There was a newness in the air. One unemployed man said, "They made me feel like I belonged somewhere."

A number of things began to happen almost all at once, the chief of which was the Grace Church Relief Association—the Unemployed Self-Help Co-operative.

The Co-operative

Unemployment swelled into a huge tidal wave no one could ignore. Myriads of human faces looked more and more as if they expected soon to be executed. In retrospect, we know that most of these people had exhausted themselves in a futile search for work. They shared the belief of the culture of the times, that every able man should work for a living. They could not accept the fact that this was impossible. They wanted work and not relief. The Bureau of Public Welfare was paying only seven dollars per month per person. Few seemed to realize that money had to be raised through government. This condition caused more alarm than the fact that people were destitute and hungry through no fault of their own. Furthermore, our society underestimated the idealism and aspirations of the poor—of all human beings. The whole society discredited itself in resisting adequate plans to rebuild itself in order to provide for human welfare.

Most of the unemployed who came to Grace Center wanted work, and, short of employment, self-help. That is why the Grace Self-Help Co-operative was formed. A group of men gathered together in Grace Center day after day to explore ideas, write a constitution and bylaws, and develop a program, including picking up unsold products at Farmers' Market; working for farmers who couldn't pay wages, for a percentage of the crop; making a deal with city for firewood by trimming and cutting down trees; picking up stale bread at bakeries; establishing a shoe repair shop, barber shop, sewing room; handling skim milk and whole milk from the commissary; working for part of the potato crops; moving members when necessary.

An early report between October and May:

    4,291 vegetable tickets given out
    7,819 grocery tickets given out
    4,760 loaves of bread given out
    5,241 gallons of skim milk
    1,173 sacks of flour given out
      888 pieces of used clothing given out
    1,638 shoes repaired
    1,821 garments made, also quilting and repairing
      649 haircuts and shaves
      252 loads of wood delivered
   28,631 tickets issued

John Evans gave me money each month to be used as I saw fit. I recall that the first gift was a wooden leg for a young man. Another task was repairing the gymnasium floor.

We had a wonderful grocery man two doors from the parsonage. He shared with me the fact that a gang of boys would come into the store to buy a nickel's worth of peanuts while the rest of the gang would steal as much food as they could. Mr. Ripp said, "I don't want to turn those guys in. They're just hungry, but I can't stand the loss." I said, "Okay, make an estimate and I'll pay"—not knowing for sure that I could. He said, "No, not that—I want half the fun." The boys were in the church at the time enjoying stolen food.

Coming through the Center one day I ran into my neighbor who was carrying two pails of water. She lived in the small house next door where there were seven people living, including a baby and a grandfather. She said, "The city turned off the water because the landlord hasn't paid the water bill." I went over to city hall and with a little pressure the water was turned on. I gave Mr. Ripp, the grocer, a credit of $25 for groceries for her and ordered a ton of coal from the *Denver Post*. I found that the house was cold.

The John Evans family helped in other ways. A father collapsed in our building while waiting in line for food, and at the same time his girl broke down suddenly in her class in school. A children's luncheon became imperative. Mr. Evans supplied the money; his sister Katherine managed the menu and purchases and helped serve every day. The Self-Help mothers cooked the food.

There was a Henry Porter Foundation in Denver administered by a marvelous person, Mrs. Ida L. Gregory. The foundation was generous in time of need but gave only three items: flour, beans, and slabs of bacon. Mrs. Gregory gave us all I requested just so it was bacon, beans, or flour.

The most ambitious undertaking of the Co-op was to harvest and transport to Denver around 100 tons of potatoes. Some of the men worked for farmers who gave them room, board and one dollar's worth of potatoes a day. Others worked for farmers who selected certain fields and gave the produce outright. However, there we had to furnish room and board. The National Guard furnished the trucks, tents and equipment or the job could not have been undertaken. The story broke in the *Denver Post* October 2, 1932.

This work was often under surveillance by officers and Red baiters. I was the president of the state co-operatives that had joined together. Three or four policemen were present every time that I spoke in Longmont, Colorado Springs, and Pueblo. One of our drivers was stopped at the county line as he crossed into Denver. He was ordered to empty his truck of garden produce and his clothing was searched. I saw the chief of police and he shrugged it all away and said, "It was a coincidence." I said, "Your coincidence is a habit." He said, "We are informed that a lot of Red literature is getting into town and we can't be too careful." To which I replied, "If you are so eager to get Red literature I can see to it that you will get it. It might do you some good."

The significance of these self-help experiences was the goodness of people. They put it all together in the bylaws: "It is the purpose of this organization to promote a program of human welfare directed first of all toward meeting the immediate and most necessary needs of the people. Secondly, it will be the purpose of this organization to create individual and collective responsibility for making social conditions such that all the needs of life may be met in a constructive way."

The commanding officer of a military installation west of Denver called and asked if we could use some discarded shoes. Every employee was issued a pair of shoes with metal caps over the toes and was required to return the safety shoes when the work was finished. Most of the shoes were in good condition; some had been used a week or less. We brought back hundreds of pairs of shoes each month. Our lone shoemaker was patching, as best he could, shoes that should have been discarded—often using worn-out rubber tires for soles. We dumped the shoes into his cubbyhole to size them up and get them ready for distribution. There were enough shoes so that quite a few outside the co-op membership also received them. Unfortunately, they were mostly shoes for men, although some of the smaller sizes were worn by women in need of them. I was invited about twenty years later to address the Cosmopolitan Club of Denver. An old man took my hand and said, "Thank you, Wallie." I asked, "For what?" He said, "My shoes—don't you remember? Look at them. I don't wear 'em much any more. They are a keepsake and I shall always hold onto them."

The Self-Help Co-operative thought we should do something for older people who lived alone in rooming houses. We began a tradition of keeping our facilities open on Thanksgiving day and Christmas with programs designed to have plenty of food and lots of fun. I volunteered to procure the turkeys, trimmings and necessary equipment. The response was electric. A simple appeal was sent out to a few people, who provided the funds. We passed the word around the neighborhood and there were nearly 200 men and women— mostly women. Some of them wanted to help cook and put things together for a happy time. In future years these lonely people did all the work and those of us in the Center caught a glimpse of another unmet human need— loneliness.

A fortunate side result took place. The story broke in the newspapers and a wealthy lady sent me a check for $100. I took the check to her lawyer and returned it, saying, "Give it back. Tell her to come down and see for herself what is happening. I think she would like to get in on the action." He said, "This has never happened before, but I'll do what you've asked." I gained a friend who enjoyed helping people help themselves.

Too Much Cabbage

We were always in short supply of the essentials, but there were times when we had too much of a good thing. We had an understanding with rabbit hunters, who could leave their surplus at the Center. What to do when a hundred hunters would pile up 1000 rabbits? Nothing was wasted, but there were times when we had too much.

Take for example the use of truckloads of cabbage. Everybody in and out of our center had all the cabbage they needed, and there were piles left over. We couldn't sell them as we did some surpluses. The menu committee discovered that there were eleven ways to prepare cabbage, but after all is said and done—cabbage is still cabbage. Then the committee came up with a great idea—*we would make sauerkraut.* We had two people who knew how. The problem was where to get barrels and other sundry items.

We went to a pickle factory and the owner became intrigued with the idea. He gave us seventeen barrels and delivered them to the church.

The committee came to my office with a startling question. "Now that we've got the sauerkraut, where do we store it?" I thoughtlessly said, "There is a small basement under the platform and a door behind the sanctuary; you might try there." They came back and said, "We need more room for four barrels." I recalled a back room in the basement of the parsonage. It was a good thing that my family was absent for a few days!

Our custodian saw me on Friday and asked, "Have you been in the church?" I followed him into the sanctuary and got his meaning loud and clear. The place smelled like a pickle factory! He said, "Them saints ain't goin' to like that." Our church was dubbed the Sauerkraut Community Church. I went back to my office to meditate. I heard a quiet voice as if from God. "It will be okay. A preacher who can get into a mess like that is okay. I've had my problems with some people, too."

We lost two good and substantial families on Sunday. They had been opposed to having the unemployed in the church, but had been somewhat tolerant up until the cabbage episode. They expressed their fears that the unemployed would infect our padded church pews with bedbugs and filth, which expressed the image that many people have about the underprivileged. They were not opposed to doing something for the poor, but not inside their own church. They announced their intention of leaving. One of them said, "We intend to join a respectable church."

Some years later there was a sequel to the sauerkraut enterprise. I received an urgent message to call on an old man who lived in a back room of the third floor of an old building occupied mostly by abandoned aging men. I recognized him as a former member of the Self-Help Co-operative, although about ten years had slipped away. The Co-op was all but abandoned because most of the members had found jobs in the pre-war period. I found that he was not long for this world. He looked up at me through eyes that were dimming with death. I told him who I was and he rose to the occasion. I took his had very tenderly. He said, "You are the minister of the Sauerkraut Community Church." I gasped because I thought our image had changed with the years. I leaned over so he could hear me and replied, "Yes, I guess you are so right." He whispered, "Thank God for you and your church—because of you and your church I am entering the portals of glory today."

Cause of Death—Starvation

Few people realized the seriousness of the Depression in terms of actual starvation. When people died of malnutrition, there were contributing ailments. One of Denver's leading physicians explained to me that doctors rarely stated the reason for death was actual starvation. Instead, they named one of the contributing causes. This practice helped to obscure the awful truth of suffering. The terrifying spector of starvation came dramatically to my attention when I was called upon to officiate at the funeral of a little boy who had starved to death. The doctor in this case was outraged to the point of truth when he gave the cause of death as "starvation." The father and mother were not far removed from a similar fate. This boy was an only child. The parents were in their forties. The husband lost his job in a tobacco shop where he had worked for many years at a low wage—barely enough to support his family. He tried in vain to find any kind of work. They struggled to get along on the few hours of employment that he did get now and then. They had never received charity and never thought of it. They bought mostly beans and the barest of necessities until the husband was so weak it was impossible for him to get around. The mother and father favored the child as best they could. They lived in one room in a house occupied by people in like circumstances. They owed several months rent and the electricity had been turned off. There comes a time in the lives of those who are deprived when they are not fully aware of what is happening to them. Neighbors entered the room and called a doctor. Actually, all three were dying. It was too late to save the boy.

A dull and bitter silence spread through the house and the neighborhood. Neighbors had done what they could but had little to contribute except to share their silence. If they were on relief the most they received was seven dollars per person a month. Agencies were unable to cope with the gigantic needs of the early thirties. Deficits were paid for by those who had to go without assistance.

A mortician offered to provide a *Christian* service. The Ladies' Aid of a Baptist church brought supplies and the first new suit the boy had ever worn. I walked into the chapel where the parents and neighbors awaited the final words of the minister. There was a ruthless and devastating resignation that made all of us feel naked, bare and ashamed. That new suit didn't help. The parents, seemingly, saw nothing at all. I felt that I stood before a judgment that was ready to cut me down for murder. This took place in my own neighborhood over which towered the proud steeple of my church. I had met hungry people, but I didn't know little children were starving to death. My ritual book was in my hand but it had no meaning at all. What possible use was there for ritualistic prayers, scriptures and admonitions which had been read a million times? I felt like a hypocrite trying to cover up reality in the priestly functions of my ministry. The scene was cold and utterly godless. I could not read anyhow because of my tears, and my mind was blurred with sorrow.

I walked out of the chapel without saying a word. I found that the attendants were watching and waiting to hear what I had to say. (Morticians are not too concerned usually about what the minister has to say.) I said, "I can't do it. I just can't." The mortician replied, "But you have to do it. They expect—they need something." I looked back into the room. No one noticed that I had disappeared. They expected nothing.

I returned to my place close to the parents and whispered words that came to mind. I said, among other things, "God did not do this. It was God's will that this boy and every child should live. It was God's will that these parents and all parents should have the privileges and the means with which to live. God created a universe in which this is possible. Man has perverted this world in selfish pursuits which favor some and destroy others. We need a new and loving economic and social system which takes everyone in and throws no one out. This is once again the crucifixion—caused by the headlong unheeding, senseless and selfish perversion of the will of God in which man has neglected to build the Kingdom of God on earth. Man did this—not God. It is the will of God that mankind should heed the teachings of Jesus and follow Him—not crucify Him or His teachings."

I then read a few verses of Scripture about the love of Jesus for little children, and the 23rd Psalm. I paused and asked, "Can you hear me? Do you understand what I am saying? Does it make sense to you?" We then paused in silence.

I said, "Amen," and asked, "Is there anything special I can do?" The mother answered, "That was fine. Will you read about Jesus and the little children again and will you conclude with the 23rd Psalm? I want it read again. You see, our boy is one of His children, and we need the Shepherd so very, very much." I was astonished how articulate she could be in spite of bitterness and heartache.

I have witnessed poverty and starving children in Egypt, Greece, South America, China, Colorado, California, Michigan, New York, and other places. But I shall never forget the little boy who received his first new suit after he starved to death.

Homeless Men

Among the dark shadows of the Depression years were the haunted jungles of homeless men, to whom were attached the cruel images related to the poor, and especially to men without any means of support. We lived in a dream world of a frontier civilization committed to the idea that anyone worth his salt could find something to do. Our culture could not imagine that men were unemployed through no fault of their own. Unemployment was correlated with laziness and shiftlessness, improvidence and immorality, unworthiness, and lack of initiative. To make things worse, those who were out of work shared this philosophy. They had been brought up to believe this folklore about our so-called way of life. Few people could admit that our economic system had exposed its weakness and that being out of work was not their fault. They bore the injustice of rejection and misunderstanding.

These men were heroic. They severed their ties of home and family to seek new frontiers, only to discover that there were no new frontiers—no jobs anywhere. They had exhausted every resource in their home communities. Many lost everything they possessed and their families suffered humiliation and poverty. Unnumbered thousands of men joined the migrations in search for jobs—any kind of work—and for opportunities that did not exist. There were no welcome signs. They were confronted with the damp chill of employment offices that had stopped hiring. Freight trains hauled as many out of town as came into town. Men learned to insulate their bodies with newspapers, froze, starved, became ill, and died in an endless stream of despair. They lined up in long queues where a bit of food was ladled out, sold apples, searched for food in garbage cans, congregated and huddled together, and moved on. There were angry voices and demands, but for the most part these men were not revolutionists. Few people understood or communicated with them. These men did not understand themselves. Some felt betrayed. Many lost their self-respect. They were poor candidates for a revolution. They struggled with a hopeless dream about America and kept moving.

Many of these men came to Grace Center. We did not ask them to tell their stories, repeated so many times across the land. They received a welcome, a meal, clothing if we had any, perhaps a bed, and a little money if we had it. Work that was available was reserved for those closest to us, so there wasn't much that we could do. Most wanted to do something for what they received. They were of all ages and from many walks of life. There were school teachers, former executives, farmers, skilled workers, salesmen, professional people. Many had families and were worried about them. Some would use our facilities to write letters.

One of those who insisted on telling his story was a young man who said that he had a wife and two children in Kansas. He wanted to get back to them and asked me to help him with a few dollars and decent clothing to replace the rags he was wearing. He explained that his family received a small relief allowance and that his wife made a few dollars, now and then, for doing housework—that he had given up trying to get a job and thought he might do better in his home town where he was known. He also needed a shave and a hair cut, which we could provide because we had our self-help barber shop.

His story did not quite ring true with me, so I said to him, "I am intrigued with your story and with you as a person, but I detect that there is something more to your story that you have not exposed."

He said, "Why do you say that?"

I answered, "I don't know. You seem to have something else on your mind, other than your need. There is something else about you."

He replied, "I'll level with you. I am a theological student and I am working on my thesis. I have chosen to study the problems of homeless men, who they are and the ways they live. I have been doing this for three months and I am as bad off as they are. I have, among other things, been trying to find friendly and sympathetic persons in the towns and cities of the United States.

This kind of thing gets around. I mean other than the usual soup kitchens and missions. I got my information from the men themselves. This has led me to restaurants, taverns, a few churches, and to sympathetic individuals. There aren't many, one or two in each place, sometimes not any. You are one of two in Denver."

This young man did live in Kansas and he did have a wife and two children and he did need help to get back home. He did need a shave and hair cut and a change of clothing. I invited him into our home where he stayed for several days. He invited me to join him in making the rounds of the missions and the soup kitchens and the places where the unemployed were allowed to congregate in Denver.

I allowed my whiskers to grow and donned shabby clothing and went with him—first to a soup kitchen operated by a local relief agency. Hundreds of men were lined up and each one was ladled out a bowl of pigsfeet stew. It was a greasy, watery concoction of mangled pigs feet and lima beans. The odor was of steamy grease and began to gag me before I received my helping. There were a few tables around, but most of the men ate while standing, forcing the mess down their throats. I said, "Bill, do I have to? I don't think I can do it. A man next to me said, "I haven't eaten for two days. If you don't want it, I'll take it. It isn't good, but after all, it is only intended to keep you alive." We gave up our bowls and moved on.

The Salvation Army was closed to any additional customers. They were providing their full capacity and could take no more that night. A friendly officer explained that they were sorry. We were invited to attend the service and told there might be something to eat after the meeting.

We visited the City Mission, which was reputed to have the best facilities in town. They had a de-louser, showers, and good beds, but we were told that we had to attend the service before anything could be done for us. The place was crowded with men who reluctantly filled the seats. There was a song service of the old fashioned religious type led by a song leader who knew all the tricks to get people to sing. The response was anything but enthusiastic. Then followed a salvation and "come to Jesus" type of sermon—quite long. The men were told that if they were truly saved they would find work. Jesus would look after them. The solo was, "Where Is My Wandering Boy Tonight." The audience sat in sullen waiting. The man next to me said, "You're low too, aren't you? Anybody come to a joint like this has to be low. It is hypocrisy. I know. And every city has one, provided by the so-called good people."

Then came the invitation "to be saved by the blood of Christ." Quite a few went forward to kneel at the altar. The reason was obvious. Each one was given a ticket which provided for de-lousing, showers, food, a bed, and breakfast. The man next to me said, "If you need to get cleaned up and eat, now is the time to go forward. You seem to be new at this." I asked if he was going. He answered, "I came in here expecting to go but my stomach can't take it. I am no longer hungry like I was. I guess I got too much self-respect."

My friend and I waited. The service came to a close and someone announced that those who remained would have to wait. There were about fifteen of us. Some were impatient and began to grumble. We were told to keep quiet. A few walked out to take their chances somewhere else. It was a cold night. Two of us waited a little longer and then got up to go, saying, "We would rather sleep in the jail." One of the mission attendents said, "Okay with us—two less bums to care for."

We went to the Volunteers of America—housed in an old building. We went up the rickety stairs into a large room filled with men. There was a human warmth that was lacking in the other places. Volunteer workers ladled each one a bowl of delicious beef stew. We enjoyed the stew as we chatted with the men. After all were fed, we were told that there were no more beds but we could grab up some newspapers from a pile nearby and sleep on the floor. They were sorry that this was the best they could do. The men quietly prepared themselves for the night.

Bill and I went back to the parsonage, weary in body and sick in mind. He said that this was the way it was all over the United States.

Hoboes

Once on my way to Dallas, Texas, I talked with an unusual delegate returning to Fort Worth from attendance at the American Federation of Labor Convention. He showed me his card as a continuous member for 42 years of the Fort Worth Labor Assembly.

The thing that interested me most was his membership in the International Itinerant Migratory Workers' Union, in other words, "Hoboes of America" organized in 1907, with national headquarters in Cincinnati, Ohio. This organization was his joy. He explained that he had traveled six times around the world. Twelve of his 73 years had been spent in foreign countries including Scotland, his homeland. He stated that "America was the best of them all," and among other things, he was a Presbyterian.

He allowed me to see a token of special significance, a card which in proper language pointed him out for "Distinguished Honor and Esteem" in the order to which he belonged. He glowed as he fonded over the words, "Knights of the Road," "Distinguished Honor."

My friend showed me his membership card on the back of which was the "Hobo's Oath." It read as follows: "I solemnly swear to do all in my power to aid and assist all those willing to aid themselves. I pledge myself to assist all runaway boys and induce them to return to their homes and parents. I solemnly swear never to take advantage of my fellow men; or to be unjust to others, and to do all in my power for the betterment of myself, my organization and America—so help me God." This membership card was signed "Jeff Davis—King" over the printed words "King of Hoboes" and was also signed by the International Secretary.

I recalled my visit, years ago, to the Chicago Hobo College where the men sat on planks listening to the lectures. The primitive benches were called "Anti-snooze, Anti-booze pews." Someone reminded me of the difference between bums, tramps, and hoboes. Bums were men who wouldn't move or wouldn't work. Tramps were folks who moved but wouldn't work for a living. A hobo was the highest order of life. Hoboes were men who moved from place to place in order to find work.

I had never seen such a membership card nor had I read the "Hobo's Oath." I have since wondered about these travelers on the road. Where did they begin? Who really practices their vows now? Surely this is a higher order of life that assists "those willing to aid themselves"—and helps runaway boys and America—"so help me God." Has America understood or desired to understand these "Knights of the Road"? Migratory workers deserve a better and more permanent security. It was good to know this strange delegate who took pride in saying that he had attended a "grand meeting" of the American Federation of Labor. Can you hear him say it? Is there a way America can really help people who do such necessary work? Who are so eager to help themselves?

Suffering

Our work in the Grace Center Co-operative brought into focus the desire of people to help themselves. Unemployed Co-operatives were organized in various parts of Denver and throughout the state. It was soon clear the unemployed could not do the job by themselves as thousands of men converged upon us and demanded that we get together and bring our plight to the attention of authorities and especially the lawmakers. I had been elected chaplain of the Colorado House of Representatives and felt crushed between the needs of the people and a legislature that did not respond readily to human problems, and seemed to be confused as to what should be done. Some preferred to do nothing, fearful of welfarism and socialism. But hungry parents with hungry children could not wait, which I clearly said in my prayers.

I prayed at the legislature for the unemployed. I was called into a meeting and was told to stop lobbying in my prayers or I would be fired. It seems that these nine men felt that I had influenced the passage of two pieces of legislation. I responded by pointing out only what I thought God wanted me to do, and walked out. This was my first assignment as chaplain and I was elected to two more sessions in the House and two in the Senate, when I voluntarily withdrew.

My power base was my church and I preached forthrightly. The press was sometimes supportive. I felt that people should speak out—not once but many times. I dealt with the seriousness of the conditions, and said, "If we wait, violence is the only alternative. I am interested in a revolution without violence...." I thought the plans being formulated in Washington, though inadequate, were a step in the right direction and said, "I think we are morally obligated to give them a chance." I raised the question, what is adequate relief? I read from the text of the NRA document which sounded reasonable but was never realized. (It built permanently into our society a humiliating process of social agencies and social work, however.) I announced, "Anything less than adequate relief cannot be long tolerated. We cannot long save taxes at the expense of less than minimum standards of living...." A second step was work relief, long associated with alms programs. People do not want make-work but real work. Self-help programs were better, but under the circumstances can help only a few.

"Men must be economically secure on the basis of regular and creative employment," I read. "This can be done only through a planned and cooperative institution affecting all of the nation's resources and the welfare of every citizen." I stopped in the text after the words, "Because he anointed me to preach good tidings to the poor." I added, "What are good tidings to the poor? Certainly more than annual campaigns for relief and for Thanksgiving baskets and soup lines. What is really good news to the poor in this hour as we face the problem of relief?" No less than an adequate annual income.

Bishop Rice

There was a character in Denver popularly known as Bishop Rice. He had been a minister and had become disillusioned with the church. He appointed himself bishop and organized his own church, naming it the Liberal Church. His purpose was to reveal the hypocrisy of the church and if possible to destroy it. His meeting place was in an alley room back of Larimer Street near the old Windsor Hotel, the Skid Row of Denver. He catered to the down-and-out and many businessmen believed he did much good. He openly announced that he served beer and sandwiches following his church services, which were not regularly scheduled. He ordained ministers and appointed bishops and cardinals for a price and issued the proper certifications. He often elaborated on his legislative program on his church stationery and in pamphlets with ecclesiastical authority. He had his committees help the unemployed, promote gambling and support the liquor traffic.

I was chaplain in the legislature at that time and observed that the gambling and liquor lobbyists made good use of what seemed to be communications from a legitimate source. Rice received considerable financial contributions from business elements in the community. His family lived well in a good neighborhood. At the time of the Mooney-Billings trial in California, the bishop boarded a train dressed in sack cloth and carried a suitcase filled with ashes which he sprinkled on his head. I understand that the railroad conductor forced him from the train in Salt Lake City.

I was inclined to believe his motives were sincere and that he had convictions about social problems and a great concern for the deprived and underprivileged. He decried the cowardice of the churches to accept any part of the responsibility.

One of his parishioners died in the squalor of a skid row room of starvation. Bishop Rice announced that the funeral service would be publicly held in Civic Center, a spacious park across the street from the new city hall and one block north of Grace Church. His announced purpose was to give the public an opportunity to know the truth about starvation in Denver and to charge all public officials with neglect of their duties. The mayor and other public officials were given summons to be present. He invited them on his personal stationery by the authority of Bishop Rice and God.

The funeral procession consisted of an ancient hearse owned by a struggling alcoholic mortician, and several hundred followers who walked the two miles behind the hearse. The police prevented the gathering from taking place, which added to an accumulating resentment and protests against the police for interference with the rights of free speech and assembly. (I had not heard about the proposed plans and probably would have advised the authorities to allow the service. This was an unusual proposal, but Civic Center had been used for many other types of meetings. There was no law denying its use for a funeral.)

Bishop Rice was undaunted and led the procession to Grace Church, where he requested the use of the church for the funeral service, which was granted. The service consisted of a number of rabble-rousing speeches about unemployment, relief, starvation and the neglect and abuse by public officials. No public official was on hand. Bishop Rice notified city hall that the services would continue until someone representing the city viewed the remains—which had been prepared to look its worst—an emaciated corpse fully exposed except for ragged pants and a shirt. I called the mayor and asked him to send someone so that the ordeal could be concluded. He sent a social worker, who was immediately asked to show his proper respect by making a speech.

The service was scheduled for civic center at 10:00 a.m. and was concluded about 1:30. The procession took its weird and dismal journey down the street, with the mourners dispersing along the way until after a few blocks the hearse proceded alone with the tall, thin mortician and the robust minister in the seat. It was said that the minister got out when the show was over. The mortician drove alone to Potters' Field where the corpse was deposited without a committal service.

New Year's Eve, 1933

It was a hard Christmas season. I was physically, emotionally, and spiritually exhausted, burdened with grief as I thought of people's needs. Our Christmas services and programs, attended by over 1,600 persons, helped a little. I was aghast at our failure with the General Assembly, but no one talked about it as we shared a holiday.

The bishop had instituted a tradition of having a New Year's Communion Service for his ministers to provide a spiritual uplift for the New Year, but I was more concerned with an uplift for thousands of disappointed men and women. I was conscious of the little boy who had starved to death, the children who had collapsed from hunger, and fathers and mothers stretching every morsel to keep their families alive. I foolishly (as it turned out to be) went to my bishop and with tears unburdened my thoughts and soul. I requested that the Communion service be dedicated to the needs of the unemployed and their families and prayers offered for the enlightenment of Christians, so we might join with the anguished prayers of those who were suffering.

My request was ignored. The bishop explained that the service was for the purpose of creating peace and goodwill and he didn't want anything controversial injected into the service. I was amazed at his lack of feeling for what was transpiring in the dark, cold world outside his domain. I sat through the service watching the priestly worshippers file from the pews to the chancel and back to their seats. I was offended at the eating of the body and drinking the blood of Jesus. I remained in my pew throughout the service.

Winter of 1933-34

The winter of 1933-34 drove people to desperation—they lived in a vacuum of suffering and fear. No revolutionary movement gave leadership or direction. There were many splinter groups and more would emerge. Thousands of people would appear to be members, but they were not going anywhere. This may have been one of the most tragic years in our history, when people who supposedly lived in a democracy had no representation and no place to direct their grievances. The demonstrations and demands of the unemployed were primarily spontaneous. The Communist Party was caught off guard and except for being an irritant in the body politic, played a minor role. The dangerous elements in our society were those who might have given decisive action but were themselves afraid and appeared indifferent. It was clear that for a third of the people the system had failed, but no one had the courage to admit it.

The unemployed were unhappy, some hostile and many proposing violence. We had many mass meetings in Grace Church to help think through the dilemma of the times and come up with constructive ideas on what could be done. Our positive stance was the Unemployed Co-operative and a community-wide organization, the National Alliance. We sought the cooperation of public and private agencies and the legislature in behalf of immediate help and adequate plans for the future. The unemployed, who met with grim opposition on the part of officials and police, were feared as radicals who had to be observed and controlled. For the most part they were not radical or revolutionary, but people caught in a holocaust of economic failure and ignorance.

Some of the best-intentioned persons felt that the unemployed would remain anonymous until they took matters into their own hands by using violence to frighten society into doing something. This kind of talk sounded logical to many who were out of work. I recall a meeting in which a well-intentioned social worker felt that this was the only weapon. She felt the problems could be dramatized by taking over grocery stores. All I could see in such proposals was that helpless people would be shot. The police were already alerted. The social worker got a big hand. I then suggested that if this was what they wanted to do, that they wait until the social workers themselves were willing to lead the fight—even then it would be one-sided. The unemployed in our part of the town restrained themselves.

We had a school children's luncheon prepared by unemployed mothers. The next step was a lunch for the unorganized unemployed. The Bakers' Union began a noonday meal for their unemployed members. Food was provided in the nursery for children of employed mothers and some who came from homes of the unemployed. Except for the nursery, those who came to eat—many of them, not all—brought paper with them and wrapped as much as they could in the paper and took it out with them to feed someone at home.

We have heard, "They get along somehow." The answer is, "They don't get along at all—except get sick and die—unless some way is found to continue living." The way it was done was disgraceful and shameful while at the same time it was noble and sacrificial.

We met with groups of unemployed and discussed every possible method of survival. Men scounged the railroad tracks and yards for bits of coal, and sometimes the yard guards would walk away or look the other way so the men could fill their sacks. Butchers supplied us with immense amounts of bones, and sometimes neglected to cut away all the meat. Milkmen delivered all their skim milk and sometimes quarts of whole milk for the children. A foundation supplied us with three hundred quarts of milk a day. (Skim milk had no value in those days. It was called "ditch milk.")

I spent sleepless nights thinking of things to do. Many unemployed groups all over the city and in neighboring towns and cities called me to discuss what could be done, and most of these meetings extended far into the night. One night an idea hit me and the next day I went to see an acquaintance who operated a stable. I asked him if he would charge me for a ton of oats. He was surprised and said, "I didn't know you were interested in horses." I told him we would package the oats for breakfast food. He responded, "That's for horses. Hell, if that is what you want, I'll give you the damn oats and deliver them." Which he did. The oats were packaged and soon disappeared as people lined up to get them. There were many puns about human beings eating oats. One man said, "We ain't humans no more—we're animals."

In those days, dog food was pure horsemeat and sold mostly in packages. There was also canned dog food that was pure horsemeat. The grocery stores found it difficult to keep up with the demand. One grocery man remarked to me, "There sure must be a lot of dogs in this neighborhood, poor as it is." I pointed out that for the time being it was human food.

Poor people turned to using kerosene lamps which could be picked up cheaply in second-hand stores. One dealer found that he had eleven lamps tucked away, and gave them to me. He had never expected to sell them anyway.

Unemployed men cut down trees designated by the city. One farmer gave us a cow and another a pig, which they allowed to be butchered on their premises. One old farmer let us use his chicken farm to raise chickens and eggs. Some unemployed searched the garbage cans of the more affluent people living a few blocks from the church. Rabbit hunters left thousands of rabbits in the courtyard of the church and Center which were often picked up before daylight. We repaired our own shoes, sewed and repaired our own clothing, and gave ourselves haircuts. The women had their own beauty parlor and sewing room. We received hundreds of pairs of discarded shoes from the military and an abundance of bean sprouts from American Japanese as well as other foodstuffs from the Farmers' Market and special donations.

We had our own social service and employment office which made thousands of referrals to other agencies and to those who had odd jobs to give out. We had procured an old truck we repaired and used to haul all manner of things to the Center. The potato project was a bonanza. Friends would stop me on the streets and donate a few dollars to keep us going.

The governor called a special session of the legislature to get action by Christmas. This gave us hope and we looked for help by Christmas, but the legislature adjourned and went home for the holiday without an enabling act. The legislature would reconvene on January sixth. It was winter and our resources were dwindling.

Tempers flared and hard words were spoken. One thing that had plagued the unemployed throughout the ordeals was that we were always under surveillance by policemen and plainclothes men. This was demeaning. The unemployed felt that they had a right to go about their honest business like other people. Surveillance increased when the legislature went home for Christmas. There were more meetings—a few in vacant lots—to discuss what could now be done. I was never aware of the presence of any organized revolutionary organization. There were splinter groups, incapable of any significant action, that scorned any group concerned with palliatives. Violence could have broken out if some hotheads had prevailed and perhaps they had exchanges with certain authorities, but almost anyone could understand why. I was in an open field meeting early in January when three policemen shot over our heads and we were ordered to disperse. We remained silent and I went out to talk to the police and they walked away. Nothing else happened. We went about our business, part of which was to meet on the Capitol steps when the legislature reconvened. We passed the word around to councils of the unemployed, labor unions and others. I notified the governor what we planned to do.

The Governor

The press made it seem I was attacking the governor for playing politics with human suffering. I liked Governor Johnson and we were friends. He wanted to do the right thing, but had difficulty rising above the level of the politicians with whom he had to work.

I received a call from the governor's office Monday morning following a sermon entitled "Playing Politics with Human Suffering" and was told that the governor wanted to see me right away. After some comments about the weather Johnson said, "I understand that you had something to say about my playing politics with the relief problem, which I wish to deny. You know me better than that."

Fortunately I had a copy of my sermon, which he read and then said, "I agree with everything in that sermon, but some people have the idea that you were after my hide."

I asked him to come to the church Sunday morning and make a rebuttal. He couldn't come the next Sunday but agreed to come the following Sunday, October 3, 1933, to speak on Colorado's plan to end human suffering.

He was not in my pulpit to refute anything I had said, he explained, but to agree; he hoped we could work together to end some of the suffering. "It is not politics, but red tape, the inevitable by product of a government honeycombed with bureaus, that is responsible for the delay in moving forward the state's program to relieve human suffering.... We are living in a democracy, and the more democracy we have, the more red tape there seems to be. Russia has its Stalin, Germany its Hitler, Italy its Mussolini, the United States its NRA—all sailing uncharted seas. For the first time in history the government has been forced to assume responsibility for relieving human distress. . . .

"A greater need exists today. The legislature met for one hundred days and did nothing. Washington read the riot act to us. An extra session was called. All taxes are unpopular.

"I am not here to defend the UR tax on automobilists. We had to find a way of raising money with which to match federal grants. Wealthy people, people with jobs, own most of the automobiles."

Looking into the future, Governor Johnson said, "We who are in authority know we are sitting on a keg of dynamite which may explode any minute. . . . The thing crashed down on us suddenly. We were unprepared. . . .

"In spite of vast sums spent to relieve distress, we are one-fourth million dollars in the red and the federal government, through its relief administrator, Harry L. Hopkins, has shut off funds.

". . . Colorado automobile owners feel they have been placed under a grave injustice by being made to carry the relief load. . . ."

He closed his remarks with praise for the self-help program inaugurated by Grace Community Church and promised his full support.

The UR tax on automobiles was declared unconstitutional, so the struggle went on into the next year. Some proposed a graduated income tax, but the legislature came up with a sales tax. This meant that the poor received two per cent less than their already inadequate support. The legislative dam finally broke in January, and Washington began to provide money for the unemployed in Colorado.

Starvation 1936

The Depression dragged on for six long years. Agencies developed to assist the unemployed continued to try, inadequately, to relieve the problems of millions of good people. It was not because of a lack of money, food and other resources. It was a period of hunger and starvation in the midst of plenty. There should have been enough for everybody. Great piles of oranges were destroyed in California. Fruit rotted in the orchards and food went unattended on the farms. The Grace Co-operative salvaged a small amount, but there was no universal program of salvage and distribution. People found it painful to admit basic facts about our economic life—that it was the system that had failed, not the people.

There was a stalemate in understanding or wanting to understand. The Depression was no respecter of persons. The more fortunate froze in their tracks, held on to what they had, and insulated themselves against the facts. There were those who continued to profit, and some even prospered. Grace Church and Center tried to reach out to the public and to responsible citizens, exposing the inadequacies of the system and the shortcomings of both private and public agencies responsible for helping human beings. Society, represented by its government, did not come up with an adequate program to rectify its weaknesses. It turned instead to the alternative of war. There were piecemeal programs, temporarily and inadequately supported. The process was degrading to the recipients and the public that gave it.

We had a public meeting in our forum, a mock court hearing on the conditions of people on relief rolls. It was a trial in which members of my church were arrested and brought to trial for the criminal offense of needing assistance. The topic was "Is There Starvation in Denver?" The church was packed with quite a few officials and businessmen. A stenographer made a transcript of the hearing, which was reprinted and sent to thousands of persons. I was the prosecutor and the congregation was the jury.

Here's how *The Rocky Mountain Churchman* reported on this program:

IS THERE STARVATION IN DENVER?

Can People Live on $7.00 Per Month Per Person?

This statement is a stenographic report of a Public Hearing on relief, held in Grace Church, Sunday evening, January 19, 1936. We hope you will take time to read it. These people, with one exception, are members of Grace Church. They are good people. Each one represents a type of need for which there is little sympathy from the Public as a whole.

Report of Meeting on Relief, Held at Grace Church on Sunday Night, January 19

Testimony of Mr. V. (age 61)

Rev. W.: Mr. V. has been a member of Grace Church for a good many years. How many years?

Mr. V.: About sixteen.

Rev. W.: What is your business, Mr. V.?

Mr. V.: Well, I have been a carpenter and a transfer man for a number of years—occupations that I cannot now carry out due to the condition of my health.

Rev. W.: When did you go on relief for the first time?

Mr. V.: Somewhere the last of May when I left the hospital. The Head Nurse at the Medical Center saw that I got the relief in May, 1935.

Rev. W.: What was the reason?

Mr. V.: My physical condition and not having funds and unable to work.

Rev. W.: Have you been pronounced as unemployable?

Mr. V.: Yes.

Rev. W.: How long were you in the hospital?

Mr. V.: Seven weeks; five weeks the one time with diabetes; out three weeks and went back again for high blood pressure.

Rev. W.: Have you owned property in the City of Denver?

Mr. V.: Yes.

Rev. W.: Have you paid taxes?

Mr. V.: I have in times gone by. In the last five years I have lost everything—a home and one-half section of land.

Rev. W.: Well now, about this being in the hospital seven weeks. As I understand, it takes $18.00 a week to keep a man in the hospital. What have you been receiving on relief?

Mr. V.: When I first went to the hospital I was receiving $25.50 a month. That included transportation, all the medicine I had to buy. A 400 unit of insulin costs $1.50. The last cost $1.25. It is very expensive and very powerful medicine which I must inject.

Rev. W.: Was that $25.00 enough to cover all your needs?

Mr. V.: No, it didn't cover all my needs, but I never said a word.

Rev. W.: What is your present relief allowance?

Mr. V.: A little less than half. The last check was for $5.82. I took it over to Mr. Beasley. Beasley said he didn't see how in the h—— I could live on that.

Rev. W.: $5.82 for two weeks. What do you have to pay out of it?

Mr. V.: My room at $6.00 a month.

Rev. W.: You get a room for $6.00?

Mr. V.: It is a nice room for a bad neighborhood on lower Curtis. That is what I have been paying all along. That is what the relief is supposed to allow me, $6.00.

Rev. W.: Do you live in this neighborhood by choice?

Mr. V.: No. People on relief just have to make the best of it. Before my wife died I lived in East Denver, north of City Park. I guess a man my age can live in such a neighborhood and get by. I used to think where a person lived was important, but none of these things count much now. At least relief workers don't seem to think so.

Rev. W.: When you left the hospital, did they give you some directions?

Mr. V.: Yes.

Rev. W.: What were they?

Mr. V.: A diet.

Rev. W.: Have you followed this diet?

Mr. V.: As nearly as I could.

Rev. W.: Are you following it now?

Mr. V.: I can't on what I'm getting, although I try. My life depends on it. Things go black in front of my eyes when I don't. I don't feel well tonight. If they don't help me I'll soon be back in the hospital.

Rev. W.: He says that the hospital has given him a diet to follow, but that he can't with the money he is getting. It is a very sensible diet including eggs, milk and vegetables, and some meat. How many steaks did you buy last week?

Mr. V.: None.

Rev. W.: A point worth observing is the fact that the city pays $18.00 or more a week per person to rehabilitate hundreds of people, of whom Mr. V. is one example. The hospital puts them on their feet and gives them careful instructions which, if followed, will maintain health. Relief allowances are so low that healthy people soon break down. This condition is a paradox opposed to common sense. The city could actually save thousands of dollars in hospital expense by giving more adequate relief. It is certain that Mr. V. will soon be back in the hospital on his present relief budget. Which is better? To pay $80.00 in hospital expenses or, say, $30.00 in relief?

Mr. V.: I don't want to seem ungrateful or unfair. They just got me a brand new set of teeth. They must be worth $30.00.

Testinony of Mrs. R.:

Rev. W.: Mrs. R. has lived in Denver since she was five years old. I might say that Mrs. R.'s folks have been prominent in business circles in Denver and have seen more fortunate days. Mrs. R. is the survivor of a substantial family in the city of Denver. When did you go on relief, Mrs. R.?

Mrs. R.: November, 1933.

Rev. W.: Why was it necessary for you to go on relief then?

Mrs. R.: I lost my property and lost my husband.

Rev. W.: Did you save anything?

Mrs. R.: No.

Rev. W.: Mrs. R. had gotten down to her last 13 cents before seeking relief. Didn't you even save out funeral expenses?

Mrs. R.: No. Didn't save out anything, and this worries me greatly.

Rev. W.: What is your present relief allowance?

Mrs. R.: The last month the checks were $6.60; the very last one $6.37 for two weeks.

Rev. W.: What is your monthly rental?

Mrs. R.: $10.00 a month.

Rev. W.: $12.74 is your allowance per month. Out of that you must pay $10.00 for rent? Don't you think that is too much for rent?

Mrs. R.: I don't think so. It includes heat and light, and a woman of my background just can't live in a poorer neighborhood.

Rev. W.: She lives in a back room on the upper floor of an old house on Cherokee Street. That leaves you $2.74 a month for food and clothes and everything else. Can you get by on that?

Mrs. R.: No. How can I?

Rev. W.: Can it be done? (To audience)

Audience: No.

Rev. W.: Have you ever been really hungry?

Mrs. R.: Yes, and I don't need much to eat, either.

Rev. W.: I happen to know that Mrs. R. received $5.00 as a Christmas gift with which she hoped to buy a much needed pair of shoes. Did you buy them?

Mrs. R.: No, when my relief was cut I had to spend it for food.

Rev. W.: Mrs. R. began her life in this neighborhood, moved with the people who moved out of this neighborhood into the better sections of the city. She is back to spend as best she can the declining years of her life. I think that is all I need to ask. She has no relatives and so she is on her own and at the mercy of the responsibility of our city.

Testimony of Mrs. M. (Landlady)

Rev. W.: Do you happen to be a landlady, Mrs. M.?

Mrs. M.: Yes.

Rev. W.: What is your address?

Mrs. M.: 1152 Bannock.
Rev. W.: Are you one of these hard-boiled landladies?
Mrs. M.: I don't think so.
Rev. W.: I would like to know if you have found people on relief refuse to pay their bills?
Mrs. M.: No.
Rev. W.: Do you infer that people on relief would like to pay their just debts?
Mrs. M.: Yes, I do.
Rev. W.: Have you lost any money in rentals to relief clients?
Mrs. M.: Yes, I have. $25.00 in the last month.
Rev. W.: Do you expect to get it?
Mrs. M.: No.
Rev. W.: Were these people chiselers in your opinion?
Mrs. M.: No. It wasn't their fault they could not pay.
Rev. W.: Are they unemployables?
Mrs. M.: Yes. Two very fine elderly people. The lady is sickly. Both were worried to death.
Rev. W.: What are you doing about it?
Mrs. M.: I had to have them evicted.
Rev. W.: That wasn't very nice.
Mrs. M.: It wasn't nice, but I have to pay my rent and depend upon our tenants to make a home for us. When we don't receive our rent, we can't pay ours. These folks couldn't pay their rent. They owed one and one-half month's rent when asked to move. They were desirable tenants, but the relief didn't allow them enough to pay the rent. It was only $15.00 a month. They really cried when they left. They knew my circumstances as well as I knew their circumstances, and were sorry to go. They have been back to see me several times since they left. They are no better off now and their budget is less.

Testimony of Mrs. W. (Grocer)

Rev. W.: Mrs. W. is sincerely loved in this neighborhood. She and her husband run a little grocery store on Fox Street. Have you lost any money, Mrs. W.? Do people owe you money at the present time?
Mrs. W.: Oh, yes.
Rev. W.: A lot of money?
Mrs. W.: I would call it quite a lot in these times. My husband and I depend on what little business we have for our living.
Rev. W.: Did you tell me that people on relief owe you as much as $600.00?
Mrs. W.: Yes, that is putting it small. We have lost much more in the last four years.
Rev. W.: Do you expect to get much of it back?
Mrs. W.: Not unless conditions change. I believe if conditions would change and these people were getting more money, they would eventually pay it.

Rev. W.: Do you mean to tell me people still aim to pay their bills?

Mrs. W.: Many of them do. They are the good people who have always lived here. They are mostly good citizens and good workers.

Rev. W.: I have heard it said that they are deadbeats. You don't believe that?

Mrs. W.: Not all of them, no.

Rev. W.: Can you think of people on relief who have held up their morale and who usually try to meet their obligations?

Mrs. W.: Oh, yes, I recall many who have; some few have given up hope and now simply don't care. But everyone isn't like that, and you can't blame them.

Testimony of Mrs. L.

Rev. W.: Mrs. L. has had charge of the distribution of clothing for Grace Church and she knows where to put them and knows how to use them. How many people are in your home, Mrs. L.?

Mrs. L.: Six. Our oldest girl, who is in high school, is working and mostly takes care of herself.

Rev. W.: What is your present budget?

Mrs. L.: The last month was for $42.00.

Rev. W.: That is an average of $7.00 per month per person. Do you mind if I get a little personal?

Mrs. L.: I don't mind. I think Rev. Wahlberg knows my family.

Rev. W.: I don't know how to begin, Mrs. L. I do know your story. Have your children been sick because of the lack of food?

Mrs. L.: Yes, we had, in eleven months, eight cases of scarlet fever, not counting colds and headaches. The two girls had scarlet fever very bad the second time, and we had to have relief to help us out. We fought to keep off relief—sold candy and papers and did anything we could to keep from asking for relief. Finally we had to ask for help.

Rev. W.: And finally you just had to ask for relief?

Mrs. L.: That was a year ago last August.

Rev. W.: Up until that time you had gotten along by selling candy, etc. Anything else?

Mrs. L.: We got relief through the Co-operative of the Grace Church when it was first organized, and later they gave me pillows, pillow tops and clothes.

Rev. W.: At the present time do you pay any rent?

Mrs. L.: $15.00 for rent and $1.00 for lights.

Rev. W.: How much do you pay for coal and wood in a month?

Mrs. L.: At the very lowest, $7.00. We can't make it reach on less.

Rev. W.: That leaves $19.00. Does that take care of everything for five people for a month?

Mrs. L.: There are kind friends who have helped so that we have gotten along, but that does not buy any clothes whatsoever.

Rev. W.: What do you have to eat?

Mrs. L.: Plenty of beans. One meal is beans and soup and then some more beans. Then sometimes these kind friends bring in some vegetables. We usually cook enough at one time for several days to save fuel. We have very little meat or milk and never such things as pie or dessert.

Rev. W.: Do you buy your clothes?

Mrs. L.: No sir, I haven't had a boughten garment for so long that I can't remember when.

Rev. W.: Haven't you bought a new dress, Mrs. L.?

Mrs. L.: No sir, those things come from where my daughter works at Grace Church. That is where my clothes come from. My children's and my husband's, too.

Rev. W.: Has your husband done anything about the Depression?

Mrs. L.: Well, he is now in a position that, if he gets enough work, he can support his family by the trade he has learned through the Grace Center Co-op.

Rev. W.: What trade is that?

Mrs. L.: Shoe repairing.

Rev. W.: Is he making a go of it?

Mrs. L.: Yes, he is. He started out in the shoe repairing after we had the scarlet fever. Before that he had been handling the fruits and vegetables that came through the Grace Church Relief, and rather than sit down and do nothing, he started in the shoe work and has been at it ever since.

Rev. W.: The L. family is a splendid example of courage and self-respect. Previous to the Depression, Mr. L. had a steady job for sixteen years with a firm that has since failed.

Testimony of Mr. C.

Rev. W.: Mr. C., have you ever been on relief?

Mr. C.: No, sir.

Rev. W.: Are you married?

Mr. C.: Yes, I have a wife. She isn't well.

Rev. W.: Do you love her?

Mr. C.: 'Course I do!

Rev. W.: What is your trouble?

Mr. C.: My trouble is that I can't get back to work because I hadn't been on relief.

Rev. W.: Where could you get a job if you had been on relief?

Mr. C.: Well, I don't know that.

Rev. W.: You have a feeling if you had been on relief you could get a job?

Mr. C.: Well, yes.

Rev. W.: P.W.A.?

Mr. C.: Yes.

Rev. W.: Can't you get relief? Have you tried?

Mr. C.: Yes. No use—they say they are not putting it out.

Rev. W.: Do you know the reason why?

Mr. C.: No. I have ideas.

Rev. W.: How are you getting along in the meantime?

Mr. C.: I have a few friends who help.

Rev. W.: Are you paying your rent?

Mr. C.: Haven't paid any rent since December. Paid up to December.
Rev. W.: Evidently, you are living with a good landlord?
Mr. C.: I believe so. He hasn't said anything yet.
Rev. W.: Have you ever been in the hole before in your life?
Mr. C.: Yes.
Rev. W.: Did you get caught up?
Mr. C.: Yes.
Rev. W.: Paid your bills?
Mr. C.: Yes. I also owe a grocery bill right now.
Rev. W.: How do you expect to pay?
Mr.C.: If I ever get work I intend to go back and pay it.
Rev. W.: The Depression has had its regular monthly toll. Each month a new group has finally exhausted its resources and as a last resort has asked for help. These last months we have most severely penalized those who have held out the longest. That doesn't make sense.

Testimony of Mr. B. (One child)

Rev. W.: Mr. B. is a member of this church and a respected citizen. You have seen better circumstances, have you not, Mr. B.?
Mr. B.: Yes, sir. I have mostly had good positions. Part of the time in business for myself.
Rev. W.: What do you think is the reason for your wife's being in the hospital?
Mr. B.: Worry over economic conditions. That is all.
Rev. W.: Have you really been up against it?
Mr. B.: Pretty tough.
Rev. W.: Have you had enough to eat?
Mr. B.: We lived for fifteen days on $2.75. We had a little bread, oatmeal and rice for a few days. The bread and rice gave out at the end of fourteen days, and we had a cup of oatmeal.
Rev. W.: You attribute the reason for your wife being in the hospital to the economic situation?
Mr. B.: Yes.

Testimony of Mrs. K. (Two children)

Rev. W.: Mrs. K. is a type for which the city as a whole has no responsibility. She is a transient. How long ago did you come to Denver?
Mrs. K.: Nineteen months ago.
Rev. W.: Why did you come to Denver?
Mrs. K.: Because of my husband's health. He has since passed away.
Rev. W.: Why can't you go back from where you came?
Mrs. K.: Well, Dr. Beggs says I shouldn't.
Rev. W.: Have you been cared for at all during this period?
Mrs. K.: I was at Sands House (TB Sanitarium) for four months.
Rev. W.: Has any public agency given you any relief?
Mrs. K.: The Transient Relief. That stopped in October.
Rev. W.: How have you gotten along?
Mrs. K.: My sister-in-law sent me a little, and I have made a little.

Rev. W.: In the meantime have you been in need?

Mrs. K.: Well, Mrs. W. has let me have groceries, and the church has supplied me with vegetables.

Rev. W.: Have you and your babies been hungry?

Mrs. K.: Yes, Mr. Wahlberg, but I don't like to think about that.

Rev. W.: Did you move out of one house into another?

Mrs. K.: Yes.

Rev. W.: You just won't go back to Minnesota?

Mrs. K.: No.

Rev. W.: Isn't it simpler to go back home?

Mrs. K.: Well, no. My mother has since died; the family has broken up and there is no home now in Minnesota.

Rev. W.: Your husband died here and you believe you would like to settle here.

Mrs. K.: Yes, and one of my babies died here.

Rev. W.: You have been told by the doctor to stay here?

Mrs. K.: Yes.

Rev. W.: You would like to work out your future here?

Mrs. K.: Yes. Also Billy has a spot on his lung and he should stay here.

Rev. W.: Here is her only hope if she is going to have life for her two babies. Mrs. K. is a talented woman; among other things, she is painting pictures and selling them. There is something fine in her as we can all see. Have they allowed your babies to be sick without help?

Mrs. K.: Dr. Beggs said I could bring them to the Clinic. I have been refused help by local agencies. I am glad my children haven't been sick this winter.

Rev. W.: When we think of transients, we think of people with long whiskers and dirty. Many are refined, whose homes have been broken up and who have good reasons for remaining where they are. Does America intend to perpetuate a class of untouchables? What are we going to do with Mrs. K. and her babies? Just kick them out? In this case the government, for a year and one half, was a party to helping Mrs. K. adjust herself to Denver, and then overnight reversed its policy. Human thought patterns are not as quickly or as easily broken. As long as people are human they cannot be swept away as we sweep rubbish from one place to another.

There Was No Revolution in Colorado

It is a long distance from a revolution to a visitation of concerned citizens upon their representatives in the legislature. This is a right of all citizens and is guaranteed by the Constitution. The idea to appear on the Capitol steps emerged from a meeting of the unemployed and I was asked to be their representative. I was careful to notify the governor about our plans, and we received permission for the gathering—though unnecessary—as the governor explained, "It was their right." Our right to meet was never questioned and there was no coercion from any authority. U.S. Congressman Wayne N. Aspinall, not retired and then a state legislator, was a close friend of mine and I relied on him for advice. He was present when we urged the governor to speak to the crowd. He described the event as "a visitation by some hungry, dissatisfied people following their right of petition." There may have been about 5,000 persons in the crowd.

I don't know how or what brought Frank Clay Cross into the picture. His mother was a member of our church and was a highly intelligent and concerned person. Cross may have been visiting her at the time. He made himself known to me before he left Denver but did not discuss the article he wrote with me. He congratulated me on the role that I had played.

He forcefully and negatively described the Twiddling Twenty-ninth, which is a term he did not coin. This session was known as such throughout Colorado. I had a higher appreciation of most of these legislators than he did. I worked with them every day throughout the longest session in the history of Colorado. Many of them were sorely unprepared for the problems they confronted. They felt that individualism was going down the drain and that they might create a class of second-rate people who would intentionally depend on the state for support. They were uninformed as to the nature of our society or what was happening to our economic system. Rather they blamed individuals for what was happening and could not comprehend that our system had failed for some 30 percent of the people through no fault of their own. They constantly pointed to themselves as examples of what people could do if they were willing to work and follow the rules. There were some among them that did fail and suffered the ills of the unemployed. One of them, to my knowledge, committed suicide.

I had little respect for many of the lobbyists who used every legal and unfair practice to influence the legislators—especially the "loan sharks." I was gathering information from the poor as to their debts and what they owed the loan sharks. One man couldn't go through Christmas without buying his children some Christmas joys and toys. He borrowed five dollars and had to pay twenty-five cents a week for over six months or be threatened with foreclosure. I told him to forget it and refer the shark to me—which he did, and nothing happened. We organized a committee and were successful in getting a reasonable law passed—with the help of the press throughout the state, interested citizens, and one of the finance companies that appreciated the rightness of our cause.

Mr. Cross wrote in *The Nation,* February 4, that on January 3, "the halls of the Capitol were thronged with people milling, shouting, hurling threats," and I had failed to guard against "Communist leaders" who had seized control of the mob and held a Communist meeting in the Senate chambers. He said, "A genuine Communist meeting followed—the first Communist meeting to be held under the dome of any capitol in the United States."

I wished that Mr. Cross had not used the word "mob." I was not aware of any activity on the part of Communists in or out of the Capitol building nor was anyone else as far as I could learn. The unemployed were gathered on the west-side steps of the Capitol—mostly waiting for the governor to appear. Some few may have been wandering around the halls as curious people would do on their first visit to the Capitol. Our committee made up of two congressmen and three unemployed had free access to the office of the governor where we discussed what should be said. We told the governor to say anything he thought should be said. We walked down the hall through the west doors where the speeches were made. The governor was warmly received all the way.

The Senate chambers are on the east side of the building and were none of our concern. Mr. Cross reported that the press did not say a thing about the Communist meeting in the Senate chambers. How could the press say anything if there was no meeting? I asked around after the article appeared. One senator said, "Yes, there were a few folks around as could be expected, but I saw no semblance of any kind of meeting." I talked with a leader of the Communists, William Deitrick, the owner of the Auditorium Book Store. He said that some of the demonstrators had entered the chambers and sat in the vacant chairs. Nothing much was done because there wasn't anyone to talk with, so they soon departed and joined the crowd gathered on the west side of the building where the action was.

I am asked in my correspondence: "Did Colorado Communists storm the state capitol in January 1934 and disrupt government?"

I don't know what Mr. Cross saw or what he thought he saw, but the answer from all the evidence that I possess is, no one stormed the state capitol or had a meeting of any kind except the one that was planned. There were no placards of any kind, largely because we hadn't thought about them and probably didn't have the money to prepare them. There were some catcalls while the crowd waited.

The governor made a short speech deploring the delays in action on behalf of the unemployed and was certain with the help of all present that action was on the way. His speech was roundly applauded. The governor then invited everybody to come inside, saying, "It is your building as well as mine. Fill up the galleries in the House of Representatives. I am sorry, but there probably won't be enough room for all of you."

A meeting was called in which House and Senate members were present. Speaker Twining did indeed stay calm. There were catcalls and jeers from the galleries as these people were finally confronted with the representatives. Why not? They were only expressing themselves as they had heard others do—including the general public. There was not a single instance of meanness. People returned to their homes as quietly as they had come, but with new hope. They had themselves participated in the process of government.

Another meeting was called for both Houses to listen to leaders in the community. Bishop Johnson of the Episcopal church was the last speaker. He concluded his remarks with, "If I were a swearing man, I would say it is a damn shame."

The Denver Labor College

The Denver Labor College was an institution of learning for many years. Newly organized workers had a deep hunger for learning, since many had been recruited from people who had little schooling. These centers of learning cropped up throughout the country, especially where there was union activity. The Denver school was under the auspices of the Denver Trades and Labor Assembly and encouraged its affiliates to send their members to the college and encouraged the unions to pay the enrollment fees, which were minimal.

Adult education in the school system gradually replaced the need for these schools—the one in Denver probably lasted the longest in the country. Courses were taught by experienced union leaders and by teachers from the public schools and the University of Denver. Classes were large and total enrollment would sometimes be as high as 400, meeting twice a week with a labor forum following classes on Monday evenings.

The courses were down-to-earth: American history, the trade union movement, labor law, English, public speaking, legislation, the union label and union support, writing, running a union, the rights of labor and subjects dealing with current problems and issues. I generally taught public speaking and for awhile was president. Teachers received no salary. As the new minister, I was eager to continue this program. The unemployed were invited to attend without paying the small tuition charge. We included a course in cooperatives and credit unions.

William Dietrick

I became acquainted with a number of persons who publicly acknowledged they were Communists. One of these was the aforementioned William Dietrick, who operated the Auditorium Book Store. He was a genuine idealist and had entertained the thought of becoming a Protestant minister if the church had accepted his passion for social justice, and if the church had been free of anti-Semitism. He was married to a Jew, as kind and compassionate as he. I always found "Bill" honest, sincere, and understanding. Bill ran for mayor in each campaign and participated in the Mayors' Night Program of the Denver Open Forum. He was kind and warm, without malice or deceit, and treated me honestly in every situation in which our paths crossed.

Communists on occasion embarrassed us by passing out literature and provoking dissension. One of them was a young man who was a walking library with a rack hung over his body filled with Communist pamphlets. He circulated along the sidewalk and the courtyard and even walked up and down the aisle during forum meetings. We dealt with the literature problem by providing a literature table open to all, to give away or sell. I explained this to the "walking library." He called me a Fascist and urged me to "call the cops." Pamphlets were thrust into the hands of my parishioners. I believed in pamphleteering, but I thought some Communists took advantage of us. I caled Bill, who understood the situation and we had no more trouble.

Mr. Dietrick called me on a Friday and sadly informed me that his best friend had died, and wondered if the funeral service could be held in the church. I hesitated a moment and wondered about the consequences. I assented. "Yes, Bill—sure, it's okay. When do you want the service and what do you want me to do?" He explained that he would have to talk to the wife and said that he would call me back. I thought about my uneasiness as I awaited the call. Why was I fearful? Death is a leveler. Did it make any difference that the deceased was a Communist? Why should I readily accept such calls from others and hesitate in this case? I felt foolish because after all, I was dealing with human beings.

Bill called me and said the widow wanted me to have charge of the service. She requested that a friend be allowed to say a few words and that her musician friends be allowed to play some appropriate musical numbers, classical rather than religious—favorites of her husband. I agreed. Bill added, "Perhaps you would rather not have the service. I can see where some people might not understand."

I asserted, "Well, you are right, there are people who don't appreciate these situations. However, I had a service for a Republican last week, and I am sure that God is just as willing for me to bury a Communist."

I quite forgot about it and turned to a busy day and didn't think about it again until Sunday afternoon. I thought about what a minister can say or read in a Communist service. I felt insecure and decided to visit the family—which was always my practice—why not this one? I met a gracious and fine woman of Spanish origin and her son. Her husband had been born in Greece and had a small restaurant. She talked about her love for her husband, enumerated his kindness and spoke tenderly of his devotion to his family. I turned to the purpose of my visit and said, "I understand that your husband was a Communist. I would like to have you tell me what you expect me to do." She asked, "What do you usually do? We are no different from other people." I explained that there was a funeral ritual with Scripture and prayers and that I often used passages of poetry. I pointed out that I sometimes made a few remarks about love, that sorrow is love so deep that it hurts—that this was an experience in love, that love transcends death—that we cannot lose what never dies, that love may be a clue to immortality.

She sobbed, "Why don't you say it? A Communist is human no different from other human beings." She explained that her husband was an idealist, a former member of the Greek Orthodox church, and that she had been a Roman Catholic. They had tried to attend other churches together but were disappointed in the churches' lack of concern for the needy and a reasonable faith for the problems of the day. She added, "You know, we have never renounced God."

She couldn't terminate her overflowingness as she continued, "I accept the evidences of God as revealed in the teachings of Jesus. I know that we hunger for spirituality. I am inspired in the love I shared with my husband and family and friends. Your remarks seem to encompass these feelings and perhaps in all of this, a finer fellowship with mankind and God."

I was shaken by her guileless faith. The service was attended by about eighty persons—probably the total membership of the Communist party in Denver. It was a religious service in which the few remarks by the party leader seemed to blend. The service in the cemetery was short, with the casket draped in red.

Some called me a fellow-traveler. Aren't we all?

Youth

A major problem were boys and girls who seemingly had no future. They were also problems to the police and the juvenile court. They became our keenest supporters and assets as we slowly built youth programs that received wide support.

The people in and out of Grace Church warned us about the "Alley Rats," a gang of boys in their early teens following the pattern of an older gang of boys who had gotten themselves into a great deal of trouble and notoriety. They were called the "Banana Peelers."

We went ahead with a recreation program which included a number of games played in the courtyard that was open to the street. One of the games was called tether ball, an arrangement of a six-foot pole set in a stand with a cord tied to the top end of the pole and a ball on the other end of the cord. I noticed that the Alley Rats were watching the action from across the street and I wondered if I would be around when they would come into the court and steal the outfit and run away with it. And so they did!

They pushed the boys aside who were playing and took the paddles, the stand and pole and ran down the street and up an alley about two blocks away. I ran between some houses and met them as they gathered in the alley. I grabbed two boys by their arms. We regained our composure and I asked if they knew how to play the game. They admitted that they did not, so I proceeded to teach them. I asked, "Do you like it?" They were enthusiastic in saying that they did. I said, "Okay, you can have it." This stopped them cold. The leader of the gang said, "But jees, we swiped it." I said, "I know you took it, but just the same, you can have it—it's yours."

I joined in the fun and the boys took me in. I asked them if they knew that we had a gymnasium. They said, "Sure, but we got kicked out." I was careful to suggest that it might be arranged so that they could play in the gym an hour or two a week. Nevertheless, after they got inside the gym, they acted as if I had given it to them for their own private use.

It wasn't long before the wrath of the parents and authorities was directed toward me. I called together a group of men to discuss the "Alley Rats." I was told, "You got them in—you get them out." One man was quite incensed and barked, "Who do you think you are—playing God to a bunch of ruffians? Those boys don't want help. They ought to be locked up for good." I explained that perhaps our usefulness as Christians depended upon what we were able to do for these boys. A young man by the name of John Harcourt agreed with me. He proposed that we organize these boys into a Boy Scout Troop and scouting would change them. He was wrong. It was the other way around. The boys changed scouting.

John agreed to be scout master. His patience lasted about two months. He said, "These boys aren't really bad. They are impossible!" I was harrassed beyond my flexibility and was ready to give up on the Alley Rats. It was in such a mood that I walked into the Center building one evening. I heard a crash and the scuffling of feet. I rushed down the hallway and into the room from which the noise was coming. It was the Alley Rats. One boy had thrown a chair through a window and just as I entered another boy threw a bottle of ink across the room, leaving a streak of black ink along the floor and two walls.

I grabbed this boy and yelled at him. I stopped for breath and discovered that he was using language that was far more colorful than mine. "Let go of me you —— —— ——! If you don't, I'll get my folks to beat up on you." I yelled louder and told the boy to "SHUT UP!" The other boys were amused. They had not seen the minister in such a role.

Now, when you start yelling at anyone and find that your words are unheeded, the logic of what you have started requires that you hit the object of your wrath. I slapped him. Fact is, I hit him hard enough to knock him down. He came up like a ball, raging and tearing at me. I stopped, because the logic of my behavior was dead wrong. The next step would be to kill him.

The situation was no longer amusing to the other boys. I was confronted with nearly twenty boys who were angered by an unfair fight. They were ready to fling themselves at me. I could think of nothing else to do but to walk out of the room, still holding on to the boy. We walked out of the building to the sidewalk. The others followed silently, ready to look out for the welfare of their gang member. The little boy at my side said, "Where in hell are you going?" I said almost without thinking, "We are going, just like you said, to see your folks and have them beat up on me."

It was about eight p.m. when we started walking. We walked up and down the street and the same way across the street. We walked in and out of alleys. The gang followed until they were satisfied that no harm would come to their pal. My companion stopped at 10:35 p.m. and asked, "Ain't you tired?" I told him that I was. He retorted, "Why in the hell don't you go home?" I restated my determination that he should take me to his home so that his folks could beat up on me. We resumed our walk at a slower pace. Then, at last, at 11:30 p.m. he stopped in front of an alley shack two short blocks from the church—all this time to walk two short blocks.

He said, "Here's where I live." I replied, "Okay, take me in." He pleaded, "They won't beat up on you—they'll beat up on me."

I was defeated. I was sorely tired and in the stillness of the night knew that violence of any kind would do no good. I hated to walk off without some understanding. The boy saved us both from humiliation. His eyes looked into my own eyes searching for something. He spoke softly and pleadingly, "Honest, mister, I got *good insides.* Honest I have."

Saying this made all the difference in the world for both of us. I put my arm around his thin body and he snuggled up to my side. We walked slowly back to the church and into my office where we sat down and looked at each other. I found that in his mind he had no reason to trust people of any kind— certainly not church folks who said bad things about him and his friends. "They called us Alley Rats, we didn't. I guess we got the idea that we wouldn't amount to much anyways." His father was out of work and was angry at everybody. He said, "Things aren't going good at home. They just beat up on me." He wondered what kind of a racket I was in. He said, "We ain't half as bad as people say we are. We just get blamed for everything. This makes us mad as hell at everybody. How would you feel?"

It was getting very late, although not later than most nights for this boy and his pals. Home was no place to go. Six people lived in two rooms so no one paid much attention as to who was in or out. We stopped talking. I said, "How about it, do you think I've got good insides?" He quickly responded, "Sure, mister." He took my hand in his and said, "Put 'er there. Do you think

I got good insides?" Then he was lost in thought. I waited. He turned to me and said, "What do you say we start the club of the good insides? I mean the Alley Rats. They are as good as anybody. Let's make them the club of the good insides." It was after two a.m. His folks weren't worrying about him, but my wife was concerned about me. I walked the boy home.

I have always believed that this was a turning point for Grace Center. This neighborhood at the time was the second worst delinquency area in the city. I received a letter seven years later from Captain Edmund C. Young of the juvenile department of the police department. It read, in part, "Dear Wallie: I don't know what has done it, but seven years ago the Grace Church neighborhood was the second worst delinquency area in the city. Today, it is the second best. I know that it is largely the work of your organization. Congratulations! Keep up the good work."

One of the most satisfying experiences is to grow up with a gang of boys, such as I did with a gang who became known as the Ramblers. The Ramblers earned an unsavory reputation in the neighborhood, but as the years passed gained a mature comradeship and a reputation for doing well that survives to this day. They seemingly aspired to nothing more than to accept each other and to stand by each other, and to live and let live as best they could. The Alley Rats had more or less dissolved in the activities of the Center, and some of them joined up with the Ramblers. They were teenagers of the Depression and were confronted with the problems of those years. Most people who knew about them predicted that they would turn out "bad." All except three have made good: as teachers, policemen, a deputy chief of police, salesmen, custodian, plumbers, musician, patrolmen, owner of a furniture store, railroad yard master, clerks, supervisor of a country club, bartenders, insurance agency owners and agents, cabinet maker, supervisor at Mountain States Telephone Company, supermarket manager, and a farmer. Of those who did not succeed, one became ill from rheumatic fever and suffered from brain damage, and the other two died of alcoholism.

One of them married our older daughter, while he was in the navy during the Second World War. I was serving with the United Nations Relief and Rehabilitation Administration in Greece at the time and he wrote me a letter for my consent. I replied that he would have to propose to Lois and if it was all right with her, it was okay with me. He completed his degree after the war. He was well established in his business and had an enviable reputation for his honesty and integrity, and was a good husband and father. He is typical of what happened to this teenage gang.

These boys, for the most part, had their problems. Some had hardly a place to stay—out all hours of the night. We analyzed over twenty of their families and found that most of them suffered from emotional and physical maladies. Some of the parents in these families had disappeared—in one case, both parents had fled. They could not buy sufficient food or clothing. It was difficult to pay for housing, so they lived as best they could—often in miserable, crowded and limited conditions. It is no wonder that these and other boys became attached to the Community Center. It was a place of security and to some the only home life they really knew. They were in and out of the place day and night. They played basketball, pool, ping-pong, and at times seemed to run the place. Some of them took advantage of the children's luncheon. They would break into the buildings at night and sleep, either on the cushioned pews of the church or on the mats in the children's day school for working mothers. They shied away from church services and activities. It is strange that so many of them are now devoted church members.

There were fifty-three Ramblers when the Senior and Junior Ramblers somehow merged. They chose their name because early in my career I took the pioneer members into the mountains for a day. They rambled away and I didn't see them except for lunch and after nightfall. Every member had to earn his place in the gang by committing some daring act against society to prove his worth and obligation to the gang. They did not respond to instruction or allow the gang to be structured. Gang leaders emerged without an election. They would not inform on each other. They were not always together, but whatever anyone did by himself or with a few others was anonymous. They learned responsibility as a group. They didn't trust anyone outside of the group. If one person did something wrong there was no way he could be tracked down through anyone in the gang.

There were perilous days when we despaired about these boys. Our only inroad was to be accepted and trusted by them. We had to meet their standards of acceptance. They resented most being blamed for everything. The police would sometimes pick up one or more of these boys and pin whatever happened on them. This gave the gang a feeling of self-righteousness which was hard to get around. It took time and many incidents, but at last, when they thought that we could be trusted, John Moore, the Center director, and I became members of the gang. We didn't know exactly when this happened, but it did.

Some years later, when all of these boys were in military service and they learned about military chaplains, they took for granted that I was their Rambler chaplain.

We initiated the concept of *group responsibility*. We never tracked down an individual. We left the responsibilities up to the gang and no single name was ever mentioned. They gradually accepted the idea and policed themselves and we had no more trouble. They went so far as to control the Junior Ramblers, and were far more severe in their treatment of them than we would have been.

The boys petitioned us to provide them with a room of their own. We gave them a room on the third floor on the alley side of the Center building. One condition was that it would be solely their own room and no one but a Rambler would have keys to the room. I knew that they were busy decorating, but it was quite a time before I was allowed entry. I was surprised at its appearance: it had been painted a bright red, white, and blue, and furnished with their prize possessions and pictures. It was, for as long as it was needed, their very own home and escape from the world.

A few of the boys belonged to parents who were sufficiently mature to survive the hard years of the thirties. Part of them belonged to the Co-operative where they eked out a bare subsistance and enjoyed an abundance of fellowship. They formed a measure of the spirit and wisdom that gave meaning to life in spite of adversity. The church congregation committed itself to a Christianity that was down to earth. These people were especially tolerant of the way we worked with boys and girls and helped to create an environment in which it could be done.

Our theories would seem to have been both Christian and in line with modern psychotherapy. Jesus treated the thief as if he were honest, and accepted the prostitute as pure and holy. He accepted the little man as if he were like other men, and received the Samaritan as a brother. We believed that our young people were good, and worked with them on the basis of their potentials and growth.

It wasn't always easy. I was called to the police headquarters time after time to front for my boys. I recall one time when three of the boys were confined to the city jail for four days before they were released to me. I met them at the cell door and led them through the corridors and through a side door to the outside air.

One of them raised his nose upward and said, "Jeez, what is that I smell?"

I asked, "Could it be fresh air?"

"Believe me," he said, and all three agreed, "this is what we will smell from now on."

There was no word of appreciation—just a good feeling that I belonged and had done no more than was expected. I came to believe that there were no bad kids. They were spontaneous and did what came naturally according to the circumstances. Humanity has the capacity for goodness, and if it doesn't turn out that way it is because the world in which human beings live warps their destinies.

My frequent visits to juvenile and other courts brought me friendships and working relationships with judges and related officials. The result was that many boys were paroled to me. I recall one boy who was sentenced to attend church once a week for three months. He came to my office and I could see that he didn't like it one bit.

He remarked, "I ain't going to no damn church just because a damn judge makes me do it."

I waited for him to think about what he said and then commented, "It can't be that bad. You've been to church today, and I'll sign your slip that you were here. Drop in once a week and if I'm busy just yell 'Hi' and I'll okay you just the same."

He seemed quite surprised and said, "Is that all there is to going to church?"

"No, it doesn't have to be that way," I replied. "A church has services and youth meetings. We have a gym and a game room with pool, ping-pong, checkers, and things kids like to do. But you said you didn't want to go to no damn church, so I am making it easy on you. The judge will understand—you don't have to tell him about the way we fixed things up."

The boy got interested and became a regular participant in all our activities.

Stealing was a common misdemeanor, but ordinarily because of necessity. I think one reason for the gang's own room was to have a safe place to eat the food they stole from the kindly grocer next to the parsonage, with whom I came to an understanding.

The boys made their rounds and often ran into tradesmen who were less kindly and totally without understanding, who thought of them as criminals. One of our boys was caught in one of these places. He and a friend went into a bar under the pretense of selling a newspaper and he stole a loaf of rye bread and a carton of cigarettes. The proprietor was furious, refused to listen to me, pressed charges, and brought the boy to trial with the purpose of putting him away for good. The boy had been guilty of some minor infractions of the law, one of which was riding double on a bicycle down a sidewalk. Members of the gang had irritated the bar owner on other occasions, and he insisted that it was time to stop them. He intended to make an example of this unfortunate youth.

The boy's mother had fled to Kansas, unable to face reality. He and his father lived in a single and desolate room, which was used as little as possible. The boy rarely saw his father, who was unemployed and not present at the hearing. I was his only defense. The decision had to be made by the judge, who invited me into his chambers.

He said, "It looks like I'll have to sentence this boy. He really has no parents. The prosecution has presented a hopeless condition—that it is clear the boy has criminal tendencies and it is best for society that he be taken out of circulation. What alternative is there? He has no one—"

I quickly interrupted, "But he has me and Grace Community Center." I might have added, "And he has the Ramblers," but the judge might not have understood.

The judge was resolute. "I'll be severely criticized for this, but he is paroled to you. I can't sentence a boy for stealing a loaf of bread, regardless of what seems to be his behavior record." The bar owner was most unhappy and cursed the court. I was aware that he would have taken the last dime from the boy's father for a drink.

We had a lovely neighbor who lived across the alley from the church. She took in female boarders to provide for her living expenses, and was a staunch and loyal member of a Presbyterian church. I never blamed her for her hostilities to our boys. As it turned out, she became one of their best friends.

Boys, among whom were the Ramblers, would frighten the roomers in many gruesome ways. They would walk on her little patch of struggling grass, and her flowers never had a chance to grow. The Ramblers' room was across the alley about one hundred feet away, and sometimes they would be overly noisy. It was bad enough to have hundreds of people going by her place to Grace Church and Center. The problem was that she would call the police with every provocation, which made matters worse.

One night at three a.m. two poorly dressed boys rang her doorbell. Hurriedly she put on a faded dressing gown, opened the door and asked what they wanted at this time of night. They explained that they were poor and had a sick mother, and that a man had promised to give them work at eight a.m. but they didn't know where he lived. They thought that she might know.

Out of her goodness, Mrs. Berg responded that there was no man—she had only women roomers. "Why did you come to my place?" she asked the boys.

They answered, "He said he lived in a house where the landlady was a real 'battle axe,' so we thought of you." They ran away, with Mrs. Berg shouting after them. She called the police to have them picked up.

One day as eleven of the boys walked down the alley, someone remarked that Mrs. Berg owned the garage they were passing. They broke every window in the garage. I heard the glass break and rushed out. I rounded them up and walked them to the juvenile court, a block away in the new city hall. Judge Gilliam was available and ushered us into the courtroom. We explained what had been done and promised to replace the glass. We were certain that Mrs. Berg had called the police, who were already on the scene of the crime.

We discussed our problems with Mrs. Berg and proposed that the court bring us together—we believed we could make a friend of her. The judge sent two of his best employees to have a conference with her. The results were miraculous. Whenever she needed a job done, she hired one of the boys. They replanted the plot of grass and zealously guarded it against all harm. She learned to know some of the boys by name and often passed out cookies. She never called the "cops" again—there was no provocation.

Boys are the products of their families and the community in which they live. Parents are what they are for the same reasons, and often the obstacles are almost insurmountable. Law enforcement agencies cannot enforce human behavior. The problem is to get all concerned parties together to find new perspectives and a way of life which are acceptable and understandable within the framework of a decent society.

We worked out an arrangement with the courts to have preliminary hearings in the Center which brought together parents, offenders, police officers, social workers, counselors and others who might assist in a creative discussion—and if possible, avoid a punitive attitude.

Many problems were solved in this way without official hearings or appearances. Why take a child to a police station and book him if it can be avoided? We also had success in adult offenses by these means. An alienated person is hard to reach and cannot be forced to do something he cannot do by reason of limitations within himself and his attitudes toward the outside world. Why try to scare people to death to make them good? The church has tried to do it through fear of the devil and hell, and has failed. People cannot be good because they are afraid to be bad. Punishment is apparently no deterrent.

During World War II we corresponded with more than two hundred young men in service, asking the congregation and others to help us. New Year's Eve was set aside to write our boys.

The following are a few excerpts from the many letters we received in reply:

"It looks to me Wally like this war is going to be just as tough on some people, when it is over, as it is now. . . . The 'yellow-dirty Japs' and 'filthy Germans' mouthings are surely but slowly creeping into the minds of the

American people. . . . The common people, the ones who had nothing to do with the war, will be the ones to suffer. . . . Love, Eddie."

Eddie Allen was one of my best correspondents. He answered my letters as soon as he could so that I would be under obligation to write him back. All six of his brothers were in the service. Eddie wrote often about life and death, and God:

"When a flower wilts and is ready to blow away, it drops seeds which grow and blossom into beautiful flowers. It is the same with every natural thing and everybody. We are all given the opportunity to deposit a seed, and we do. . . . We never die, we keep on living . . . that to me is God in action. I've tried praying when there was something besides love in my heart, with very little or no results. Therefore when you have love and kindness in your soul, you know that you are spiritually in contact with those you love.

"I'm beginning to think that environment has *everything* to do with the way a person turns out. These Arabs, for example—even in their filth, brutality to animals, dishonesty, and their very low moral standards, no one should blame them; because we too would be the same way under the same circumstances, the same conditions that they have to exist in."

Carl Allen wrote:

"I'll leave you with the thought that we have no fear or hatred of things to come, but only that we are waiting for the light which will bring peace and happiness for everybody on this earth."

Donald R. Finney described the enemy:

"We are fighting an enemy here that obeys a couple of the rules. In everything an American does from childhood to manhood he is taught to play, work, and if need be fight, but always obey the rules. . . ."

Eddie Foster was the first of our boys to die in action and wrote me his last letter from a hospital bed:

"Your letter arrived here on time, but I am indisposed. It is next to impossible to answer as I would like. Because of conditions, we don't have the facilities we used to have. I am sure you understand.

"I remember most the beautiful candlelight service at Christmas. It is a good picture to have in my mind at this time. . . . We are fighting hard to get the war over so that as citizens we can build not only a nation of freedom but a world of freedom."

Dick Finney described a church service in an interesting way:

"For singing—they show the words on the screen after drawing the curtains back, and then we stand and *sing*—that's what they call it. You'd probably call it hog calling."

Swatkin was impressed with what he saw among the missionaries on some distant island:

"I like the natives very much from what little I've learned about them and these islands. I owe them for teaching me. I have a nice collection of their craft work—they are still quite primitive, as they have been from the beginning."

Lou Joplin had a special slant on his location:

"One thing about here that helps is a fellow doesn't have to stay so close on the beam as in garrison (camp). We can have a goatee and handle-bar if we want it—that makes us shave only about once a week. Also our work clothes and leggins don't have to be kept so clean. So you see this life has its advantages."

Hubert Moore was our only conscientious objector:

"There is dissatisfaction among the CPS men everywhere. They are anxious to get out and 'heal the wounds of the world'—feed Europe, relieve suffering, do *important* work.... One's alternatives at present are few; it seems to be a choice of the lesser of several evils, with the good behind the clouds temporarily.

"We are witnessing the beginnings of the decline of our so-called Western Civilization in that we are infected with the sickness that brought down civilizations in past history ... We are committed to the principle that we must discuss mutual problems through strength—meaning military power. One thing that the world or nation can no longer afford is a military establishment. It is the greatest drain upon our decreasing resources.... Another war would gun us all down. I imagine that every civilization that has failed was confronted with these problems. We have much less daring in what needs to be done."

Another meaningful comment was:

"I don't know why I'm here, I ain't mad at nobody."

I Go South

I was elected dean of the Pinecrest Epworth League Institute and held that job six years. This was a campground program serving the young people of the Methodist churches of eastern Colorado. Many of these churches were in small communities with few cultural and recreational resources. We set about providing music, crafts, folk-dancing, games and religious dialogues. A student council met between institutes to decide what was most suitable.

I was also a member of the council of the National Methodist Youth where I met Dr. Timothy B. Echols, who was working with young black people in the south. I asked Tim to spend a week with us in Colorado, which he agreed to do if I would spend two weeks with him in the South.

My first assignment with Echols was the Epworth League Institute in Pelham, Texas, where I was entertained in the home of Square Porter—the venerable saint of a substantial black community. My presence was subject to an investigation by the sheriff of the county who chatted for a few minutes and left, saying, "What is okay with Square is good enough for me." He was the only white man I saw during my stay in Pelham.

Square and I had a number of talks as we sat on his spacious porch. It was 1935, the year of a great drought in Texas. The earth had opened up into wide cracks like mouths gasping for water, and people in almost every section of the country were on relief. There was no one on relief in Pelham. Square was in charge of relief and was called upon to help people in neighboring communities. He described his philosophy. "We folks live by the Bible. It say, there was seven good years and seven lean years. We has had seven good years. We knows there can be seven bad years. We just saved our extras and we will have enough."

It was an entirely black community in which the farms, stores, a cotton gin and a cooperative canning plant and other facilities were owned by the blacks. They had a telephone system long before their surrounding white neighbors. They had their Farmers' Improvement Society and owned a bank which closed in the Depression; the bank was in such good condition that most assets were recovered. Each family owned a farm and lived in an adequate house. There were good school buildings built by the members of the community. There were three churches: Baptist, Methodist, and African Methodist. All cooperated and joined forces in the Epworth League Institute to provide discussions, study classes and evangelistic meetings at night.

This community began a few years following the Civil War. Grandfather Porter had the responsibility for three small grandchildren, whose parents had disappeared in the days of slavery—having been sold out of state somewhere. According to Square, the grandfather said, "They say we are free, but there is no freedom without a farm, owned by us. We are free to starve until with our own hands and lives we get a farm. God will help us. The Bible is our guide. Let us go into the wilderness and like Moses, get a farm."

The four of them took over a piece of "free land" and worked themselves a farm. When this piece of land was producing they took over another plot of land and invited a black family to take it over. All of them in turn took over more land and invited other families. The farm in each case belonged to the new family. This experience continued through the years until approximately one hundred families belonged to the community.

The Porters had definite ideas which were respected and provided the unwritten laws by which they were governed. They were told to respect the white man but have as few dealings with him as possible. They believed that they could provide for their own security and work out their own problems and that they must avoid the exploitation of the whites. Their basic institution was the church. Their textbook was the Bible, from which they selected the lessons relevant to their needs. Square Porter was eighty years old and stone blind, but he continued to advise and guide his people.

They built their own cotton gin "to get rid of arguing all the time with a white man about how much and how good. They say figures don't lie, but they do when a Negro does business with the whites if they do the bookkeeping. We always ended up in the red. Now that we have our own gin we end up mostly in the black."

The young people wanted a less emotional faith and one that addressed itself to problems of racial humiliation and lack of employment and human dignity. They respected their churches because they had been their only point of communication, understanding and action. No blacks held any kind of political office. The community was sufficiently prosperous to send their young people to black colleges and to give generous support to education. They would have been persecuted if they had talked as openly in the presence of white people as they did to me.

Square Porter outlined to me the growth of the community as we sat on his spacious front porch in the cooling breezes of the evening. He pointed to the original cabin that stood as a shrine to the labor of years. Though blind, he knew where everything was. He told me about their first act of charity, which was to take care of the sick wife of the man who had owned them as slaves. The house in which I lived was the third and largest built for the family of Square Porter. The three brothers who were the original grandsons were still living.

Neighbors told me about "the dividin' up day." The three brothers had held some things in common throughout the long years, "just as the Bible says." As they grew older, they felt it was necessary to bow to the conventions of ownership in order to protect the interests of their children. They made an inventory of their possessions and divided them equally between the three brothers—tools, stock, land, buildings, chickens, hay and many other things. Finally, everything was divided except one bale of hay. Each urged the other to take it. Each refused and then Square Porter solemnly slashed the bale in thirds. The brothers embraced each other in tears as the ordeal ended.

I walked hand in hand with a five-year-old great-grandchild of Square Porter as I went to my classes and lectures. Dressed each day in her starchy best, her hair was carefully groomed.

She asked me, "Are you all goin' home tomorrow?" I told her that was true.

She said, "That's too bad."

"Why is it too bad?" I asked.

She replied, "Cause if you'd stay down he-ah awhile, we'd low'n you to talk."

I returned to Texas in 1936 to work with Tim Echols in two institutes— Rocky Crossing and Dennison. I gave talks, taught a class, and shared in discussions on building a youth program in the local church. I had discovered in Pelham that these Southern youth had concerns of their own, different from the youth of the Northern states. They were much more militant about human rights.

My friends met me in Mexia, Texas, where the countryside was almost completely depleted by white operators who had purchased or leased most of the farms in search of gas and oil; the black farmers were homeless and poor. Tim Echols told me that feelings between many people were bad and thought it best that I have a room in a white hotel in Mexia. I would be picked up to go to Rocky Point, a distance of seven miles. I refused the suggestion and said I would prefer living with the campers.

We passed through the black section of Mexia and I noticed that a Methodist church had been burned to the ground. A group of white youngsters having a drunken brawl decided to have a dance in the black Methodist church. The minister protested the intrusion and pleaded with them not to desecrate his church. They became angry and burned it down.

I asked what had been done about it and was told that the sheriff was called but did nothing; he had made no effort to apprehend the violators. But the white Methodist church had given $197.00 towards a new church.

Many of the young people here were physically and mentally undernourished, confined by the limitations of a bare existence of sharecroppers. My first assignment was to lead a discussion on the dilemmas of youth. One of the dilemmas had to do with shouting parents, grandparents and preachers who constantly disturbed the church services.

Evening services were camp meetings attended by young and old from nearby farms and communities. Young people dominated during the day, so there was a wide contrast in emphasis and procedure. The evening services were gospel songs, several sermons, altar calls and enthusiastic shouting and "amens" that had characterized the old fashioned revivals of my own youth. I was invited to preach each night and found I couldn't compete with the fervor of my colleagues, although shouts from the audience spurred me on. They cried, "Tell 'em, brother!" "Yes, dear Jesus!" "Praise the Lord!" "That's right!" "Sure 'nough!" accompanied with the clapping of hands and a rhythmic stamping of feet, and hundreds of "amens."

Following one of these services a dark hand was placed upon my shoulder and I looked up into the face of a large fellow-minister. He said, "That was a fine rendition, what you spoke, but what was your crownin' point?" I could not tell him, but his sharp remark helped in the preparation of future sermons.

The high point of the conference was the appeal on race relations by a young man who had attended the National Methodist Youth Conference. He concluded, "The youth of today, in an understanding spirit of Christian love—working with God for a new world, without discrimination and prejudice—will do what the older and bigoted generations have not done."

The air was hot and dry and the ground was parched and dusty. I needed a bath and asked Tim where I could get one. He told me that everybody washed and swam in a nearby stream, and invited me to go along with him and another person. The river pool, under fragrant southern foliage, was a refreshing interlude. I neglected to bring soap and towel so I borrowed from Tim. I noticed some white faces looking at us from downriver.

I took a walk along one of the roads and noticed the shanties in which some of these people lived. I entered a little church with an earthen floor and planks for benches. Later I heard a young minister of one of these churches preach, and I was certain he could have equalled in eloquence and thought any of the great preachers in our church. His salary was $175 a year, plus what he could raise in his garden.

After one early vesper service I returned to the camp grounds to find everyone disturbed and frightened, cold fear gripping the crowd of nearly a thousand. Three white men were searching for me and accused those present of hiding me. They demanded I be delivered to them at once or they would take action against them.

I approached the white men and welcomed them to our camp, only to be rudely interrupted and grabbed by all three. I heard, "He's our man. Come on you, we want you. I'm a deputy and he's a deputy, and he's the assistant district attorney. Now come clean—what are you doing here with these niggers?" I was pushed and shoved and threatened with violence. I answered questions, but they weren't listening. I explained my mission, gave my name, address, position, church, and a dozen more items.

They said, "Are you a Communist? A radical? He's here for no good! Don't you know that whites have nothin' to do with niggers? You're stirrin' up trouble. First thing you know we'll have a revolution with yer damn talk of love and brotherhood. We whites work out our salvation and the niggers work out theirs. We don't have nothin' to do with each other except to keep them in their place, and we don't need the likes of you."

I tried to explain that there was no law against Christian brotherhood and that these people were members of my branch of the church. They said, "No, we are taking you as a vag. You got no business here with all your damn talk of equality." It was obvious that our meetings had been under surveillance. One of the men guarded me while the other two held a secret conference.

I urged the guard, "Let's look at this sensibly. Let me go on with my work." He replied, "You can't go. If we don't do something, the whites in this neighborhood will lynch you within six hours." The others returned and announced, "We are taking you in." I asked where that might be. They said, "To the county seat, Grossbeck."

The crowd was milling around, anxious and fearful. Some had fled, believing the camp would be demolished. A college president tried to intercede. The officers flatly refused to talk to anyone and roughly pushed my friend away, knocking him down. One officer said, "They are all liars."

I spoke loud enough so that all could hear, "Don't worry. I'm sure everything will come out all right. No one is going to get hurt."

I was pushed into the back seat of their car with one deputy next to me and the other two in the front seat. I overheard them say, as we passed hundreds of people on their way to the evening meeting, "Who are those damn niggers trying to talk to us? God, what a lot of niggers. There ought to be a law against them meeting. This religion of theirs is a waste of time. Who knows what they are planning to do?"

Prospects seemed ominous as we rode through winding country roads. I tried to talk to the man next to me and was told to keep my damn mouth shut. I learned later that my friends were following and they expected that I would never reach the courthouse.

I was ordered out of the car and into a hearing room on the second floor of the courthouse and told to sit down. They notified the sheriff and district attorney that they had their man. The interrogation began before the sheriff's arrival. I was asked to produce credentials, give my reasons for being in Texas, and explain about personal letters that I had in my possession. Their questions were liberally interspersed with profanity.

"What is this?" "Who is that?" "Do you know anybody in Texas?" "Do you preach to a nigger church in Denver?" "When did you arrive?" "What did you say to those niggers?" When I tried to talk they said, "Shut your damn mouth."

I insisted on asking why I was arrested. They shot their reply at me with hatred: "For eating and sleeping and going swimming with niggers."

The sheriff arrived, impressive and hard looking, with two revolvers exposed on his hips and a belt full of bullets around his waist. He glared at me and turned to his deputies and said, "You all got him, I see." We had a second session going over everything that had gone on before—repetitive questions and profane comments. It was increasingly difficult for them to appear important, as the evidence seemed less than incriminating. A clergy transportation ticket stamped "clergy" was confusing. The Colorado Conference minutes weren't quite the radical literature they had expected to find—all my literature was safely stowed away under my bed.

They turned their questioning to immorality. The sheriff asked, "You were sleeping with niggers?" I pointed out that I shared a tent with three important people, all males and leaders of the conference. They probed, "They were niggers, weren't they? Don't you know what a nigger is?" The sheriff asked his deputies, "Were there any women in the tent?" They answered that they had not seen women in the tent. "Were there?" he asked sneeringly. I didn't reply. The sheriff commented, "Sure queer—whites that associate with niggers are all radicals." He went on, "In the South, we think only one thing about whites living with niggers." This seemed to be humorous as all laughed and the sheriff gave way to a grin. One of them laughed and said, "Ha, if I was in a tent with a nigger, it would be with a damn good looking nigger wench. No women in the tent! Ha!"

The district attorney arrived. His questioning was more analytical and deliberate, perhaps because he was irked with having been brought into the situation. He asked me, "Know anyone in Denver I can wire to identify you?" I gave him several names, including the mayor of Denver and my district superintendent. They sent a wire to the mayor with the following message: "Is there a minister named Edgar M. Wahlberg pastor of a white church in Denver. Notify his whereabouts immediately." They were convinced that I was an imposter. They said, "No white folks would listen to a minister that works with niggers."

The telephones began to ring, interrupting our conversations. These calls were from my friends, and were disconcerting and deflating to my accusers. The district attorney was taking a dim view of the importance of the proceedings, and was embarrassed with the crudeness and profanity of his associates. It was clear to him that I was not a vagrant and perhaps was a person of some importance. They considered what could be done. I suggested that I could be tried under a criminal syndicalism law and discover if it was unlawful to be a Christian in Texas. I promised to furnish sufficient evidence out of my files to convict me. The district attorney gave me a knowing look, thought about it for a moment and said that it wasn't a good idea.

One of the deputies whispered to the district attorney, "Get him down here"—meaning the local Methodist minister of the southern Methodist church. They called him out of bed. There wasn't anything to do but wait for him. I listened to the rambling conversations, some of which were for my benefit. Some of the discussion was rather easy and good-spirited. They talked about how the South handled race problems. They said that Negroes were stupid and ignorant and that the white race was superior because that is what the Bible said. They said, "White folks go to their churches sometimes for curiosity and fun, because these niggers make a mockery out of religion."

They repeatedly warned me that only "Communists, radicals, and immoral whites" mixed with "niggers." I asked if the church people of the South ever cooperated with the Negro churches. The answer was, "Hell no, it just ain't done in the South." I saw that the district attorney was listening idly and not agreeing with what he heard. He kept silent throughout this period and waited patiently for the preacher.

The Methodist minister arrived and was detained in a whispered conversation I could not hear. He felt that he was on the spot and seemed quite shaken and fearful. It didn't take him long to identify me as a minister in the Methodist church, north. He felt that I had been imprudent largely because I was unacquainted with the culture of the South. He added, "If he insists on being a martyr, that is his responsibility—but that is a horse of a different color." He advised me to "accept the psychology of the South and keep him out of trouble." I think his own words stunned him. He went on, "On the other hand, he hasn't broken any legal statute." The sheriff frowned and said, "No, I guess not—but we could make the vag law stick and get him out of the state." The preacher countered, "He does have authorized official status and business with these people who are members of his church, assuming that all the facts we have heard are true."

They brought in a message from Mayor Ben Stapleton of Denver; there followed an uneasy and embarrassed apology and a half-hearted effort to create goodwill. The district attorney adjourned the hearing. The deputy sheriff warned me to get out of Texas and stay out. I reminded him that I had unfinished business in Texas and would return immediately to Rocky Crossing. He said, "Okay, it's your life. The white folks around there will get you, sure." No one seemed to know what to say or do.

Finally the district attorney said, "Aw hell, leave him alone and let him go. He is just preaching and teaching religion. These Negroes sure need religion, like all of us."

It was about two hours until daybreak. The sheriff gave me a room and breakfast. The minister lingered until we were alone. He apologized, but explained that he had to do what he did if he hoped to retain his church. He knew that relations with the Negroes could be improved. He hoped that I wouldn't write an article about what had happened. (I did write an article and sent it to a leading Methodist publication. The editor sent it back. He said that ordinarily he would have been glad to print it, but due to the possible unification of the northern and southern Methodist churches, Methodist editors had agreed not to use anything about black issues that would upset the southern church. He hoped I would refrain from getting my article printed in any other channel of communication.) The minister asked me to convey his goodwill to the people in Rocky Crossing. I told him that he was obliged to do this in person, that I couldn't do it for him. It occurred to me that I had no transporation, so I asked him to drive me to Rocky Crossing, which he did.

We arrived in camp about ten in the morning. Breakfast was untouched. Most of the young people, the ministers, and many others had kept a vigil all night. Everyone threw arms around each other, clapped hands, shouted hallelujahs, sang spirituals and gospel songs with prayers of thanksgiving.

There was a young man named James Farmer (age 16) at this Institute. It was a turning point in his life. He became the organizer of C.O.R.E. and its national leader through a most crucial period in the struggle for dignity and freedom.

News about Rocky Crossing traveled quickly among our black churches and constituents. I was asked to speak in the Dallas church on Sunday morning and the Fort Worth church in the evening. Each church was packed beyond capacity, in spite of hot, humid weather. The minister's home in Fort Worth was overcrowded so I suggested that I get a room in the YMCA, which I had noticed was just around the corner. Dr. Haynes explained to me that the "Y" I had seen was the Negro YMCA, but he would be happy to drive me downtown to the white YMCA. I chose to pick up my suitcase and walk to the "Y" around the corner and presented myself before the registration desk. I was promptly informed that the white YMCA was downtown. I questioned the man in charge and asked if there was any law or prohibition which might keep me out of any YMCA. He said, "No sir, all the constitution say is that you be a man." I had a comfortable room and ate my breakfast at the YMCA lunch counter. I wrote letters in the lobby until it was time for my bus. I asked the secretary if he would mind calling a taxi. He asked with a smile, "Do you want a colored taxi?"

I found that Sherman, Texas, was on my bus route, so I stopped off there. A mob had recently burned down the courthouse in this town, making it a funeral pyre for the body of a human being. The sheriff had tried to protect the man from being lynched. I wondered what kind of a community this could be. I walked around the central block where the courthouse had stood and wondered at the darkness shadowing the goodness of mankind. I boarded a bus for Dennison, and the last thing I saw in Sherman were the words over the Masonic Temple door, "Let there be light."

I arrived in Lubbock for my next appointments and hastened to the post office to cash a money order. I presented it to the clerk, who asked if there was anyone in town who could identify me. I gave the name of the Negro minister who was serving his fifth year in Lubbock. I was told he was unknown. When it was revealed that he was a Negro I was told, "We don't allow niggers to identify whites in the South." I asked for my check, but received the money without further comment—wondering if the clerk was about to commit a federal offense.

A Negro postal employee told me stories that were hard to believe, one about an innocent man who was lynched and burned and his remains dragged behind a truck through the Negro section of Lubbock. It dawned on his pregnant wife that this was her husband.

The Lubbock Institute proceedings were without similar incidents. I am sure that the white people and white ministers did not know there was an important meeting in town. The meetings were not reported in the press. I called on the white minister of the Methodist church and he did not know the name of his Negro co-minister, who was as well educated and had had more years of service.

Unification of the northern and southern churches came about in 1939. I voted against unification, not because I had a grudge, but because I believed that we could have come together on a much higher level. We voted "Jim

Crowism" into the church by putting all the blacks into one jurisdictional conference covering the whole United States, and the whites into five geographical conferences. The black jurisdictional conference has since been dissolved.

Holmes and Adell

I hesitate to write about personal friends without including all of them, but there are two men who in terms of devotion to each other can be described in a special context: Dr. Clarence Holmes, a black dentist, and Robert Adell, who was born of Jewish parentage in New York City. Each one has a different story, and age-wise, we aren't far apart.

Clarence began his practice in Pueblo, Colorado, and moved to Denver about the time I arrived at Grace Church. He heard about our work for all people and our belief in only one race—the human race. He came over to see if this were true, because his primary concern was interracial cooperation. He was ineligible for membership in the Dental Association because of his color, and suffered the humiliations of his race. He liked what he found and became a familiar figure in and around Grace Church and Center. He belonged to a black Episcopal church, but Dean Roberts of the St. John's Episcopal Cathedral changed that some years later and Clarence became a vestryman of Dean Robert's church.

He opened up a small clinic at Five Corners, the center of the black neighborhood, and for some time found it impossible to make ends meet. He came regularly to our church services and forum activities, particularly those that dealt with racial issues. He was my first black usher. He was jovial, intelligent and outgoing, and loved all people. He was a man of potential leadership. He greeted each one near the doors of the church, and with a smile reached out to shake hands. When some parishioner hesitated he would say, "Ah come on, shake hands, it won't come off." People soon forgot his color and enjoyed his fellowship.

It was following a discussion group in our Co-operative that Clarence said to me, "A lot of those folks need dental care. Their mouths must hurt something terrible." Dental care was hard to provide. Dentists didn't seem to be very charitable. The best I had been able to do up to that time was to get dental plates through the Bureau of Public Relief for an aging man who had to have a special diet which required teeth—and then he couldn't get sufficient food for his diet.

Clarence remarked, "You don't have any money and I don't have any money, but I have time, and I would be glad to help with dental care. All I need is money to buy the spare parts, wholesale." We were in business, because I could use some of the money that Mr. John Evans was providing. Hundreds of men, women, and children were served.

Dr. Holmes and I arranged for like-minded people to meet in the parsonage for the purpose of organizing the Denver Cosmopolitan Club. We developed a program to include all ethnic groups, and were entertained in turn by each group. We enjoyed their kind of food and entertainment and worked constantly for better human relations. We had a "Heroes for Peace" service every Memorial Day. We would seek out a woman who had died in childbirth, a fireman or policeman who had died in the line of duty, and other persons and would decorate their graves. A noteworthy individual was asked to give an address. Some people thought it was a shameful idea, but after a few years it became accepted and popular.

The public bath house was scheduled to serve whites most of the time; blacks were given a limited time a few hours a week. There was a lot of friction about this, but this changed when the color line was erased. This was also true in the outdoor beaches, but trouble stopped when discrimination stopped. The Cosmopolitan Club played a great role in human relations in Denver, and Dr. Holmes was the genius. Denver is a large metropolitan city now and quite different, but it is good to recall some of this heritage of the past.

I became acquainted with Robert Adell in a series of forums dealing with economic problems of the United States. I discovered that this young man was perceptive and knowledgeable and always pursued the subjects in which he was interested.

He inquired about the nature of our institution and discovered that I was a Methodist minister. This turned him off completely. He said he knew all about ministers who used every device in the world to get people into something or other, so that they could be proselytized and become members of the church—which was historically known for deceit and falsehood.

I stood my ground and said, "Did anyone ask you to come to the forum? Has anyone asked you to attend church services? Believe me, they won't. You had better take a look around and find out what is going on. If you don't like what you see, don't come back. If you like what you see, you will be welcome. You might want to give us a hand." He walked away without saying a word.

When I went into my office the next morning, there was Robert Adell, as I had expected. I liked this guy from the very beginning. He said he had come to look the place over. I told him that he was late because the milk station had opened at 5:30 a.m. We made an inspection of the Center building, purposefully staying away from the church sanctuary. He discovered the nursery school, which was in business at 7 a.m. I noted that he had a fondness for children. We observed the ladies preparing food for the school children's luncheon. I introduced him to Ray Lowderback, the business agent for the bakers union. Then I had to leave and told him to wander at will.

He was unemployed and had diligently tried to get any kind of work. He was humiliated because in order to survive, he was selling cheap sheets and pillowcases and other things, going from door to door selling his wares for what he could get. He lived in a miserable room and could hardly pay the rent, and sometimes he didn't get much food.

He became a familiar person in our fellowship, but we never mentioned the church. He remarked one day, "You are having trouble with some individualistic teenage boys. Would you mind if I tried my luck with them?" Bob worked wonders with these boys. It was a person-to-person type of service which, because of lack of funds, we had never been able to get started.

Time went on and the NRA organized a camp for jobless men. I was asked if I could recommend a director of recreation. I called Bob into my office and told him about the proposed job and informed him that I had recommended him. He paused in thought and said, "Wallie, I don't know a damn thing about recreation." I replied, "Don't tell anybody and they won't know the difference." I knew he would make an excellent director. He took the job.

Bob returned when the camp was closed. He came immediately to my office and after warm greetings and an embrace he informed me, "I've saved $1,200. You have advised me about a number of things—what should I do with it?"

I replied, "There are two things I won't give you advice about—your money and your women."

Bob had a friend with some money. They bought a garage and went into the car repair business, and succeeded. Bob sold out his share and purchased a garage in the middle of the central district of Denver and did a whale of a business.

Then one day Bob came to my office and burst out, "I've got a girl, and I want you to marry us." Zella was a psychiatric social worker for the state of Wyoming and a remarkable person—just the right girl for Bob. I said, "I'll have to see your girl first before I can promise to do the job."

They came to my office in the fragrance of a beautiful companionship and love. We talked happily about marriage. Presently I said, "Bob, you know how we feel about each other—nothing will ever come between us, and I am sure Zell is just as fine as you are. But I've been thinking. You have wonderful parents and a tremendous heritage, and I am sure that you want your parents to be especially proud of your marriage. I have talked to my good friend Rabbi Kauvar about the whole thing, and I believe in the long run your happiness will be enhanced if you let Rabbi Kauvar celebrate the marriage vows with you. It would be a marvelous milestone in my life to marry you— but I'll always be your friend, perhaps closer than ever." They were married by Rabbi Kauvar, one of the greatest of men.

Bob sold his business and went into real estate so he could have more time to spend with his wife. They traveled together around the world. Bob is still in business, but he is leisurely about it. Zell passed away in 1981.

Housing in the Thirties

Housing was a primary unmet need of poor people in the thirties. There was a myth that the less thrifty should suffer the consequences of their way of life and would naturally have to live in undesirable neighborhoods. Each would find his own level. A committee which went into the problem of housing for the underprivileged was told that those who did not have bathtubs would not know what to do with them if they had them—bathtubs would be used for coal bins and trash receptacles. In the end everyone was content, each happy in his own place, some clean and rich, others filthy and poor. Neither would enjoy changing places with the other.

This ready explanation in the thirties did not go unchallenged. Fully

37 percent of the houses in America were not in good condition, and by any standard, at least 5 percent were unfit for use. Twenty-three percent did not have indoor plumbing. Only 38 percent of the houses in the United States were in good condition. At least 20 percent should have been condemned and torn down, being either uninhabitable or in need of such major repairs that neither private nor public enterprise would repair or remodel.

The plain facts were that no really decent housing was ever built for the low income urban or rural worker. The building industry had never tackled this problem because it offered no profit. Low income families could not pay the price, and probably would never be able to pay the sale costs and rentals necessary to make their housing an attractive venture for private enterprise. The end result of this economic stalemate are the vast slum areas in every city.

If anything were to be done to provide housing for low income people, it would have to be done through a government agency, either local or national. Almost every country in Europe had recognized the necessity of government participation in building adequate and standard housing.

The most persistent critics of the work of the Denver committee were the realtors, who believed that any government activity was unfair to private enterprise. They claimed that any such program would threaten their legitimate business. We urged them to look at the facts and that they had no more right to traffic in inadequate houses than a butcher had a right to sell contaminated meat. One area in Denver had the highest infant mortality rate in the world. This section in the river bottoms was demolished, but nothing was done to find housing for those displaced.

Captain Richard L. Reiss, a member of the housing committee of the London County Council, had said, "... far from putting private enterprise out of business, public housing activity ... indirectly stimulated the demand. As the lowest income groups became better housed, people with higher income demanded better housing accommodation, thus creating an additional demand which private enterprise could provide."

Many people didn't like our research, which covered the statistics on a number of American cities revealing the same general pattern as Denver. Our forums at Grace Church included many meetings with people of all points of view, including realtors and members of the building industry.

Governor Teller Ammons was concerned and asked me for suggestions. (Ed Johnson had moved to the U.S. Senate.) I was appointed chairman of the Colorado Housing Committee by Governor Ammons on February 23, 1938.

President Roosevelt had authorized the 1937 Housing Act, so the committee was enthusiastic and immediately went to work. On January 3, 1938, the committee presented a report of its first year, the first report of its kind in any state of the Union. There was a tremendous demand for this report when it appeared. Page 24 had a spot map on typhoid fever, and showed that a large portion of the state's cases appeared in rural districts due to inadequate housing and unsanitary conditions.

We provided a bibliography on housing, pamphlets, and a petitition for a local housing authority which could be used in any city of the state. We bore down on the city of Denver. Matching funds from the government could provide sufficient funds to begin significant housing projects.

The city council had several hearings on a proposed Denver Housing Authority, and finally voted to ask the mayor to set up an authority. Mayor Stapleton asked me for four names as possible appointees. I asked why four names, when there were to be five members. He said he hoped that I would be chairman and be the fifth person, but I had to decline. Members were to select sites, draw up plans, work out directives, select occupants, and work out tenant relations—perhaps form a co-operative store. My choice for chairman was James Quigg Newton, Sr., a liberal, well liked businessman. The fifth member was Father Mulroy, who had a parish in the inner city and was concerned with the welfare of people. We had worked together on many projects. He was also the priest who took me to task for having a planned parenthood clinic in Grace Center. I agreed to serve as chairman of one of the subcommittees, the tenant selection committee.

The first site was about eight blocks west of Grace Church, and I watched the buildings take shape. The housing committee had selected Ira Lute as the first manager, for many years the executive secretary of the YMCA.

I recall one of the tenants, a widow with two small children, who had lived across the alley from the parsonage in a made-over alley stable. Rats were common in this neighborhood and she could never get rid of her fear of them. I heard her scream several times as a rat ran down the alley. She often expressed her gratitude for living in an apartment in the project. The housing committee built three additional housing units. I was critical of only one of them—the one built for Spanish Americans—because it was smaller and inadequate.

Japanese Americans

It was said that Japanese Americans all looked alike and were regarded as potential traitors. This idea was stimulated by selfish political and economic interests which had fought what they called "the yellow menace" for many long years. They used the war as a way to make their bias a national policy.

I recall an incident in our Grace Center Quigg Newton Camp. Someone donated a new flag and we had a celebration for the flag raising. The Ramblers made the pole and set it in its proper place and took care of the guests as they came, parking their cars and showing them the way. The boys sat back on some rocks and watched the proceedings and listened to the speeches. I overheard a businessman saying as he observed these teenage boys, "I don't care what you say, they all look like toughs to me."

At the Japanese Young People's Christian Conference, held in Grace Church November 27-29, 1936, we began to organize Japanese young people of Colorado. This grew to include all faiths and became a large organization. They had no suspicion of what lay ahead on the west coast. They could not imagine that their country would take action against law-abiding people.

The first violence in Denver came when the windows of the Japanese

Methodist church were destroyed. The Pastor's Union of Denver unanimously voted to replace the windows and urged the police department to stand guard to prevent additional damage.

The War Relocation Authority issued a bulletin on its responsibility in May, 1943: "During the spring and summer of 1942, the United States government carried out, in remarkably short time and without serious incident, one of the largest controlled migrations in history. This was the movement of 110,000 people of Japanese descent from their homes in an area bordering the Pacific coast into ten wartime communities constructed in remote areas between the Sierra Nevada Mountains and the Mississippi River. . . . In the weeks that followed, both American-born and alien Japanese residents were moved from a prescribed zone comprising the entire state of California, the western half of Oregon and Washington, and the southern third of Arizona."

The pamphlet clarified the difference between relocation centers and civilian internees. The internees were handled by the Department of Justice. Residents of the relocation centers, however, had never been found guilty—either individually or collectively—of any such acts or intentions. [Subversion.] They were merely a group of American residents who happened to have Japanese ancestors and who happened to be living in a potential combat zone shortly after the outbreak. I visited several of these centers and called them concentration camps. If they had been living "in a potential combat zone"—why weren't all citizens removed?

This military action was bounced on the American public with such suddenness that there was no way for American citizens to provide legal defense for civil liberties or the rights of citizens. At Grace Church we were alerted by letters from friends on the west coast and what documents I could procure from my friends in Washington. Japanese Americans who had the means and who could qualify might choose to move on their own initiative. Military orders were that a community willing to receive these more fortunate people had to provide a letter of authorization from an elected state or city official to guarantee that they would be welcome and that work and housing were available.

Before the evacuation orders, the Japanese American population in Denver was approximately 250, and in the state of Colorado about 3,000. Those who took advantage of the compulsory evacuation deadline and voluntarily emmigrated to Colorado doubled these figures.

My first job was to get an official to consent to being the authority required in Colorado. I went to the chief of police, who didn't like the idea at all and wasn't about to help bring "Japs" to Denver. I asked him if he had had any trouble with any of them. He recollected not. The governor had given an address to our open forum about being friendly to the Japanese Americans and helping to ease the stress by refusing to believe rumors. He gave me a gracious reception, and I presented my request for a letter of authority to expedite the movement of Japanese Americans to our state. He thought it over and said, "Wallie, my friend, you are always on the right side and I would like to give you such a letter, but it would be political suicide for me to do this. Did you know that the legislators are being pressed to support a bill to prevent the Japanese from buying land in Colorado, and I don't like it. To respond to your request might muddy the waters a bit."

I went to my friend Benjamin F. Stapleton, mayor of Denver, from whom I had asked a number of favors, and thought I would not ask him for this letter of authority. He listened to my request and said, "Can't you get someone else to do this? It could be political suicide, feelings being such as they are." I told him whom I had approached and then suggested that I write the letter on his behalf saying, "I am authorized by the mayor of the city of Denver to say ..." His eyes glistened as he said, "Go ahead, and I hope it works. I trust that we won't get into trouble over it." I wrote many letters with these words and no one ever questioned them. Good people were so eager to help people who had been wronged that a letter like this from a minister was sufficient clearance—thanks to Mayor Stapleton.

The pressure on our offices at Grace Center became extreme as the first Japanese Americans arrived in Colorado. We were not the only ones who were doing their best to help these fellow citizens. Approximately 8,000 evacuees were financially able to seek shelter in other parts of the nation. Three thousand could not get clearance, so were forced to go to relocation camps. Many who were financially able chose to go to a camp rather than be separated from their families. Many of those who managed to escape the relocation camps despaired over their separation from loved ones and friends, and spent much of their energies to find and reunite their families. Much of this effort was futile. No one had a blueprint for such emergencies.

When all was said and done, these people had left nearly $3 million in assets, much of which was never recovered—real, commercial, and personal property. The War Relocation Authority tried to conserve some of these assets. The first Japanese Americans who left voluntarily disposed of what the they had in quick sales that frequently involved heavy losses. All the others tried by lease or sale or the support of friends to conserve their holdings. One of my friends owned a hotel in Portland and leased it to an acquaintance. He returned to find his hotel in shambles, not worth renovation. Most of the furniture had been stolen.

Those who came within the period of voluntary evacuation sought jobs and a place to live in order to prepare a place for members of their families detained in the various relocation centers. Many of these people were businessmen, skilled workers, technicians, professional people and farmers. They were willing to take any kind of job until something better showed up.

Finding jobs was possible, but finding places to live was difficult. Many communities resisted any effort to have Japanese Americans move into their neighborhoods. Those who could afford to buy homes often discovered unfriendly neighbors. We called on their neighbors to reassure them and even stayed overnight to prevent violence. There were always friendly people who welcomed stranded strangers.

I visited a center to see what I could do about reuniting a family, part of which was in Denver. The relocation center served over 12,000 people, 3,000 of them children. The evacuees had just recently arrived. Soldiers were stationed around the camp. The leader of the camp was a civilian and seemed to be distraught—perhaps with responsibility, perhaps with inner conflicts—

caught up as he was in a human catastrophe. There was not enough lumber on hand to finish the barracks. One evacuee had been arrested because he had picked up a piece of lumber to make a table.

The West Coast states had prevented the Japanese from purchasing and owning land. They could rent or lease, but at extra cost. By a narrow margin, we managed to defeat the Japanese Land Act in Colorado. It took the cooperation of churches, unions, businessmen, Farmer's Union, and women's clubs who brought pressure on every candidate of the legislature. Here and there, people changed their minds and attitudes.

The most painful part of the ordeal for the evacuees was the constant attack in the press upon their motives and integrity, attacks provoked by the Congressional Committee on Un-American Activities. In Germany the military committed genocide upon a whole population, but we did the same thing in principle. We did not physically kill Japanese Americans, but we sacrificed our principles of civil liberties and human rights.

The War Relocation Authority maintained a measure of sanity and defense of human decency as a human tide of hatred and ignorance crashed against the interned. The War Relocation Authority had to appear before the Committee on Un-American Activities to defend itself and its wards against countless rumors and unwarranted charges and suspicions. The committee gathered together an array of tawdry witnesses of discharged and emotionally disturbed employees. All allegations were proven false. Nevertheless, the reports in the press kept the public misinformed, fearful and divided. The morale in the centers was at the lowest possible level.

A representative of the WRA before the committee said, "It is difficult to carry on a program of Americanization behind wire enclosures among a group of people who find themselves ceaselessly branded as un-American in the press and over the radio by certain officials and private organizations." Dillon S. Myer, director of the War Relocation Authority, said before a subcommittee of the House Committee on Un-American Activities July 7, 1943, on the constitutional principles involved in the relocation program, that he believed in civil liberties and wanted to give his people, at least, a leg on which to stand: ". . . detention within a relocation center is not, therefore, a necessary part of the evacuation process. It is not intended to be more than a temporary stage in the process of relocating the evacuees into new homes and jobs. The detention or interment of citizens of the United States against whom no charges of disloyalty or subversion have been made, or can be made, for longer than the minimum period necessary to screen the loyal from the disloyal, and to provide the necessary guidance for relocation, is beyond the power of the War Relocation Authority."

One case involving the civil rights of those imprisoned got to the Supreme Court. Myer said, "On June 21, 1943, the Supreme Court of the United States handed down its decision in the case of *Gordan Hirabayashi* vs. *the United States*. Hirabayashi had been convicted of violating both the curfew orders and the evacuation orders applicable to Japanese Americans. The Court held that curfew was a valid exercise of the War Power. Although the question of the validity of the evacuation orders was directly presented to the Court in that case, the Court did not decide the question. There is evidence in the majority and concurring opinions of the Court in the Hirabayashi case that, although it found the curfew to be valid, it believed that the evacuation orders present difficult questions of constitutional power, and detention within a relocation center even more difficult questions. Mr. Justice Murphy, in his concurring opinion said concerning the curfew orders: 'In my opinion this goes to the very brink of constitutional power.'

"Mr. Justice Douglas, in his concurring opinion said: 'Detention for reasonable cause is one thing. Detention on account of ancestry is another. . . . Obedience to the military orders is one thing. Whether an individual member of a group must be afforded at some stage an opportunity to show that, being loyal, he should be reclassified is wholly a different question. . . . But if it is plain that no machinery was available whereby the individual could demonstrate his loyalty as a citizen in order to be reclassified, questions of a more serious character would be presented. The United States, however, takes no such position.' The chief justice in the majority opinion was careful to point out that the Court was limiting its decision to the curfew orders and was not considering the evacuation orders or confinement in a relocation center."

Grace Church and Community Center helped thirty-nine families come to Colorado during the period of voluntary evacuation. One letter we received was from the brother of Ben and Mimi Matsuda; he was confined to the camp in Poston, Arizona:

> . . . In these troublesome days, we Americans of Japanese ancestry feel lost and without an aim in life. Surely we feel that we are not to blame for the present world crisis, and it bewilders many of us to see our former American friends turn against us or forget us completely. It is doubly gratifying and encouraging to know that there is one among many, who without knowing us, is willing to turn his efforts to reunite a family, separated by the results of this war. No matter whatever the outcome, we shall always remember your kindness and shall be deeply indebted to you forever. I am looking forward to the day when my family and I can meet you in person. If that day comes it will fulfill the old quotation, 'It is an ill wind that blows no good.' For surely the pleasure of meeting you will compensate for much of the hardships that we have gone through these last three months.
>
> Sincerely yours,
George Yugi

Planned Parenthood

Father John R. Mulroy, who had an inner city parish, was well known for his liberal social work and views. I had worked with him on many problems and had suggested his name to Mayor Stapleton as a member of the Denver Housing Committee. He represented the Roman Catholic position on birth control. I was sorry for our differences on this subject.

Past incidents also disturbed me greatly. We had Margaret Sanger who founded the planned parenthood movement, and had been sentenced to prison several times in her long career. The Catholic press protested her appearance in Denver and attacked the forum for presenting her to the public. The result was that quite a number of Catholics attended the forum, and more Catholic women made use of the clinic which had offices in Grace Community Center. Fully 50 percent of our patients were Catholic, and perhaps more—they hesitated to make their affiliation known.

The Denver Antithesis Club was a small group of well known people who had specific points of view in various areas. Two Catholic priests in the membership threatened to resign if I continued to be a member. I offered to resign, but the club felt that my resignation would be contrary to its purposes. A Catholic layman, the president of the Loretto Heights Academy, took the place of the priests and continued to represent Catholic views on various subjects.

The Denver Open Forum

We had a program which included three open forums: the Denver Open Forum, organized in 1920 by Dr. George L. Lackland; the Sunday Afternoon Argue Club, attended mostly by lonely men who had nowhere else to go; and the Denver Labor College Forum, part of the Denver Labor College, that met every Monday evening following classes during sessions of the college. The Women's Labor Auxiliary had an annual Sunday morning service in Grace Church.

The forums had a great influence in bringing understanding to people of differing views. Forums were far less sophisticated than they are today. It would seem to me real forums have gone out of style. We invited discussions as well as question periods, and were quite informal. It is possible that television has changed the manner in which we discuss public questions and issues.

We tried to get widely known authorities for the Denver Open Forum. We had occasional panels, involving several points of view; we had political candidates nights during elections years for senator, governor, and mayor. All parties were represented, right as well as left. The Republicans refused to participate in the first program unless the Communist candidate was dropped. When the Republicans realized how popular and well accepted the programs were, they joined up.

During the Depression many groups emerged who had ideas on how to solve our national problems: the Utopians, the Technocrats, the Townsendites, the Workers' Alliance, the National Alliance, the League for Peace and Democracy, the League for Industrial Democracy, and many other groups. All were eager to express their ideas and were heard in our forums. Dr. Townsend, a doctor from Long Beach, California decided that aging people needed food and medicine and crusaded for old age pensions. There were thousands of Townsend Clubs throughout the nation. There was a competing old age pension group in Colorado called the Annuity League, under the direction of O. Otto Moore. Judge Moore provided the political leadership such an organization required so that Colorado became the first state to provide a pension of $40 per month.

In fifteen years, we had some 1,800 meetings. Some popular speakers were Margaret Sanger of Planned Parenthood; Governor Edwin C. Johnson; Senator Edward P. Costigan; Josephine Roach, president of the Rocky Mountain Fuel Company; John Lawson, who led the strike of the southern coal miners in 1914; the Annuity League for Old Age Pensions; Judge Ben Lindsay, the pioneer in juvenile courts; Norman Thomas, candidate for president of the United States on the Socialist ticket; the Socialist delegation from Spain during the Spanish War; and Clarence Darrow, famous lawyer.

Norman Thomas was a popular speaker but received more votes from non-Socialists than from his own party members. The Socialists couldn't get along among themselves. Norman Thomas told a story in which he said that you couldn't give artificial respiration to a drowning man at the bottom of a lake—you had to get him on shore first. I have always wanted to know where that shore was so that we could provide artificial respiration. Seemed like we were all drowning with no place to go.

The three men who did us the most good were Dr. Harry F. Ward, a professor in Union Seminary, New York, and executive secretary of the Methodist Federation of Social Action; Dr. Orrin W. Auman, national treasurer of the World Service agencies of the Methodist church; and Scott Nearing, who had been dismissed from his university professorship during the First World War for being a pacifist. These men stayed in Denver long enough to hold seminars so people had sufficient time to think and really discuss the problems of the day.

We had problems with some of our forums, especially where emotions were stirred up intentionally. The most difficult program was the Spanish delegation on which was a Socialist Catholic priest from Spain. The Catholic weeklies attacked the proposed forum, and phone campaigns were worked out to get our best supporters to force us to call off the meeting. Heavy pressure was brought and many people threatened to withdraw their support if the meeting were not called off. I stood my ground in defense of free speech. I asked Dr. Ben Cherrington of the school of international studies at the University of Denver to be the chairman. That night I walked into a packed church, and saw Rabbi Kauvar sitting in the front pew. I asked him why he was present. He said, "To give you and your meeting respectability— and, of course, I want to know what is happening in Spain."

One of the very fine morning church services was planned by Noble Sissle of musical and orchestral fame. His orchestra was playing at the Lakeside Amusement Park, and he was invited to take over our morning service. He and his team were very religious people. He preached the sermon and the orchestra sang and played. I shall never forget the woman soloist who sang the Lord's Prayer. It was jazzed up a bit—but good. Mr. Sissle, Dr. Holmes and I went fishing the next day. Mr. Sissle gave the rest of his life to finding talent among young people and to giving them a chance to grow.

Webb Waldron

Early in 1942, a Webb Waldron dropped in to see me. He explained that he was a writer for the *Reader's Digest*. He had done a story about a Catholic church and was now searching for a Protestant church that was serving people in time of need. My church was one of seven that he intended to visit; he would write about one of them for the *Christian Herald*, and it would later appear in the *Reader's Digest*. He explained that he was not interested in traditional churches carrying on as usual, but in churches concerned about helping people. He was not looking for the best preacher in town, but for those who were sensitive to human needs. He said that there were too many traditional churches and too few with social conscience. He added that he was not a churchman and would not be attending church services or activities. He wanted me to recommend certain contacts, and would ask me to introduce some of them; but for the most part he would be on his own. He didn't want me to tell anyone that he was around, or describe his purpose or what he was doing. He wanted complete freedom to come and go as he researched our program in and outside of the Center. He was a very serious person, and never offered a smile or word of encouragement until the end of his stay of about eight days. He wished to remain completely incognito. He would be displeased with any effort to set up any activity "to make us look good" other than what was scheduled, or to influence anyone in our behalf. He said that he would terminate his stay at any moment he felt inclined, but if he approved he would remain as long as it took to do a good job in line with his assignment. He did not reveal how or why he came to Denver. I accepted his ground rules, and was tremendously curious as to the outcome.

I was hardly aware that he was around after the first two days. I did not know where he stayed. I was inclined to believe that he had come and gone, until I saw him in a Sunday morning service. After the service he became talkative and offered his first smile, which was to my wife. Her curiosity got the best of her and she asked if any article would be released. He smiled and said that it was almost finished. She asked, "Who will decide?" He replied that he would. The article in full length appeared first in the *Christian Herald* and in condensed form in the *Reader's Digest,* April 1942.

Mr. Waldron was quite warm as he conversed with us before he left. He said that there were five places on his list but he had found the one he wanted, and that we had saved him a lot of time and effort. He related that he had never before met anyone who was welcome in almost any circle, whether they be Communists, radicals, liberals, Democrats or Republicans. I explained that my politics were basically human needs and hunger. He told about one writer for a large daily newspaper who said, "Sure, Wallie is okay, but sometimes I think he believes he is God for this whole damn town." Mr. Waldron seemed to like this. He said, "Maybe there is a God after all, you know what I mean? By the way, I liked your sermon—you were down to earth."

He referred to meeting a few ministers. No ministers were on the list I had provided. One minister was in my corner with the highest praise. (I thought this one must have been Dean Roberts of St. John's Cathedral, who gave us both encouragement and assistance.) One minister said that I had gone too far out on the limb and had sacrificed a promising future. (I thought that this one must have been my district superintendent or bishop—both of whom knew their middle class constituencies much too well.) Mr. Waldron went to a prominent rabbi—who I am sure was Rabbi Kauvar—who praised me to no end. One minister accused me of being a publicity seeker, and Mr. Waldron couldn't see this at all—he had searched through the files of the newspapers and felt that the publicity was deserving.

I told him about an encounter with Mr. Fred Bonfils of the *Denver Post*. He had invited me to his office where he congratulated me on being the minister of Grace Church, formerly held by Dr. Christian F. Reisner, a friend of his. Mr. Bonfils wanted me to preach a sermon on corruption in Denver, and would give me two reporters to dig out the information—to be used against Mayor Stapleton. He promised that he would make me the outstanding minister in Denver. I informed him that I thought Mayor Stapleton was the best man in the coming election, and intended to vote for him. Mr. Bonfils ordered me out of his office and said that my name would never be mentioned in the *Post*. He relented some two years later when we had an Indian Night with Chief He-wan-chee-cha of the Utes as speaker. Mr. Bonfils was an honorary chief and member of the Ute tribe and had to get in on the act. Everything went well from then on. I felt that he became a sincere friend and gave our program tremendous support. He even allowed me to pick out what books I wanted from his shelves, which were sent to him free of charge as was the custom. He said, "Take what you want, I don't read them anyway. It's a good way to get rid of them."

Mr. Waldron thanked me for a stimulating week and went his way. He was a tremendous person. I sorrowed when he passed away. Few men had his perspective on people and their feelings.

A Church for All People
Condensed from Christian Herald
by Webb Waldron

(Copyright 1942, Christian Herald Assn., Inc.,
419 Fourth Ave., New York City
Christian Herald, April 1942)

In his home town, Denver, people everywhere greet him with: "Say, Wally, you did a swell job with that kid!" Or, "Wally, we got a fight on our hands—we need your help!"

To newsboys, judges, bank presidents and janitors he is Wally. The Reverend Edgar M. Wahlberg, round-faced, spectacled, small but tough as nails, is a 42-year-old Methodist preacher who has made his church a vital instrument of social good and a magnificent example of what a church can do.

Not a temple of cold doctrine, but a radiant center of human brotherhood; that is Wahlberg's idea of a church. To encourage people to stand on their own feet, to stimulate the community to shoulder responsibility for its own welfare, to help those in need, to open wide the church to every worthwhile activity of the people; that is Wahlberg's idea of a church's job.

Stand any day at the door of Grace Church and watch the human tide. Working mothers leaving their children at the free nursery. Women attending the Mothers' Clinic. People going into the job-finding office. In the evening the Rambler Gang—young fellows Wally brought in from the streets—playing all sorts of games. In the parsonage the Denver Labor College holding a class in public speaking. In the Community House a Czech group putting on a folk dance, and busy classes in cooperative buying, homemaking, first aid, citizenship.

Attendance at Grace Church activities, apart from religious services, last year exceeded 200,000, including people of 26 denominations. Not one in 20 was a Methodist, and many belonged to no church. Often there are 240 meetings a month, with some crowded rooms running four shifts a day. In the recreation rooms many of the youngsters are delinquents paroled in Wahlberg's care. Only two such boys have fallen back in the clutches of the law, and both were mental cases. There are 32 Grace Church basketball teams, and what had been one of Denver's toughest boys' gangs won the inter-church tournament last winter.

Wahlberg was born in Denver, the son of a Swedish immigrant. He graduated from the University of Denver and soon afterward went into the ministry. He has three children of his own.

Early in his career he proved the value of incentive and activity in the world of youth. Juvenile delinquency was rampant. He said to the mine manager: "You pay $2,700 a year to keep the streets and parks clean. Why not hire the boys in town to do the job—for the same money?" The manager agreed. The boys, finding an exciting sense of responsibility in doing what grownups had formerly done, pitched in and did it well. Juvenile crime practically ceased.

When Wahlberg came to Grace Church a dozen years ago, in the depths of the Depression, it was dying. Well-to-do supporters had moved away; church attendance averaged 49. Wahlberg tried pulpit pyrotechnics but the people wouldn't come back. "Finally," he says, "I realized that the church wasn't offering anything that interested people. So I turned the church over to them—to the whole community—and let them do what they wished with it."

Invited in, the neighborhood started a self-help cooperative which raised vegetables and made clothes. In "Problem Meetings" hundreds vigorously discussed poverty, relief, jobs, and the role of the church in the crisis.

Church membership took a jump. Wahlberg discovered that when he stopped pushing the church *as a church* in the narrow traditional sense and made it a community affair, the church *as a spiritual force* multiplied in power.

Alarmed that one district was breeding potential jailbirds, citizens asked Wally what to do. He suggested a community center. They got hold of an abandoned firehouse; old streetcar seats were made into chairs; folks gave tables, stoves and lamps, got up craftwork and games for boys and girls. There has since been almost no juvenile delinquency in that section.

"No corrective effort is effective if imposed from the outside," Wahlberg says. "You must find some root in the community out of which self-improvement and discipline can grow."

Four years ago a Denver businessman, James Q. Newton, gave Grace Church a 500-acre ranch. The Rambler Gang turned it into a boys' ranch. Many people had said the gang wouldn't do a lick of work. But, hauling out tons of manure, they made the cow shed into a dormitory, the machine shed a kitchen and dining hall, the hay barn a craft center. Some 30 boys are there the year round, and in summer the ranch becomes a camp for needy children.

But youth activities won't guarantee that children from bad homes will grow up wholesomely. In the three-square-mile section around Grace Church, housing conditions were among the worst in town. Denver was advertised as the world's healthiest city, but Wahlberg pointed out that part of this area had one of the world's most shocking infant mortality rates. Juvenile delinquency flourished, too. Both evils Wahlberg laid to the cold, dark, unsanitary shacks in which the people lived.

His outcry brought real estate men down upon him. This upstart Methodist preacher was a traitor to his city. Wahlberg retorted that just as there are laws against selling rotten food, there ought to be laws against renting rotten houses. The governor appointed him chairman of a state housing committee, and he saw to it that the black spot near his church was replaced by a low-rent housing development. Infant mortality and juvenile misdemeanors took a sharp drop.

Anything that hit evilly at his people brings Wahlberg up fighting. Many in his community were falling into the hands of loan sharks. Interest was sometimes pyramided to six times the principal, and borrowers often found themselves buried under a growing pile of service fees and refinancing charges. Wahlberg and his friends fought through a city ordinance which eliminated some of the evils. This battle against usury stimulated the organization of credit unions; the one at Grace Church did a $4,000 business last year. Other group enterprises started under Wahlberg's inspiration and guidance include a consumer's cooperative and a medical and dental service.

Eleven years ago Wahlberg heard that the Denver Bakers' Union was looking for quarters. He invited the bakers to rent rooms in the Community House. Nineteen Denver labor unions have been born in Grace Church, several enjoying free quarters till they got on their feet.

The strongest fraternal hand reaching out to Wahlberg in Denver is that of Paul Roberts, Dean of St. John's Episcopal Cathedral. "Wally not only talks social ideas and ideals—he lives them," says Roberts, who has helped Wahlberg get financial help for his church from wealthy citizens. The two ministers held monthly dinners that brought together Roberts' "coupon clippers" and Wally's labor people. Talking frankly about wages, jobs and working conditions, these men discovered that employers and workers were not different breeds but troubled human beings confronted by different circumstances, trying to work things out into satisfactory lives. These gatherings have spread a better feeling between capital and labor in Denver.

"The Church needs," says Wahlberg, "to rethink and restate the needs of men. Until it has done so it will be jostled out of the way by the onrush of movements that gather round those needs—that give vitality to fascism and communism. If democracy is saved in America the Church will have to take a hand. To do so it will have to know not less about God but more about men."

Our Parting Gift to you—May It Often Bring Remembrance, Too

To Our Beloved Family Wahlberg:
Who, for the past fifteen years, have lived to serve and inspire the literally thousands of people who now live and have lived in the Grace Church community and throughout the city of Denver.

Many of us came into your lives and influences during the "Terrible Thirties." We came for physical, moral, and spiritual aid. There were hungry babies then; unhappy children; a youth maladjusted; browbeaten parents with home and financial problems, too great to be carried alone; the aged; the lonely; the bereaved; the handicapped; the mistreated and misunderstood minorities; bitter racial hatreds, the unfairly paid laborer; the unemployed and the penniless.

At no time did you spare time and effort to help. Always, we were given aid, and many, many times, this was financial as well as spiritual. Never was the social or the political issue sugar-coated or set aside as "too hot" to handle. We liked your clear and accurate statement of the truth, and your firm and fearless remedy. We received a liberal education in your ably conducted forums.

Then also, came the happier days—the day of the nursery school; the mother's clinic; athletic teams; cooperative and self-help groups; the Cosmopolitan Club; christenings; weddings, birthday parties, the beautiful Christmas pageants; wonderful Easter days.

Then again, the cruel tragedy of war, with all of its accompanying tensions, fears, and grief.

All these experiences have been woven into the warp and woof of our lives and endeared you to us.

So now, because of this fine fellowship we have shared, we wish to show our love and appreciation to you by giving you this gift.

May God graciously care for you; give you new strength and inspiration for the tasks which lie before you, and grant you many happy years together in His service.

—The Members of Your Congregation

(This message was presented to us at the farewell party and retirement from Grace Community Methodist Church and Community Center, November 1945. I departed a few days later for Greece [later China], under the auspices of UNRRA).

A Letter Dating Back to Grace Church Days—9/24/68

Dear Wallie and Jimmy:
Here is another voice from back in the past—to wish you well.

Just the sight of your name stirred up so many wonderful memories. I am only sorry that it took an illness to find out where you people are.

Because it has been so many years (over twenty) since I saw you last, and because our lives have taken so many paths, I won't try to make this a newsy letter. I'll just make it a letter of thanks.

Thank you, my dear Rev. Wahlberg and dear, sweet Jimmy—

Thank you for kindness and understanding—and shoes for cold feet in winter.

Thank you for spiritual guidance, and wise personal advice, and for good wholesome food when meals were few and far between—and haircuts when barbers came too high.

Thank you for the wonderful lifelong gift of good books to read; and a very stern lecture in your library—not about books.

Thank you for prayers shared under the stars around a campfire, and in a redwood chapel; and for the experience of cooking on a wood stove for twenty-eight little boys; and painting a barn, and horseback riding, and hayrides; and for secret, (holy) words to get into the mess hall.

Thank you for the singing of songs like—"C.O.L.O. hip, hip, A RADO I'm a mile high feelin' fine."

Thank you for funny old movies, and beanbags, and pool tables.

Thank you for basketball, and dancing, and wood shop.

Thank you for knitting lessons, and day nursery—with tiny socks and T-stools—and loving care.

Thank you for our very own juke box.

Thank you for the use of your attic for ironing and mending, and the use of your basement for the sealing of home-canned fruit and jellies.

Thank you for allowing me to assist in preparing the Holy Sacrament, along with your children, and as reward, and extra glass of sacramental wine—and a beautiful explanation of what it meant.

Thank you for slumber parties, and ghost stories.

Thank you for candlelight services, and long black robes, and Christmas baskets full of food, and a present for everyone—when there wouldn't have been any at all.

Thank you for my first trip to the circus, and—of all things—ballet lessons!

Thank you for teaching me to love all people, whatever their color or creed. What a wonderful thing your unbroken circles was—and is. Just holding hands in prayer can be a very warm and spiritual experience.

I guess there is no end to the list of "thank yous" that I owe you for making Grace Church my home during my growing-up years. You were the church to me.

I guess I should give a little credit here to someone else.

Thank you, God, for letting me share a tiny corner in the lives of such wonderful people.

Get well, Wally—please get well.

I am only one of the many, many—from Denver to China—that you inspired and aided. You were always an example, but above all, our friend.

God bless you and yours,
>With love always,

Norma Jean (Mickey) McCoy

Postscript

Grace United Methodist Church and Community Center finally succumbed to what was felt to be the inevitable, sold out and was rebuilt in a new suburb. The program reverted to traditional ways and gave up most of its social outreach.

Evans Memorial Chapel was transported stone by stone to the campus of the University of Denver and rebuilt.

Grace Community Center was reorganized and relocated in southwest Denver.

The Planned Parenthood Clinic continues in a new location.

The Conifer mountain camp remains in operation.

The first truck belonging to the Grace Church Cooperative Relief Association. The truck was old but rendered all manner of services for the community.

The Commissary was the center of the Grace Church Cooperative Relief Association from which thousands of dollars of foodstuffs were dispensed. Much of this was earned by members. The faces of these men reveal the true horror of the Depression; they worked long and hard for what little the Cooperative had to offer.

The shoe shop was one of the essential services of the Grace Church Cooperative Relief Association. Mr. Lutes (foreground), a former night watchman who had lost both his job and a leg was given the job and eventually developed a sizable business.

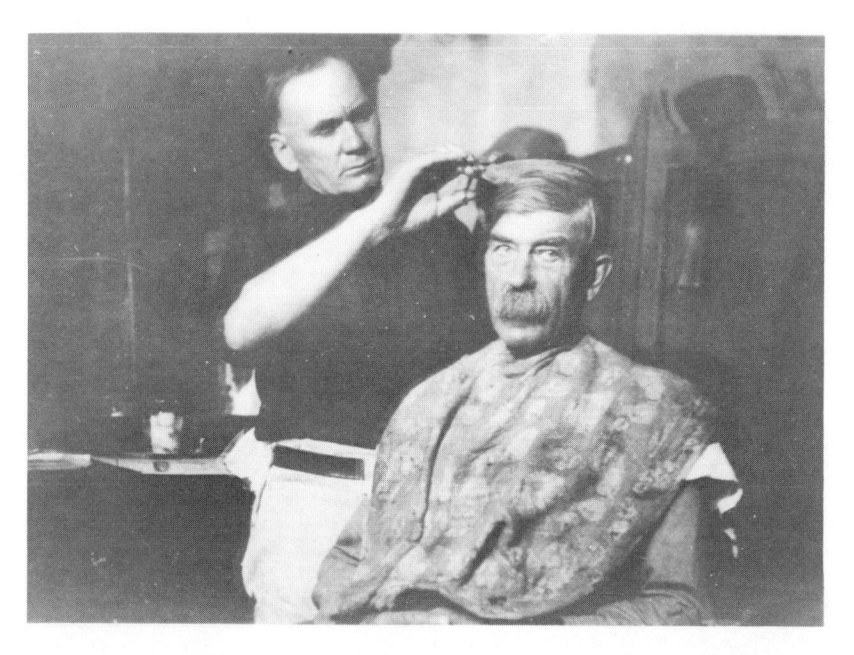

Another business that was established at Grace Church was this barber shop in the Community Center. (Women had a separate beauty salon.) After professional training by an experienced barber nearly ten men were able to work at least part time.

This was the base camp of the Grace Church Cooperative Relief Association potato project in Greeley. Tents and transportation were provided by Major Ardoural of the Colorado State Militia.

A truckload of potatoes ready to return to Denver.

Sacking potatoes.

For the men of the Cooperative, this was back-breaking work. Few of them had ever been farmers.

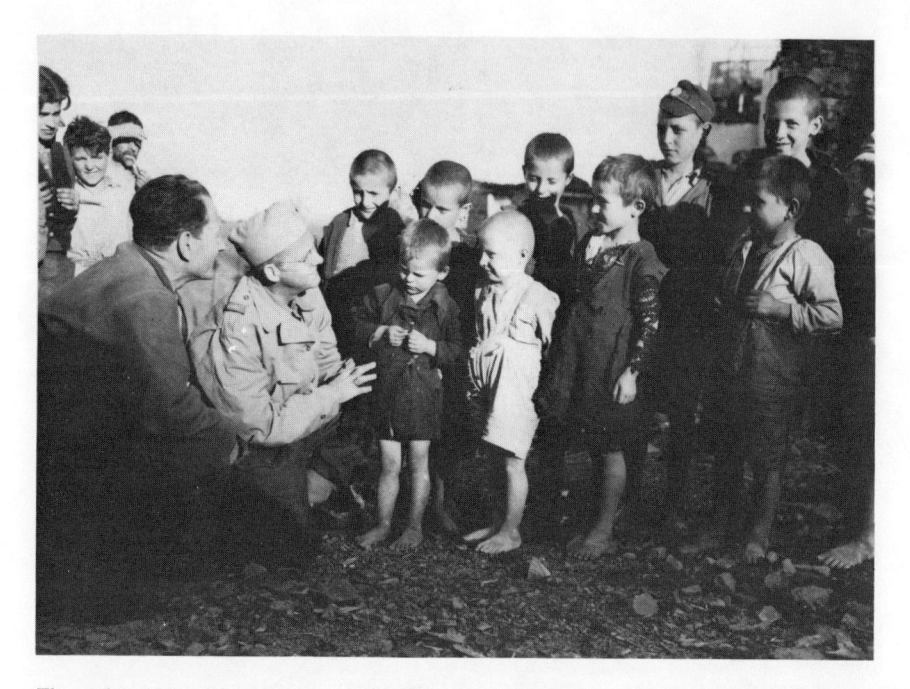

The author (second from left) as an UNRRA official in Greece.

6. UNITED NATIONS RELIEF AND REHABILITATION ADMINISTRATION, GREECE: 1944-1945

Orientation

The Second World War changed the nature of our program at Grace Community Center, but not its purpose or philosophy. There was plenty to do as we turned to the needs and problems of Japanese Americans who were separated from their families scattered in the various concentration centers. Thirty-seven of these families united with our church. Their young people needed recreational and referral services, which we tried to supply. Their morale was generally low as they were confronted with the growing anti-Japanese attitudes of many people.

We maintained our nursery school for working mothers. We enrolled one small Japanese American who had a miserable time in spite of what our teachers could do. The children liked to play war games, and this little boy was always the enemy. The children could not separate themselves from the war that everybody was fighting. This boy could only wait for his mother to rescue him at the end of the day. I called him aside and he sobbed out his story: "I'm not an enemy. I am an American!" I counseled with his mother, who in turn expressed her grief. She withdrew the child from the school and found a more congenial atmosphere with a Japanese American family. This experience grieved me and gave me insight into what suffering many people had to endure. I came in for similar antagonism. We had a Japanese American secretary, Michie Terasaki, but she could endure any kind of weather. She later became secretary to a justice of the Colorado Supreme Court, Otto O. Moore.

We served boys in military service stationed near Denver one night a week for dances, socials, and various get-togethers. We corresponded with our boys from the church and the center who were scattered around the world. Most of the Ramblers volunteered. The poverty and hunger of the Depression years faded into the background. Men and women wanted work and most of them found it. The idea that women should not take jobs slowly disappeared.

We had younger children in even greater numbers. The school children's luncheon was discontinued, and the Grace Church Co-operative Relief Association became a mere skeleton to provide assistance for those who could not help themselves. Forums were much harder to conduct because people turned their thoughts mostly to winning the war. The Denver Labor College disbanded for the duration, which turn out to be for good. Sewing circles made sweaters and socks for the boys in the service. People went out on bond drives to prove their patriotism. The Congressional Committee on Un-American Activities and similar organizations bore down on people with liberal ideas. A few intelligent people were fearful of the regimentation that was part and parcel of wartime, from which the United States would not soon recover.

I realized that we had come through a decade of idleness and depression and wondered what my role might be in the next decade. Friends in Washington D.C. suggested that I might serve with the United Nations Relief and Rehabilitation Administration. I read about the hunger and starvation in Greece and other parts of the world. I did not want to be a chaplain in any military service.

I was invited to serve in the Balkan mission to be organized by UNRRA; it did not materialize because Tito of Yugoslavia could not accept the conditions of UNRRA, which included admitting British troops, a military liaison, to occupy the country—presumably to make it safe for the work of UNRRA. After what happened in Greece, he seemed to have been wise in this decision. I was naive about the real purpose of a military liaison, which would seem to have been to make the political situation conform to the interests of Great Britain—at least this is what happened in Greece.

I filled out an application, took my physical examination, and waited for final instructions. My friends told me that I was investigated to determine my loyalty as an American citizen. My assignment was to be a welfare officer in Athens.

I received my directives on May 1, 1944, requested annual leave from my church in Denver, and reported to UNRRA offices in Washington for special training and orientation. Thus began an experience in what was supposed to be an effort to help people help themselves. I shared the despair of the Greeks and tried to do the job with equal compassion for all Greeks, regardless of their loyalties.

We left Miami, Florida, July 9 and arrived in Cairo July 18 by way of Puerto Rico, Trinidad, Georgetown, British Guiana, then over the equator to Bellau and Natal, Brazil, where we had a four-day stay. Natal was a city of some 60,000 people. The streets were narrow and crowded; the streetcars were open and overflowing with humanity, passengers standing where they could—mostly on the steps. We were told that only seated passengers paid a fare; all others rode free. We took off for Ascension Island, situated in the mid-Atlantic. It was a volcanic rock which thrust its way out of the ocean and on which the United States had carved out a landing field. It was dismal and isolated. After Waterloo the English thought of imprisoning Napoleon on this island but decided against it because it was uninhabitable. We rushed to the mess hall and ate a poor breakfast—scrambled powdered eggs. The loneliness and low morale of the men stationed there disturbed me. We left in an hour and flew 1,362 miles across the rest of the Atlantic to Accra in British West Africa, known then as the Gold Coast, now Ghana. Most of the buildings, barracks, mess halls, officers quarters, tables and chairs were mahogany.

The caste system was complete in the subjection of these intelligent natives. Wages were thirty-eight cents a day. The United States had spent millions of dollars on installations and airfields but did not own them. They belonged to Brazil, Great Britain and Egypt. Much would depend upon good international relationships after the war, and ours were none too good. We stayed in Accra two nights. I went to church at the main base on Sunday morning.

We flew again on Monday at 6 a.m. to Kana, 744 miles, and then to Maid Ugan in a British colony 308 miles further into the heart of Africa. The country did not seem to be very fertile, although we passed over large areas of forest. We arrived in El Fasher in the afternoon, another 838 miles east. A storm had settled in and we were grounded five hours. Native people and villages were all around us. Two of us ventured into one of the villages where children were naked and the women were topless and the men naked except for a loin cloth. They seemed happy to see us.

El Fasher had a ritzy dining hall named the "Fireball Line Inn." The dining hall was beautifully decorated with native decor, with native waitresses dressed in white and red and a dwarf cigarette boy. The mess captain had once operated a restaurant in Rochester, New York. It was a treat and a morale builder for all who traveled through this distant part of central Africa. There was one problem. One had to be fully dressed, including a necktie. We had neglected our ties so we were not admitted. We were told to go back to our plane and pick up our neckties, which we were not about to do. I called to an Englishman who was seated nearby and asked him to lend me his tie, and he did. I arranged the tie and was admitted. I took it off and gave it to my friend next in line, who did the same for our next companion. All were finally admitted and the tie was returned to the owner, who was thanked for this courtesy. There was no rule that said this could not be done, so the employees accepted our ruse. Everyone in the dining hall seemed to enjoy the situation.

Among others I met the Presbyterian chaplain, Ketchum. I think he must have been a champion circuit rider, flying from Khartoum to Kana and sometimes Accra on a regular schedule of church services and appointments. All his constituents were white.

We landed in Khartoum early the next morning, and hoped we might lay over for a needed rest. We had traveled another 503 miles and had had enough, riding in bare bucket seats. But in Khartoum we changed at once to another plane to fly down the valley of the Nile River to Cairo, 992 miles. This was the roughest ride of my life and I could hardly bear it. Egypt is the Nile. Countless villages which looked splendid from the air were miserable dwelling places when seen from the ground. Here is the largest and oldest irrigation system in history. We passed over Luxor and saw the Valley of the Kings, where King Tut was buried. As we approached Cairo we saw the

Sphinx, and then the three great pyramids. Finally we landed, so completely exhausted we could hardly make it to the terminal.

Cairo was everything that has been said about it, from filth and poverty to riches and modernity. I never saw a screen door or a window. The claim was that religious belief is that flies have as much right to live as people. There were millions of them and we were everywhere pestered by them, except in our own quarters. I saw flies crawling in and out and around sores on human beings, especially children. It was hideous to observe flies crawling and lighting on the eyes, mouths and ears of babies and little children. A young Egyptian was asked, "Don't your health authorities understand the danger of flies which carry all kinds of sickness?" "Surely," he said, "but there are too many of them. We have to be tolerant. We swish them away." It seemed that all better class Egyptians had "swishers." They were not fly swatters, but horse hairs imbedded in a handle. It was a sight to watch an Egyptian calmly carry on a conversation, gracefully swishing and totally unconcerned about the flies. We also learned about lizards and cockroaches.

Cairo and Palestine

The staging area for personnel in the Middle East was in Cairo. Laird W. Archer was the head of the mission and director of the Near East Foundation with its office in Athens. Our assignment was a Greek refugee camp at Nusierat near Gaza, Palestine. The trip was by train. The fact that we were Americans had its own charm, and the fact that we gave the brakeman a few dollars provided us with a compartment so we could stretch out and rest. It was a feudal land, the people regimented to the cruel discipline of soil, sun and water on the one hand and the relentless surveillance of the agents of the owners and overlords on the other. Crowds of people, mostly children, surrounded our train every time it stopped, begging for whatever they could get get.

When we arrived in Gaza, we engaged a Jewish boy with a donkey to haul our luggage to the station. He piled our baggage on top of his donkey and then climbed up himself and guided us there. We washed up and shaved at an outside open faucet and waited for transportation to Nusierat.

I talked with a Palestinian Jew who was a sergeant and had relatives in the United States. I sought information about the cooperatives and communal villages. He was an ardent Zionist and thought that Arab-Jewish relationships would work out for the benefit of both groups; he felt that the troublemakers were neither Arab nor true Jewish, but mercenary interests motivated by national politics and loyalties.

The transport hurtled us toward the Nusierat Refugee Camp more than ten miles away. There were a number of British military units stationed along the road. Our eyes rose to the three flags flying in the cool Mediterranean breeze over the entrance: the United Kingdom, the Greek, and the American. Originally there had been only two flags. I learned that a Greek family who had formerly lived in the United States, and for twelve years in Athens, had made the flag.

The camp had 10,000 persons, divided into four units. The management and services of each unit were inadequate. The commandant, Major H. H. Vrendenburg, was able, intelligent, and humanitarian. He looked toward the UNRRA for leadership and supplies. It is almost impossible to imagine the responsibilities and skill necessary for the operation of such a camp.

There were limited military personnel to keep order. There were a few social workers and volunteers and members of English pacifist organizations. They proved themselves indispensable in every situation. There was a limited opposition, especially where Americans were involved. I used every group available.

The Greeks were enrolled as they came into the camp and appointed to the various units where they were expected to organize themselves and make their lives as livable as possible. They had their own civilian leaders and committees which sometimes spent more time in discussion than work. The most popular activity seemed to be military training, especially for guerilla warfare.

I attended a program of Greek songs and music at which the audience of 2,000 people broke into uncontrollable applause when a chorus sang a song against Italy. The feeling was so intense that it picked you up like a raging, overflowing river. The applause drowned out the chorus. Men and boys accompanied by martial songs marched constantly. There was a tremendous eagerness to get the war over with and to return home, to get out of the complications and unhappiness of camp life. Refugees sometimes hate both friend and foe, and are suspicious of everyone; they can't trust each other and exaggerate all grievances, or so it seemed to those who were trying to help.

Nusierat Camp also had a boys' camp for boys who were unattached with no known parents or sponsors. Some had roamed and lived like dogs, snatching and stealing whatever was available. Some knew that their parents had been killed; others didn't know much about their parents, but hoped to find them. The Greek Jews knew that their parents had been killed and they would never see them again. There were nearly one hundred boys in the camp. Their one hope was to kill Italians, Bulgarians and Germans and they waited impatiently for the time they would be recruited for military service.

I was asked to come up with recommendations for improvements to this camp. My problem was communication. We discovered that the leader of the camp, a champion soccer player from England, could speak a little French; one of the volunteer leaders was French and could understand Greek. We worked out a communication system in an effort to talk to the boys. We discovered that knowing each other's language was not always essential to understanding each other. The soccer player's experience with boys was limited, which he freely admitted. He taught the boys soccer on the level beach, even though the boys had no shoes or equipment. There were a number of sprained ankles and broken toes. Outside of military activities the boys liked best a quiet game called "Drama," which I learned at the time. There were seven boys in each tent; they did their own work, including cooking. The camp was surprisingly well-kept and clean. There was some effort to make the tents homelike with pictures and floral wreaths. Some of the boys liked to get their bowl of stew or soup and whatever was available, and eat in their own tents. There was talk of having a mess hall where the boys could eat together, but it seemed to make them feel better to have their tents the center of their important experiences.

The UNRRA officers were asked to write out a program and make recommendations, especially about the boys' camp. We discovered that there were 1,242 unemployed men—not including the boys in camp—and came up with a few suggestions. There were few if any available materials. It is difficult to keep all men employed in an established community, without believing it can be done in a refugee camp. Unemployment led to frustrations and feelings of helplessness, although there was already considerable creative work being done. We believed that as much as possible the boys should be placed with families, and that the boys' camp should not become a fixed institution in which a group of homeless youth might find themselves permanently isolated from the community. The Greeks liked this idea because it was their custom where children were concerned. They had saved hundreds of Jewish children by claiming them as their own.

When our work was accomplished in the refugee camp, we asked to visit a few places in the Holy Land, and our request was granted. We went to Jerusalem which we knew for its many churches. I found that those churches were heedless of the poverty around them.

Bethlehem

We visited the usual places in Jerusalem—took a trip to Jericho and to the Dead Sea, where we sat in the salt-saturated water just to see if it could be done. We took a trip to Bethlehem, and on the way stopped at the well of the Magi near where Bethany existed, the home town of Jesus' best friends.

We went to the Jordan River and stopped at the Allenby bridge. I excused myself and walked down the river bank, where I found an open place covered with willows. The bank was about three feet high, so I held on to the willows with one hand while I reached into the water with the other. I filled my right hand with the water and poured the Jordan River water over my balding head. I walked slowly back to the car, where a member of the medical corps came by and asked where he might get down to the river. I retraced my steps to show him where I had been.

I asked him, "Do you wish to be baptized?"

He replied, "Yes, you are right. First time in my life I needed a preacher—but I guess I can do it myself."

I told him I was a minister and would be glad to baptize him, unless he wanted to be a Baptist—the river seemed to be too deep for immersion. He said that he expected to be a Presbyterian and wanted more than anything else to be baptized in the River Jordan. He said, "It's a damn miracle to have a minister just when you need him."

Bethlehem is five miles southwest of Jerusalem. We looked over the fields of Boaz and in the distance were the Judean hills. Bethlehem is on the top of a rolling hill, and is supposed to have been founded by the grandfather of Boaz. The Church of the Nativity towers over the small houses and narrow streets, and I suppose Bethlehem looked much as it always as. People still lived in the caves along the side of the adjacent hills.

The Church of the Nativity was erected over the supposed birthplace of

Jesus and belongs to three ancient sects: Greek, Latin and Armenian. The basilica was built by order of Emperor Constantine and another part of the church by his mother Queen Helen. Some authorities believe that the church underwent considerable restoration in the days of Justinian, 525-565 A.D. The church escaped destruction, in spite of the conflicts in which most early Christian churches were destroyed. It was restored in the Middle Ages when the roof was covered with lead. The Turks stripped the church of the lead to make bullets. The church suffered considerable damage but was again restored by the Greek Orthodox church.

After stooping to get through the low entrance, we studied the ancient floors and mosaics. At one time the church had been used as a stable, so the entrance had been raised to accommodate horses, and later lowered to make this impossible. We listened to the drone of the priests of several sects, rituals handed down through the centuries. We saw the bells, which are played over an international hookup every Christmas Eve. We were led past hoary and antique walls shrouded in the dim light, and down two flights of stairs to the underground Chapel of the Nativity, dark and dimly lit by musty oil lamps and candles.

The tiny Chapel of the Manger was three steps further down. The manger was made of marble, replacing the original manger which was said to be in the Church of Santa Maria Maggiore in Rome, where it has been since 750. At the end of the subterranean passage was a round hole out of which water had burst forth, presumably for the use of the Holy Family. A monk droned out in poor English the story of Bethlehem and the birth of Jesus.

This, it seemed to me, was the story of Christianity in a nutshell—buried under vast aging structures, stairways, darkness and fables about original mangers and miracles and a million voices droning ancient words and rituals, without relevance to our world. I turned abruptly away and found myself in the clear air and blazing sunlight. I watched the people and wondered what I could learn from them. I was startled by a statement from our guide who spoke from behind me, "I know what you want."

He led me down the street which was a little more than a crowded narrow lane, and there I saw a manger, a few goats, and a donkey. Little children were playing and shouting. A mother walked out of the door of a neighboring Palestinian house. She held a baby in her arms. This is what I had come to see—not the pyramids or chapels and churches and darkness huddled over an alleged cradle of the Christ child.

I visited a communal village to talk with Jewish friends. This community raised citrus fruits for trade and gardens for subsistence. I talked with the purchasing agent for the whole community, who had escaped the oven chambers in Germany where it had seemed he was destined to die. He was a scholarly man and had a friend, a Lutheran minister of some standing, who helped him escape. He was delighted with his job and the prospects for the future.

We took the train to Lydda (near the then new city of Tel Aviv) where we changed to the main line on our way back to Cairo. The little train, old and weatherbeaten, jerked its way around bends and curves through the Judean hills, stopping every few miles at villages and small towns. There were flocks of sheep and goats on the hillsides, terraced with strips of farmland that grew grain, vegetables, corn, olive trees and grapes. Stately women walked to and from the wells, balancing jars on their heads. I saw a mother with a baby in her arms riding a donkey, with her husband walking beside her. She was dressed in a black robe and he in a white robe. There were prosperous farms and villages as the countryside opened into valleys and flatland. A leader of one of these communities sat opposite me in the coach and gave glowing accounts of his work and of the people living in cooperative communities.

The surging power in Palestine was in the communal and cooperative farms of the Zionists, who turned desert wastelands into productive areas. Their villages and towns were centers of health, happiness and vitality, in remarkable contrast to the drab deadness almost everywhere else in the Middle East. The plains of Judea and Israel teemed with new life. It was not an easy life as people from many countries and with many dialects tried to work together for a homeland. There was new hope and old fears.

I reread the synoptic gospels while the impressions of Palestine were fresh in my mind. I had seen children like those who gathered around Jesus. Boys and girls were badly neglected, without facilities to play and grow. They grew up in narrow lanes and shadowed rooms. I had seen the proud and the rich praying in public places and poor men shy from the presence of God. I had been confronted with many beggars living in filth and rags. I had observed the lame and the blind and the sick, and had seen scribes and pharisees of many faiths. Jesus had despaired over the conflicts of the Jews and Romans and Samaritans, Pharisees and Sadducees. I was aware of the hatreds of Jews and Arabs and the disdain of Europeans and Americans. I had seen many churches (bearing no witness at all) encircled by poverty, with hundreds of priests repeating endless rituals and creeds which seemed meaningless. I had seen a wretched feudalism and its victims subjected to the mandates of the great powers. I had seen new life with a promise for a new world. I had sensed the opposition and hatred of those who believed that ideas of democracy and freedom were a threat to their special privileges and entrenched institutions.

I reread the words of Isaiah which Jesus accepted as his commission and purpose:

"The Spirit of the Lord is upon me,
Because He has annointed me to proclaim good news to the poor;
He has sent me to announce release to the prisoners
And recovery of sight to the blind;
To free those whom tyranny has crushed,
To proclaim the acceptable year of the Lord."

Greece

We returned to UNRRA headquarters in Cairo and were told that it would be some time before we would embark for Greece. We were virtually under the command of British military liaison which planned to occupy Greece for six months before UNRRA would become wholly responsible for its program. More UNRRA personnel converged on Cairo for briefing, with little real work to do. We were placed in various hotels. Later I moved to a pension, operated by an English widow, which was more comfortable and outside the noise of the inner city. A Mr. Van Tylingen from Montana became my roommate, and we spent our leisure time exploring Cairo and its environs. He was an architect in charge of rebuilding houses in burned-out villages. He had a most frustrating job because of the lack of materials. He was also the champion chess player of Montana. He played the champion of Egypt, and the game ended in a tie. I was no match for his skill in chess.

It was suggested that we spend our working hours writing "An Appreciation and Plan" for Greece, particularly as related to our assignments. My plan was accepted as the one with the most promise; for this and other reasons I was asked to join the military liaison in its staging area near Alexandria awaiting orders to embark for Greece.

While working on the plan we were given access to all literature, reports and files (including those that were secret and confidential). I read some things that disturbed me: England evidently planned to bring in the exile government with the aging Papandreou as prime minister, and later bring back the king. This was contrary to what I believed best for Greece. The majority of Greeks expected EAM to continue to govern Greece. EAM was a united party except for the Communists and the Royalists. The exile government had sat out the war in London while ELLAS, the military arm of EAM, had fought the Germans. The great powers had supported them and given them every reason to plan on continued support.

I also read that Greek sailors had mutinied (if indeed Greece had a navy). I rather believed that these men had protested the plans to bring in the exile government. .

UNRRA sent me to military liaison as an UNRRA welfare officer. Military liaison turned out to be a British occupation army that eventually fought EAM and ELLAS to their extinction.

We were billeted in the desert near Alexandria for some weeks before we were readied to leave for Greece. I kept busy with lectures to the troops about rehabilitation, about the origin and purpose of UNRRA, the United States and many other issues. Some of these men had been through the North African campaign and had not seen their families for five years. I also taught these Englishmen to play American-style baseball, which seemed to fascinate everyone. I learned to appreciate Colonel L. Lubbock of the military liaison. Our ideas seemed similar and we were both apprehensive about plans from headquarters. Lubbock had thought his job would be simple and he could turn the work in Greece over to UNRRA long before schedule.

Word came that the Germans were retreating toward Bulgaria and so we embarked on October 12, 1944. We were cautioned to keep portholes covered so no lights might be seen from the air as we crossed the Mediterranean, circumnavigating the island of Crete, where an unknown number of Germans had been abandoned. We turned back for a day as we approached Greece, due to mines and mine sweepers clearing the area. Two of these mines were exploded by mine destroyers accompanying our small fleet. Sunken vessels in the harbor kept us from entering the harbor of Pireous. Thousands of people with banners welcoming the United States, Britain and Russia, lined the shores. By means of barges we landed at St. George's dock, arriving after dark and settling down with our belongings on soggy ground.

Two of us ventured into a village nearby where hundreds of people were celebrating their liberation day. We were welcomed with great enthusiasm. There were many banners and flags honoring the three great powers and Roosevelt, Churchill and Stalin.

We entered Athens on October 17. I was the first **UNRRA** officer to step on Greek soil. We were heartily welcomed by throngs of ragged people, all relieved that the long ordeal was over. There was a special welcome from EAM. They had been ordered not to harass the German military departure from Greece; nevertheless, ELLAS continued to attack the German rear columns.

(A Swedish leader in charge of Swedish relief services in the Peloponnesus told me that he was present when the English and Germans agreed on the retreat. One condition was that the Germans not be molested. He thought that the English and Americans wanted these German battalians to join up with German forces near Berlin to prevent the Russians from occupying Berlin.)

The whole population of Greece was well versed in the Allied propaganda about the four freedoms. They believed we were messengers of peace, ready to link arms with them to build a democratic world safe for the common man. They asked most that we understand their wretched conditions and the sacrifices they had made through four terrible years of war. EAM was for the masses the political vehicle through which they could work with us. EAM, with the help of our own OSS and English personnel, had collaborated with them throughout the war and had supplied arms and other resources. For the first time Greece had a viable political organization. It was obvious that the people's government would not be given an opportunity to unify and rehabilitate Greece.

We had anchored in the Pireaus harbor near the queen ship of the Greek navy, the Avoroff. Appropriate ceremonies were held to commemorate the triumphant return of the Avoroff. Thousands cheered as the ship lay in Greek waters. But there was sadness. The ancient ship could only symbolize the days of 1910 when it had been given to the Greek navy; it was old and had nothing in common with the new—including its passengers—the exiled cabinet. There were a few who hoped the king would soon return, but he could never return to Greece except through bloodshed.

The Greeks had won a decisive war with the Italians. They were proud and united. Their moments of victory were not long, for soon the Germans moved in on a people already exhausted with war. However, many fled to the hills and with the help of the Allies built a new political and military structure sufficiently effective so that the Germans were forced to use all their available resources to remain in Greece. They burned hundreds of villages to the ground to stop the guerillas. These burned villages were a testimony to the effectiveness of EAM and ELLAS. The Germans were pinned down in Greece so that they could not join the North African campaign and help General Rommel defeat the Allies; the Germans in Africa were defeated for lack of necessary support from the men stationed in Greece.

Previous to the war Greece had a dictatorship under Metaxis. The Communist party was outlawed during his regime, which meant that all persons inclined to democracy were either silenced or suspect, and many who had no intention of joining the Communists were often detained or sentenced to prison. There was a tremendous surge of nationalism when the Italian army invaded Greece and was defeated. People donated money, clothing, blankets, medicines and other supplies to support the Greek fighters. The government was at an all-time high of popularity when the Italians gave up. Then German forces invaded Greece, found it an easy prey, and completely subdued the country; Greece became a staging area for further conquest of the Mediterranean area, especially Northern Africa. The Germans failed in these plans because of the opposition and tenacity of the Greeks.

The Italians were quite different from the Germans. First of all, they lacked the arrogance that marked the German army. Many Italians resented Germany and lacked the discipline and enthusiasm necessary to fight the Greeks. Italians fraternized with the Greeks, and many stayed in Greece to live and married Greek women. The Greeks had no deep hatred for the Italians, and thought of them as pawns of the Germans. There were few reprisals. I talked to many Italians who had settled down in Greece, who thought that the Italian campaign had been a mistake and blamed it on Hitler and Mussolini.

As much as they could, the Germans disciplined the Greeks to serve their own purposes. The Greeks reacted in a number of ways. Some who held government jobs held on to them; others fled into the hills to help organize a government in hiding, which became EAM and ELLAS. A few groups presumed to fight the Germans. Those in business either continued their work or went into hiding. Some businessmen prospered during the occupation.

Not all who remained in their places were loyal or sympathetic to the Germans. Many found ways to assist the underground. The Greek government had been for many years a puppet government without democratic policies. There were quislings, collaborationists, opportunists, and a silent minority if not a majority. Most were terribly afraid, not only for their own lives and privileges but for their relatives and acquaintances who had joined the underground or who openly criticized the Germans. The Germans organized security battalions recruited from among the Greeks, trained and outfitted them, and had them play a role in military control and information; these were the most hated among the collaborators.

Liberation opened the doors for all kinds of emotions, fury and revenge. As the Germans retreated, EAM and ELLAS took over and appointed committees with the authority of government agencies to rehabilitate the country. Towns and villages had their own governmental structures, and immediately went to work. EAM saw to it that only those who had proved their loyalty served as officers. I met with a number of these local representatives and thought that they were doing a good job. EAM and ELLAS sought out informers and collaborationists, took them prisoner and held them until trials in courts set up for that purpose. No doubt some were executed. ELLAS was after the Greek security battalions that retreated to areas of comparative safety. Under the guise of maintaining law and order, they had served the Germans. ELLAS might have easily cut them to pieces, but the English rescued these battalions for their own purposes during the so-called civil war. Police departments that had served during the occupation were suspect. However, police precincts had helped the Swedish and Swiss Red Cross, as well as the Greek Red Cross, church agencies, and other welfare projects, to help the people; so there were mixed feelings about the police, until it was discovered that they cooperated with the English forces during the so-called civil war. The problem of guilt and punishment was overwhelming; the dilemma of the alleged threat of Communism plagued the minds of many. Anything liberal was branded Communist, and many underground citizens and soldiers became suspect. Greece was confronted with the same kind of propaganda that had overwhelmed the United States. The only possible political solution would have been the British and the American Intelligence Services continued support of EAM and ELLAS, the rightful means of establishing a stable democratic government with the least amount of bloodshed. Russian intelligence services were minimal in Greece. As it turned out, with a change in Allied policies chaos broke out in Greece. The fact that Russia had been an ally was soon erased; signs portraying Stalin, Russia, and the KKE (Communists) disappeared.

Some of us in UNRRA suspected that UNRRA was being used as part of a military operation in Greece. This suspicion prompted us to write to the president of the United States in protest. We did not receive a reply, but I believe it had some influence in maintaining the original purpose of UNRRA.

Subsequent experiences freed us from allegiance to the British military orders.

Diary and Activities

I kept a daily diary while in Greece and made weekly reports to Colonel Lubbock of British military liaison and to Archer in Cairo. As the only UNRRA officer in Greece, I had freedom to follow my own judgment. Lubbock thought that UNRRA should take over all welfare services as soon as possible without any limitations of screening for political loyalty.

Tuesday, 17th October, 1944

Contacted Mr. Michaelides Scourso of the Near East Foundation and met the members of the staff. Discovered that the Near East Foundation is handling twenty feeding centers, ten dispensaries and two homes for refugee children from burned villages. Made arrangements to visit some of these centers.

Wednesday, 18th October, 1944

Attended the Liberation Meeting in Constitution Square. It is well to make certain observations of this very intense celebration. Banners scattered by the thousands throughout the crowd carried these slogans: "Popular Free Courts;" "Glory to Our Dead;" "Welcome Allies;" "Honor and Glory to the Dead Heroes of EAM;" "Revenge;" "Remember Haidari" (the worst German concentration camp); "Down with the Bulgarians;" "Democracy;" "The People Must Have Power;" "Unity and Order;" "Long Live the Government;" "The EAM Welcomes the National Government;" "Long Live the Communist Party." EAM and KKE were everywhere. The Nationalist Party did not take part in the mass demonstration, but dropped leaflets and Greek flags from the balconies. The propaganda emphasized greater Greece as a reward for their sacrifices and the people's hopes. It was obvious as one looked over the crowd that a whole population had been reduced to a very low level of existence; for the most part clothes were shabby, although people dressed in their best for the occasion.

... JRC had 35,000 tons of foodstuffs in the harbor, 2,000 tons of it wheat, 2,400 tons intended for the Aegean Islands and 3,000 tons for Crete. [It took 300 tons a day to supply Athens.] The outlining districts of Corinth are in very bad shape. The JRC had been supplying about 36,000 tons a month. 600 tons of milk per month has been supplied for the children's institutions. Fresh milk has been supplied through exchange for bran products from the milling of wheat. Almost 300,000 people have been given free rations except for bread in Athens. There was no civil registry, no departments of welfare; all welfare institutions were supported by private funds ... there was no council of social agencies and no central registry or confidential exchange. Mr. Sandstrom seemed disturbed about the situation and was anxious for close collaboration between ML and the government. Mr. Helger came in just as the meeting was breaking up. He reported that JRC prices on bread had been 50 million drachmas on Monday, 100 million on Tuesday, 300 million on Wednesday, and 600 million on Thursday. He said that the ration was 100 drams a day. As a result of this inflation in prices, one third of the people could not buy bread on Tuesday and one half could not buy bread on Wednesday. (A drachma had been worth 25 cents before the war.)

Wednesday evening had a talk with Elizabeth Mayston, formerly with the Near East Foundation, but during the war responsible for Greek Americans and American citizens. She reported that there were about 3,000 persons who had a very hard time because they did not fit into the regular agency services. By borrowing money from generous friends she was able to carry on. Also met Dr. Pandelis Choreftis. Made arrangements to visit several hospitals and dispensaries on Sunday.

Thursday, 19th October, 1944

Amalia Lycourezou (child welfare director for Greece on the staff of the Near East Foundation) arranged with Dr. de Fischer of the Swiss Commission for us to visit milk stations, feeding centers, and a special dispensary.

The people that we saw were very poor. One center is in a community in which eighty houses had been burned down less than two weeks ago. Many children are suffering from malnutrition; their conditions have improved through the services of these centers.

Met Mrs. Papastratos of the Greek Red Cross and the Wardrobe of the Students. The latter organization helped students pre-war, but during the German occupation handled clothing distribution for the Greek Red Cross (supplies from America). Talked with Mr. Wildlung, the Swedish delegate from Thebes. The Germans turned some 1,500 tons of foodstuffs over to the Swedish delegate, part of it spoiled.

Met Mr. Young and Mr. Stavrides of UNRRA. Decided that they should be responsible for looking for housing for UNRRA and that we would make the Near East Foundation the unofficial UNRRA office. Talked with two Swiss delegates, Alfred G. Boller and G. Rohn.

Friday, 20th October, 1944

Established AML office in Mistra Hotel, many inquiries about jobs, ration cards, missing persons. Attended staff meeting of HQ-One. Attended meeting with Dr. and Mrs. Person, Swedish delegates from Tripoli and Mr. Hans Ehrenstroke from Patras. They were disturbed about AML feeling that it could not be possible for two different groups to distribute foodstuffs. AML supplies have arrived at both Kalamata and Patras—and no understanding was shared with the Swedish delegate. Mr. Sandstrom came in and the delegates were referred by Major Glafka to higher level.

The Swedish and Swiss delegates differed on what the nature of representation should be. The Swedish members were appointed by the government of Sweden and the Swiss by the International Red Cross; the Swedish delegates depended on Stockholm for guidance; Swiss could move more quickly.

Relief was administered honestly, although leaks were inevitable. IRC employees received double rations because there was no money to pay them. Some of these supplies would get out on the open market as people traded for products they needed. Even people receiving regular rations traded for things that they needed more than the rations. Sometimes foodstuffs would be stolen enroute to villages by Greek factions or the Germans.

There are few trained workers in Athens. The EOXA (church) did a great deal of work, not always the best quality; they were mostly society people eager to help. Since the detention of the archbishop this work has disintegrated. The EOXA served the most destitute. The government ministries have not taken much responsibility for human needs and is more political than effective. Charitable work was left to private agencies.

The Swiss wish to leave as soon as possible. Their doctors come for six months' service and all have outstayed.

Saturday, 21st October, 1944

In conference with Col. Chiddick cleared relationship between Relief HQ and Relief HA 1. Pointed out there were areas of great need in Athens. Attended a meeting in which Major Griffin explained condition in Euboia. All the villages are at least partially burned, some only a few houses, many, almost completely. Need foodstuffs in the South. Everywhere need of clothing and medical supplies—blankets, building materials. Talked with Mr. Tino S. Balanos from Euboia of the people's organizations who is interested in boys' training centers and training classes for women.

Sunday, 22nd October, 1944

Had a long conference with Dr. and Mrs. Person of Tripoli. Advised them to be patient. Distribution to many sections has been difficult since Germans declared Peloponnesus a war zone. EAM is doing good work and has effective committees in many areas. There is little currency in the provinces. They have not seen a billion drachma note in Tripoli. Barter is their means of exchange. The government cannot charge for rationed goods; people cannot buy. Swedish delegates wish to turn over work as soon as possible to UNRRA but will remain as long as necessary.

Monday, 23rd October, 1944

Visited two homes in Kephissia for about 300 refugee children from burned villages. Children in great need of blankets; windows in buildings blasted out as result of explosion of German ammunition dumps. One little girl has leg amputated as result of German machine gunning in which mother was killed. Helped take sick child to local children's hospital. As result of Geman and Italian requisition of buildings, the hospital has very inadequate quarters (only a fifty-bed ward for sick children).

EAM megaphones broadcasting a three-point program: distribute all Red Cross supplies at once. Government must provide food for people; permission for "Andartes" to parade in Athens; punishment of the traitors hiding in the hotels of Athens.

There was a second ceremony following the liberation demonstration in Constitution Square in which the Greek flag was officially raised on the Acropolis and a wreath was placed on the tomb of the Unknown Soldier. These demonstrations were in contrast to the spectacle of a lone German lieutenant who walked up to the Acropolis at 10 a.m. the last week of the German occupation of Athens, took down the German flag and placed a wreath on the tomb of the Unknown Soldier. The people had moved back and waited in silence. When the German officer left, the Greeks rushed in and tore the German wreath to pieces.

I visited as many villages as possible. We would be able to do only a fair job at best, but the so-called civil war which broke out in December would make conditions worse and the job of helping people help themselves much harder.

Report on Island of Salmis, population 150,000

Seven villages; largest is Koulouri, the capital. Was Greek naval base employing over 3,000 men, now unemployed. Only other important work is fishing. Limited truck gardening, [cultivation of] olives, grapes and goats. Some skilled workers and wood cutters used to work on the mainland. Forty homes were damaged by the Germans, naval base completely destroyed. Lost only 10 percent of fishing boats, but nets in very bad condition. Visited Kouldouri, population 10,000, and Paloukia, population 2,000.

Met with mayor, police, priest, doctors, Red Cross workers, and other leaders of Koulouri. Total population indigent. Receives Red Cross bread. Other supplies: 3,000 portions for grownups and 3,200 for children. Dry milk cut off in September due to difference of opinion on how it should be distributed. No hospital. Trachoma, T.B., malaria and malnutrition high. One doctor claimed he had 500 cases of malaria this summer. Only four doctors on whole island. Thirty-five percent have trachoma and many children blind. Had anti-trachoma school before war. Have no drugs, cotton or bandages. Andartes have disarmed police.

Nea Sfagia, population 12,000—whole district 35,000— on road to Piraeus

Two milk stations serving 2,000 children; one special feeding center serving 300 children. A very poor district where refugees were housed during the catastrophe in 1922 with Turkey when all Greeks had to leave Turkey. Housing conditions terrible, mostly the same old shacks hastily built in 1922. Bedding and clothing nonexistent. Much persecution by the Germans. Men once worked in the factories, now abandoned, so they now have no work; lived during this period by selling firewood. Live nearly entirely on what Red Cross can distribute, quite insufficient. Need housing, need roofing and building materials, clothing, shoes, bedding and food.

Piriditopian, population 20,000 (north of Athens)

Four milk stations serving 5,000 children. One special feeding station serving extra weak children, 256, ages five to sixteen. Many more need this special food. Working people, factory workers, small shops, gardeners, wood sellers live here; were generally self-supporting. Eighty homes burned by Germans, more than 100 killed. Men were not allowed to come out of their houses but were burned in them; thirty-eight were shot in their gardens. Now they are all poor and destitute; need clothing badly, foodstuffs, housing, shoes.

We visited many villages and the story was almost always the same. I recall a tiny fishing village of about 150 people that had supported itself with fishing, gardening, and a few olive trees and grapevines. There had been no fertilizer for four years so the yield was slight. I shall never forget the bare feet, sometimes covered with rags, trudging miles to gather a bundle of wood to sell in Athens and the larger towns. They were mostly women and children. Then there were countless men with leg amputations. There had rarely been distributions of food in these smaller villages. And yet we were welcomed in these tiny fishing villages and the people cooked what they had— tiny little minnows, which on occasion tasted pretty good if the oil in which they were cooked wasn't too rancid. In most of these communities EAM had appointed working committees to get into reconstruction.

AML in Athens saw things differently as their staff worked with the inept cabinet that had arrived on Liberation Day. This cabinet was disorganized and out of touch with the people of Greece.

Militarily speaking the use of the word "Allied" was a misnomer; there were a few American officers in Greece, but the operation was totally English. The American officers privately acknowledged the position of UNRRA but kept silent. There was no reference in the reorganization paper about the work of EAM or the committees ready to work with ML (military liaison) and UNRRA. It was fortunate that I had immediately established an UNRRA office separate from ML with both paid and volunteer Greek staff. I could not condone military preparations and the undertones of ML. Armored weapons were brought into Greece and I was fearful. UNRRA was meant to serve all those in need, regardless of political persuasion, and there was no question that that policy was negative as far as the "people's government" was concerned. I had a dual responsibility, with two offices providing weekly reports to ML and UNRRA with headquarters still in Cairo. Two reports, military, short and to the point, and one to UNRRA, which went more deeply into the problems, were made. The military set up regulations and orders, while UNRRA tried to work with existing organizations and help people help themselves. When the conflict began in December, Col. Lubbock was prepared and turned the full responsibility for welfare over to UNRRA, which could serve on both sides of military lines.

We visited a number of hospitals, all in a deplorable condition. The Germans had requisitioned essential equipment and had left the hospitals more or less helpless, except to revert to primitive surgery. Walls had been torn down, so that most of the care was in wards. We visited prisons from which all those imprisoned by the Germans had been released; they were now filled with alleged informers, collaborationists and traitors awaiting trial while makeshift courts were established. Most of the prisoners depended upon food brought in by relatives and friends who were carefully scrutinized. There was a minimum of medical attention. We were never refused admission to the prisons, which for the most part were overcrowded bullpens. The ranking ELLAS officer had his headquarters in Lamia; his handyman was a youngster who had been born in Chicago. This officer refused to give up, and fled back into the hills when the ensueing conflict seemed lost. He was captured and beheaded and his head was placed where all could see, as as a warning to insurgents.

The political situation continued to deteriorate. EAM and ELLAS lost their opportunity when they welcomed ML into Greece. They had cooperated with both American and British Intelligence throughout the occupation of the Germans, and naively believed that this cooperation would continue. The Papandreou government offered EAM a few cabinet posts, on the condition that ELLAS demobilize and turn over their arms to the government. There were about 40,000 ELLAS under arms. EAM could not accept this condition; they were increasingly suspicious of the English, who had saved the German security battalions and were bringing armored weapons into Greece for which EAM saw no purpose. And there were far more English soldiers than EAM expected. They didn't take lightly the fact ML would not work with their leaders and committees. There was an armed division called EDES under General Zervos which capitulated completely. EAM and ELLAS felt that they had basic rights because of their heroism during the German occupation.

On Friday, November 17, 1944, I spent the day in conference with the UNRRA personnel who had been flown from Cairo, and knew little about what was happening in Greece. I moved in with them into the Acropolis Hotel and joined with my friend Van Tylingen. We would soon be surrounded by gunfire as EAM and ELLAS began to fight it out with the English. UNRRA personnel returned to Cairo to wait until the war had subsided. Archer warned me of this flight and told me that if I wanted to remain in Greece, "I should get lost," meaning that I should find a place to stay. The JRC had asked for my services, and Miss Lykourezou found me a room with Mr. and Mrs. Chelmi in a safe district of Athens. Mrs. Chelmi had been a great actress, known as Koutoupouli ("Little Pigeon"). I was given a supply of K rations to last about five weeks.

We soon found ourselves in the middle of furious gunfire. I went to work with the Red Cross as a truck driver, bringing food to children's homes and hospitals, and became a familiar figure to the fighters as I drove back and forth to Red Cross headquarters.

EAM asked the government for a permit to demonstrate and parade, beginning at Constitution Square and out onto the main street. Prime Minister Papandreou gave his permission and then for some reason withdrew it, warning that any demonstration would be prevented by force of arms. EAM and ELLAS were determined to show their strength and went ahead with their plans, announcing publicly that the demonstration would be held and that the people should assemble in Constitution Square to get organized, but that no weapons would be allowed. I was talking with Col. Lubbock when the action began. From our office we could see the whole square and the streets converging on it. Several hundred people had arrived ahead of time and congregated in the middle of the square. British soldiers appeared and formed lines across the streets to prevent others getting in. The police headquarters were across the square from our viewpoint, and the police also formed to prevent access to the square. The streets were filled with crowds who didn't dare push their way into the center as the soldiers raised their rifles and ordered them to disperse, but the people stood their ground in silence. Those inside the square planned a strategy. They picked the street that had the greatest numbers and pretended they wanted to leave the square. The soldiers obliged by giving them room to leave; instead, the people turned around and those in the streets followed them into the square like a river of humanity, completely filling it. Leaders gave them instructions that they would go down the main street and if fired upon, everyone should fall to the pavement. The leaders started to go ahead when the police fired over their heads, but the crowd was on the move. The next shots came from the soldiers directly into the crowd. The people fell to the ground and waited a few minutes and tried it again; again there was a volley of shooting and they went down. They stood up and marched down the street carrying the dead and wounded. That was the end of the shooting. The next day the funeral procession moved down the street and around the square with the bodies of some thirty persons.

Hostilities began in earnest the next day, December 4. ML was pretty well fenced in, but they had the military equipment—armored tanks, artillery and planes. In the long run ELLAS couldn't stand up to the power of the mountain brigades, including former German security batallions. EAM and ELLAS had been provoked into a war with those whom they thought were friends.

Relief activities had come to a complete halt, as few workers dared to be seen on the streets for fear of getting into the crossfire of the furious and indiscriminant shooting of rifles, mortars and grenades. Sentinels on both sides allowed me to cross the military boundaries. I crossed into ML territory and conferred with Archer and Lubbock. Archer said he was making preparations to fly UNRRA personnel back to Cairo; Lubbock and I assayed the situation to discover what he could do. There were beans and blankets available, and huge iron vessels in which he would have his men cook as many beans as could be delivered. He could not enter ELLAS territory where the need was the greatest. I assured him I could get trucks from the Red Cross, now in a stalemate due to the war. Helger of the Red Cross was eager to get going, if we could get the drivers. I conferred with Miss Lycourazou, who was under great strain because shipments of foodstuffs to the Near East Foundation children's homes were overdue. I talked with Alecko Adosides and George Trypanis, our driver-interpreters, and they agreed to do their part. We participated in many incidents in places that were under fire. I still have a bullet which embedded itself in the seat of my truck, after passing through the sleeve of my coat. Miss Lycourazou in her reports to Archer wrote:

"As soon as operations started on December 5th my first concern was to supply the Kifissia Eagle's Nest with foodstuffs. For this purpose I arranged with the Red Cross to let me take some food from the unique warehouse which was in a somewhat free zone, and in which there was only a small supply for the personnel. The Red Cross agreed, but there were neither trucks nor drivers available on account of the strike.

"On December 7th I asked Mr. Wahlberg ... to make arrangements for transportation of foodstuffs. Mr. Wahlberg met Mr. Helger, president of the JRC, who gave him a truck which he had to drive himself. We were told, however, that we had to have special permission from ELLAS for our truck to pass through their territories. We went to the warehouse, and Mr. Wahlberg with the help of neighbors loaded the truck and without waiting for permission, left for Kifissia. It was the only truck of foodstuffs that circulated that day.

"Going through Ambelokipos, we met three English tanks which were just bombing Tourkovounia. We withdrew and asked the Tommies whether we could proceed. 'Oh hell,' they replied, 'It's dangerous, but when passing, step on it.' We arrived at Kifissia safely; the personnel and the children were extremely happy to see us and, as they said, they were sure that someone would turn out to help them. We found the children well taken care of. I left with them 3,000 drachmas, which I borrowed from Mr. Wahlberg."

We were in Kifissia again on Christmas Day. The Greeks had not celebrated Christmas for four years under the occupation of the Germans, so we were determined to give these children something to be glad about. Miss Aravantinou had taken over 100 little Christmas trees left by the Germans. I asked that the children sing a Christmas carol, the only carol I heard that year. Another report by Miss Lykourezou:

"On December 8, coming back from Kifissia, we stopped at the Red Cross Hospital to investigate conditions there. The situation was frightful. The hospital was being used as a fortress by the mountain brigade and the gendarmerie. Furious fighting was going on. About 400 patients in a confused state crowded into the basement corridors, without food or water. As soon as they saw us they started crying out, 'We are hungry, we are thirsty!' Most of the maintenance personnel had been arrested and the few left were under control. Met with the commander, had a talk with him, recommended to him the doctors and the nurses we had to rely on, and requested him to assist them in their work. We also made arrangements with him to bring food supplies to the hospital the next morning. Early the next morning we came back with foodstuffs and water and also volunteer Red Cross nurses. I wish to make reference here to the excellent spirit the nurses had shown during this hard period."

We returned the next morning and found that conditions were much worse. Fighting had been furious and there were dead and wounded in the streets. We hesitated to get near the firing and hid behind a wall when a hysterical nurse came from the hospital and said we could go around to the back of the hospital, which we did. The mountain brigade inside the hospital did not dare show their heads to help us unload the truck. ELLAS was within firing range behind the hospital, and some of them believed we were bringing supplies to the soldiers. We had explained we were serving the patients.

We had to unload the truck ourselves. I picked up a box of canned milk and a bullet shot thorugh the box, spraying milk all over me. Then the firing stopped, as no doubt someone relayed the message that we were helping the patients. It was pitiful to see the patients that were able to help themselves eat cold beans from a can. We arranged to bury nearly thirty bodies. There was no way we could persuade the commander that he and his men should leave the hospital. There was only one thing to do—remove the patients to their homes and to other hospitals and clinics. This was an arduous task that took several days. Our helpers were Trypanis and Adosides, who were the drivers along with myself and a group of nurses. Miss Lekou, an ardent and beautiful volunteer nurse, was killed as a mortar hit the side of the truck where she was sitting. Mr. Trypanis provided a detailed account of what they did that day; he and the convoyeur were slightly wounded, and a patient in back of the truck escaped unhurt.

"... For two or three minutes we were too badly shaken to think clearly. As soon as I recovered I ran back to the car with the 'convoyeur' to see what we could do for Miss Lekou and the old woman, whom we had completely forgotten till then and who was still sitting in the back of the van. As I arrived at the car, some ELLAS Red Cross people came with a stretcher and took Miss Lekou away. I was surprised how quickly they were on the spot, as it could hardly have been more than five or six minutes since the accident happened. In my relief that some atention was being given to Miss Lekou I forgot to ask them where they were taking her. I then assisted some unknown persons to get the old lady out none the worse for her adventure, and she was taken charge of by them.

"... after having the small fragments of metal removed from our wounds we were kindly brought back in a Red Cross car to the Maraslion (the JRC headquarters). There I reported the facts and Mr. Mulder and Mr. Wahlberg proceeded in a passenger car and a truck to the point indicated in Piraeus

Street. There they located Miss Lekou's body, which they brought with them."

So it was for seemingly endless days. A right front tire was shot out from under our Red Cross truck as we were returning to the Maraslion on one of our mercy trips. I observed a large field covered with rows of naked, decaying bodies that had been shoveled out of shallow graves by hundreds of people who were searching for the bodies of their loved ones. The stench of dead human flesh was unbearable. Nevertheless, hundreds of women covered their noses with rags and went up and down the rows trying to find a loved one. The bodies were so badly decomposed that there could have been no recognition. We delivered medical supplies to medical authorities in a town some twenty miles from Athens, and called on EAM officials. A British plane flying nearby turned to strafe the main street. People ran for safety, but a number were wounded and some were killed. We had turned up a side street to escape the fire and then waited to see if we could help. Hundreds were already at work, so we went back to Athens.

Col. Lubbock kept his men at work cooking beans and we delivered the beans to what we called "bean centers." One of the centers was carried on for indigent actors in the vestibule below the apartment in which my hosts, Mr. and Mrs. Chelmi, lived. I saw hundreds of people crying for food in near riots around the "bean centers."

The war worsened for ELLAS as their troops retreated northward and into the Peloponnesus. ELLAS made a fatal mistake by taking hundreds of hostages with them from Athens. They didn't have the resources to keep them alive, and as it turned out the British would not bargain for them. Our office turned to picking up the hostages and caring for them. We had the complete support of the Greek Red Cross and the JRC and the Volunteer Friends' Service teams, that were trained and fully organized. There was an Asquith of English fame on one of these teams. I asked him why he had chosen to serve in such a humble capacity. He replied, "To do penance for my family."

We were concerned with the children's centers in Tripoli, Kalamata and other towns in the Peloponnesus, all in control of EAM. We decided on a convoy of food, and I turned to Asquith and his team for assistance in driving the trucks and rendering whatever services might be needed.

The problem was that they spoke with an English accent that might not be acceptable to EAM and ELLAS. We discussed the matter of speech and I agreed to do all the talking. Miss Lykourezou went along to attend to her responsibilities as child welfare director, to make contacts and to give us guidance. We were hardly prepared for the fact that the English military held a line south of Corinth, where we were ordered to stop, turn around and go back. We had a short huddle with our team and decided to chance it. I was in the front truck and it was agreed that when I raised my hand we would start moving. I explained to the officer in charge the purpose of our mission and reminded him that we were Red Cross and by international understanding had a right to cross the lines. He ordered, "If you defy my command, I'll have my men shoot." I raised my hand and off we went without a single shot. We came close to the ELLAS line and stopped our trucks while Amalia and I went ahead to talk to the officer in charge. He made us feel welcome, but reported that the road was mined around hills toward Tripoli; if we would come through his line, he said, he would remove the mines until we got by but it would take a little time. We camped that night and waited, and were given the order to proceed the next morning.

Conditions in Tripoli were worse than we expected, and Kalmata in much deeper straits. We were asked many questions by people who had been cut off from the world for months. There were many orange groves near Kalamata, but the oranges would not be harvested because there was no business whatsoever. The farmers told us to load up our trucks and take the oranges back to Athens for hospitals and children's centers. There was one orange called dulcha, which was the sweetest and most luscious orange I ever ate.

We were soon on our way back to Athens. My friend's English accent had meant nothing at all because we had been on a mission of friendship.

The UNRRA personnel came back to Athens with a new chief, a Mr. Maben who proved an effective administrator. Archer had resigned; he felt that he had suffered enough and wanted to get back to his job with the Near East Foundation.

Mr. Mabin promoted me to the position of coordinator of continental Greece and Rodney Young, coordinator for the islands of Greece. Rodney and I agreed to travel together for the first trip around. We were supplied with a four-wheel drive, which was fortunate as we circumvented destroyed bridges, washed out roads, and followed stream bottoms in an effort to cover all of Greece, not counting the Peloponnesus. We made daily reports of the conditions of the roads, crops, burned-out villages, the feelings and circumstances of the people, and commented on the progress of UNRRA districts, as well as the military forces located throughout the area. We met with staff, local committees and political leaders. Rodney was an archeologist of considerable reputation, so we took time to view certain areas of interest. I picked up a few fragments of marble in Philippi. Alecko Adosedes, whose father had been the governer of Macedonia, was our driver and interpreter. We stopped at Salonika to observe conditions and went on to Thrace to the Turkish border, and then along the Bulgarian and Yugoslavian borders. We tried to communicate with the Bulgarian and Yugoslavian guards through motions of our hands and eyes. One of them understood Esperanto, of which I had some slight knowledge. We returned to Athens to embark on a similar trip to some of the islands, when the hand of fate was turned in my favor. Rodney and I had tickets for a small ship to leave in the evening. In the office I was asked if I would relinquish my ticket in favor of an UNRRA welfare officer who was to serve several of the islands. It was important that he go on this particular ship because no one knew when there would be another departure. I naturally consented, so Rodney went off without me. The ship was overloaded, and for some reason it capsized. There were about 120 passengers and many drowned, including the UNRRA officer to whom I had given my ticket. Rodney was picked up after five hours in the water.

Miss Lykourezou saw in my new appointment the chance to get UNRRA involved in her plans for camps for undernourished children, which she had organized as far away as Jannina. She had the support of the Red Cross and the villagers whose children would benefit. Some were in pitiful condition, dwarfed after four years of insufficient food; some had stomach worms. These children had to be fed five times a day because of shrunken stomachs and bodies. Mothers would walk many miles to enroll their children. We took special care to provide services and supplies to these camps hidden here and there in all parts of Greece. It was my duty to keep in touch with UNRRA offices and districts. As limited as transportation was, I could drop Amalia and members of her staff off in the camps and give her a chance to look for a new location. Alecko and I slept under the jeep at times. The English had requisitioned all the desirable hotels and the accommodations in the larger towns of Greece, and Greeks were cautioned that they were off-limits.

This led to an incident in Jannina. I had made up my mind that we should have at least equal rights. We were on a mission in which we had to stay overnight in Jannina. I went to the registration desk in the leading hotel and informed the sergeant that we needed two rooms, one for the lady and one for the two men. I had explained our work and what we were doing. The officer in charge said that my request was irregular, but he would talk to a superior officer who was an Englishman. I was informed, "We can give you a room but the Greeks will shift for themselves." I was disturbed and insisted on fair treatment for Amalia and Alecko. Words became louder and more vociferous when a major from Scotland came down the stairway and coming our way said, "What seems to be the trrrouble?" I reported our dilemma. He said, "Sirrr, that is no trrrouble—I'll take carrre of it," which he did. He looked around so no one else could hear and said, "Good mon, I like what ye did. I don't like these English betterrrn an you do."

In May 1945 my interpreter and I traveled in a jeep toward the village of Laguadia. We stopped to pick up a 12-year-old boy who had two scrawny live chickens and a small sack of wheat slung over his back; this was his pay for six week's work as a carpenter's helper. He had walked fifteen hours and would have had seven hours still to go if we hadn't given him a lift. His father and older brother had been killed by the Germans and he had taken his father's place of supporting his mother and younger sisters. We asked to buy his chickens, but he said he could not sell them because they would lay eggs; after they stopped laying eggs they would be killed and his family would eat them. After some additional conversation the boy sat back in silence. I saw him cross himself three times. I asked Alecko to inquire why he crossed himself. The answer was boy-like: "Oh, I'm lucky. I got a ride."

The Germans burned down sections of cities and towns and in many cases whole towns and villages, like the town of Kalavryta, a beautiful inland mountain town of 4,500. The Greeks had ambushed a German convoy nearby and the Germans retaliated. A German battalion entered Kalavryta and rounded up about 1,300 men from the age of 15 up—all the husbands, grandfathers, brothers, grown sons of Kalavryta. They were marched out of town and shot. Five escaped out of this jumble of blood and flesh, by lying as though they were dead. Twenty-five were in the hills; thus thirty of all the men in Kalavryta survived. The Germans burned down every building and house. Women fled to the hills with their aging mothers, babies and children. They returned to search for the bodies of their loved ones and bury them, seeking out what remained of their possessions and then began to rebuild Kalavryta and first of all the church. Fellow Greeks in nearby towns rushed in to help and so did the Swedish and Swiss missions to Greece.

I felt that I had been through it all and that there wasn't much more that I could do, so my thoughts turned homeward. Anyway, I was sick with malaria. The doctor gave me a thousand attabrines, yellow pills that turned the skin yellow. I finally got a temporary release and passage back to the states in the fall of 1945. My friends helped me walk to the plane.

When I returned I reported to the Washington office and was asked if I would like to take a position in the UNNRA China mission. I requested time to think things over, went out to meet my wife, younger daughter and son, and on to Florida to visit my older daughter and new son in law.

I left Greece proud of the Greeks, who belonged to a land that had been despoiled, betrayed and manipulated by great powers and yet believed that someday they would have a democracy worthy of their heritage.

The Dilemma of the Jews in Greece

Among the inquiries that came into our offices were Jews who had been hiding and were without ration cards. We expected many more than came, because some 100,000 Jews had lived in Greece prior to the German occupation. After several months only about 5,000 seemed to have survived, and of these some 3,000 had found refuge in Athens. There were about 60,000 Jews in Salonika at the beginning of the war.

The Jewish community had begun to decline after the first Balkan War in 1912, and especially after a disastrous fire in 1917. Many wealthy and middle class Jews took refuge in other countries, so the Jewish population had declined to about 60,000 in April 1942 when the Germans took over. The Germans soon began to requisition apartments and other buildings owned by the Jews, and took over businesses, furniture, and plundered the libraries.

Some Greeks as well as a few Jews profited from collaboration and cooperation with the Germans. Traditionally the Jewish community was law abiding and responded to the German orders to register for labor assignments. The Germans collected large sums of money for the release of Jews from labor camps. The Jews were required to wear an emblem with a serial number. The census had revealed some 55,000 Jews of Greek citizenship—the remaining Jews of Spanish and Italian nationalities were exempt from these requirements. About this time the ancient and revered cemetery of the Jews was destroyed. Marble monuments were used for building materials and paving the streets. The graveyard had been a matter of controversy because it was located in the center of the city, so it is likely that local feelings had something to do with this.

Restrictions and prohibitions were leveled against the Jews until they found themselves confined to two ghettos. All Jews were required to submit detailed accounts of their possessions, which were gradually confiscated.

Then followed the methodical and wholesale deportation of thousands of Jews in box cars. Even hospitals and clinics had to be evacuated. Some 50,000 Jews were deported to Poland and parts unknown, and virtually none remained in Salonika. Few returned. Jewish property came into the possession of Greek nationals. Few Jews returned to reclaim what belonged to them.

Many Greeks did what they could to help the Jews. Children were smuggled into Greek families where they lost their identity as Jews and became members of their foster homes. Amnesty for the Italian and Spanish Jews ceased. Some Jews joined the Greek guerillas in the hills of Greece. Jews were constantly on the move to escape one search after the other, plagued by informers and living in constant fear of detection. Probably only 5,000 out of 100,000 survived.

7. UNITED NATIONS RELIEF AND REHABILITATION ADMINISTRATION, CHINA: 1945-1946

I first wanted to go to China when I heard returned missionaries in the Swedish Baptist Church in Denver. They described the awful conditions of the teeming millions in China, the worst omission in their minds being that most of them had not heard about the "saving grace" of Christianity; they worshipped pagan gods and would go to hell. Nothing was said about their ancient civilization or accomplishments. There was planted in me a desire to go out to these helpless people and teach them the truth about a merciful God. I have dropped from my vocabulary all reference to pagans, infidels, heathens, and similar terms related to human beings.

Again in my seminary training the desire to go to China emerged, and I told the board of missions I was a candidate for missionary service in China. In my senior year I was interviewed by a foreign missionary committee, and was bewildered by them. They asked nothing about why I wanted to go to China or what I was prepared to do. I was well aware of the revolution led by Dr. Sun Yatsen, and believed Americans had a stake in promoting democracy in China. The committee asked me only about my religious experiences and beliefs, questions I had long abandoned. They inquired as to the moment of my rebirth; I asked what was meant by this question and reported that I had joined the Baptist church when I was ten years old. They said, "When were you reborn?" I replied that there had been many rebirths in my life and that I was sufficiently open minded to believe that there would be more renewals in my life. They asked, "Are you committed to saving the souls of the heathen Chinese?" I answered that I wanted to learn about the Chinese and perhaps we could learn from each other so that we could build a better world.

The questions continued on this line for several hours, questions foreign to my studies in seminary and about which I had thought little since my early church membership; in fact, I had avoided so-called fundamentalist doctrines and churches and had heard little about these subjects at Illif, which was essentially liberal. The study of Jesus and the Old Testament prophets had led me to a concern for human beings. The committee rejected me, advising me to continue my studies until I learned the essentials of salvation. At the moment I wasn't about to continue my work in school. We went to the mining camp in Utah.

When I returned from Greece I found an urgent letter from Buell Mabin, chief of the UNRRA mission in Greece, to return as soon as possible; he needed me for an administrative position. At the same time I had a chance to go to China; I received a letter from Donald S. Howard, a friend of mine already in China as director of welfare, urging me to accept a China appointment. After a visit with my family we decided that I should go to China.

I resigned from Grace Church and Center and returned to Washington for assignment. We flew eastward over North Africa, Iraq, Iran, and touched down in Calcutta; we then flew over the Himalayas into China and landed at Shanghai. Conditions were chaotic; I was billeted in a hastily improvised building to which I was assigned for several days. It wasn't easy to lug my belongings to my cot. UNRRA headquarters and the Kuomintang were still in Kunming in the upper reaches of the Yangtze River above the famous Yangtze Gorge, which was difficult to navigate. The Kuomintang had fled into southwestern China before the Japanese onslaught and maintained headquarters there until the war ended.

UNRRA established its headquarters in Shanghai, a major port for UNRRA supplies. UNRRA personnel filtered into Shanghai and had settled on office space. Among them was Donald Howard, who had been in China nearly a year and had made several trips into the interior. Relief projects had already been set up where supplies were available, but many people were starving. The Kuomintang was preparing to take over in Nanking.

Shanghai was teeming with people as refugees crowded into the metropolitan area. It was chaotic, noisy and filthy. People could not move without bumping into each other. There were thousands of beggars, many in grotesque and pitiful positions and conditions, many undernourished children held in the arms of reclining and emaciated mothers. Prostitutes filled doorways and street corners. My roommate and I were returning to our hotel from the office when a rather pretty woman accosted us and wanted to know if we were available. We rejected her when a man offered us a "nice, clean woman." My companion said, "How much?" The reply was, "Fifteen dollars." When told that this was too much, he said, "I got one not quite so clean for five dollars."

The hundreds of rickshas and pedicabs found it difficult to get through the streets. I thought for the novelty I would take a ride in a ricksha, and rode behind a man for a block. I had such a bad feeling about having an undernourished human being pull me down the street that I stopped him and got out. The average age of a ricksha driver was under thirty. For the most part these men did not own their rickshas, which belonged to fleet owners who paid their drivers a pittance. No wonder the new government in China abolished this traffic. I discovered that beasts of burden, for the most part human beings, had the right of way, each one shouting as he or she tried to get through the confusion of the streets. There were many massage parlors. There were "honey wagons" to collect human excrement destined to fertilize the garden plots just outside Shanghai. The most appalling things were the vehicles that picked up the dead, like so much garbage. The poor could not pay for a traditional funeral, so twice a week they would lay their dead outside their doors to be picked up. More than 567 were picked up in December of 1946, 23 of whom were children.

The finest thing that happened to me in China was to meet and work with Benjamin H. Kizer, chief of the UNRRA China mission. He was a famous attorney from the state of Washington who had a wide interest and knowledge of world affairs, especially of China. His faith was Quaker. A kind, understanding, utterly fair (and very firm when the occasion demanded it) man, he was an excellent administrator, although his enemies tried to discount this. We kept in touch after our UNRRA days, until he died, nearly 100 years old.

Kizer and I discussed my possible role in the UNRRA organization. The problems were enormous. UNRRA had run a tight ship in Kunming where there was a lot of planning for the time when the country would be opened up, but Washington had sent personnel to Shanghai before the UNRRA headquarters could be moved.

There were many conflicting directives, and it was difficult to get reorganized. Happily, one of Mr. Kizer's best qualities was patience. No orientation or briefing of district officers or even directives could unify the fifteen UNRRA districts.

Operations in China were quite different from those in Greece. The Chinese government had the right and obligation to create CNRRA (Chinese National Relief and Rehabilitation Administration) and to appoint the officers and employees. CNRRA was the operational agency and UNRRA was in China simply to expedite the movement of supplies and then turn them over to CNRRA. UNRRA advised CNRRA, but the Kumintang had the ultimate responsibility. Mr. Kizer had worked intimately with government officials in Kunming and was aware of a number of problems. I was appointed regional operations officer, directed to work out a plan and acquire staff for fifteen regions.

Dr. T. F. Tsiang was the chief of CNRRA and Dr. C. M. Li was his assistant. Dr. C. Y. Hsiang was my opposite as regional operations officer in CNRRA. I couldn't have asked for a better man with whom to work day in and day out; I regarded myself as his assistant. We traveled together throughout China and no decisions were made without his concurrence.

China and the Kuomintang had its problems as far as the people's movement was concerned. General Marshall in 1945 tried to reconcile the Kuomintang and the Communists; my office had a representative on his staff. But the Kuomintang had no intention of reconciliation, and continued to call the Communists "bandits."

Our first job was to work out directives for the three top regional officers. Our concern was that UNRRA officers in the field might take lightly the responsibilities of CNRRA and belittle the ability of the Chinese to help themselves. Traditionally China had had its own family and village ways to provide for the indigent, ways which had disintegrated during the wars. It was hard to change old habits, thoughts, and institutions, and UNRRA personnel had not been taught much about the Chinese culture.

With Dr. C. Y. Hsiang I visited the regional offices and advised them on improvements or changes to be considered. One concern in CNRRA was the operation of the UNRRA Tsingtao office. Tsingtao was north of Shanghai on a point of land into the Yellow Sea, hemmed in by the Communists. We telegraphed our coming, and visited Tsingtao. On the first night we were lavishly entertained by the director, who was living with the wife of a Kuomintang general. He called her his interpreter. All the operations were at a standstill; there had been no effort made to alleviate the poverty outside of Tsingtao. Communist encirclement was the excuse. C. Y. and I decided that the director should be asked to resign, and asked him to prepare to go to Shanghai and confer with Mr. Kizer and Mr. Tsiang. He became very angry and threatened that he would have my job if it was the last thing he did. We returned to Shanghai and told our story to Kizer, who immediately ordered the director to Shanghai. This same man later represented American liquor interests in China. I never heard from him again.

C. Y. and I went to Hankow, where we found a very able director working out an extensive program which had put many people to work. He had one roadblock in that Chinese officials saw no reason to appoint a welfare committee; they claimed that it had never been done and that there were too many poor people for such a committee to be effective.

In Hankow I saw for the first time the devastating results of American military napalm bombing which had burned sturdy buildings and institutions to the ground, a fire that could not be quenched. The bombing had been indiscriminate, and what it had done to human life, both friend and foe, was horrendous. Victims who were not burned to death often had crippling scars that made their bodies useless to the end of their lives. Presumably the Chinese were our friends.

There was also a difference in the reasoning related to the treatment of the defeated. There were perhaps 3,000 Japanese in Hankow when the war ended who simply stopped their aggression and roamed the streets of Hankow at will, trying to adjust to peace. The Chinese thought this was natural, as they were no longer enemies (although not necessarily friends) and saw no reason for retaliation. The Japanese soldiers put aside their weapons. Their generals continued to wear their swords and regalia, but accepted defeat and offered no antagonism. When the American military entered the city they were astounded at the freedom accorded the Japanese. They immediately rounded up the Japanese, took away their weapons, and crowded them into miserable concentration camps where they gradually were forced to barter away their possessions for food. I visited one of these camps, which was short of supplies, services and essential medical attention.

The Communists seemed to hold most of the country areas north of the Yangtze River, more than 25 percent of China. They allowed the Kuomintang to hold the cities—a liability, crowded as they were with refugees and people who feared the retaliation of the Communists on landlords and were opposed to a people's revolution. This situation was true in Hankow where both CNRRA and UNRRA distributed goods in Communist-held territories.

James G. Johnson, a sensitive and understanding person, had preceded me to China. We submitted a joint report to the Shanghai office April 27, 1946.

"Upon his return from Hankow, Mr. Wahlberg presented a report on the military interference with CNRRA distribution supplies in Hupeh and Hunan. He found the military take the position that the distribution of the supplies by CNRRA in Communist dominated regions in Hupeh is contrary to military policy. The military feel that the Communists in Northern Hupeh are cut off and surrounded and should be starved into submission. The pressure on the CNRRA regional office is so great that the deputy director feels he may be compelled to resign. Mr. Wahlberg also reports that on one or two occasions soldiers have demanded CNRRA relief supplies, attempted to requisition them from their families, and followed CNRRA's distribution teams and confiscated all or part of the supplies distributed. This information has been passed along to Mr. Falconer who, upon Mr. Kizer's instructions, is collecting data on all cases of this kind, as a basis for action on the highest levels. The regional office is also pushing the matter in Hankow."

Such action on the part of the military was contrary to the understanding and agreements of CNRRA and UNRRA. The government of China made the most out of all shipments into China to strengthen not only itself but favored individuals. Only 1 percent of UNRRA supplies went into Communist areas.

There is a historic document on the subject, "Report on First Supplies Sent by UNRRA to the Communist Areas of Shantung Province":

"The desire of the China office of UNRRA to implement the basic policy that UNRRA's supplies should be sent to all people regardless of religion, race or political belief, had been delayed by civil wars, which followed the end of the hostilities with the Japanese. With the signing of the ceasefire order on 10 January 1946, it appeared that many of the difficulties which had hindered action were now removed, and plans were started immediately to make a first shipment. An agreement had been reached between Dr. T. F. Tsiang, director of CNRRA, and Chou En Lai, deputy leader of the Chinese Communist party, laying down conditions under which CNRRA could send supplies into Communist areas. In a joint CNRRA-UNRRA staff meeting on 9 January 1946 Dr. T. F. Tsiang had stated the agreement was substantially as follows:

> "Firstly, that relief be extended to needy persons in Communist areas who suffered war losses, regardless of race, religion or political view;
>
> "Secondly, that CNRRA will not interfere with the local administration of the various areas concerned;
>
> "Thirdly, the Communist party may appoint representatives to participate in the administration of relief in Communist areas;
>
> "Fourthly, that if CNRRA personnel or supply trucks are detained by Communist authorities, CNRRA will withdraw itself from the Communist areas.

"Dr. Tsiang had also explained to Chou En Lai that it was planned to make the first shipment of about 3,000 tons to the port of Chefoo." (In Shangtung Province, of which Tsingtao was the capital.)

Conditions had immeasurably improved in the Tsingtao regional office with the change of directors. The report of James G. Johnson and myself of April 1946 read in part as follows:

"Mr. Tshihatchef, regional director at Tsingtao, reports improved relations both with the Chinese government officials and with the Lin'i Communist government. This cooperation has resulted in improved road communications, especially in southern Shantung. The matter of telephone and telegraph communications and also railway conditions are being worked on.

"The excellent beginning initiated last month in activities throughout the area controlled by the Shantung regional office continued during March. We were successful in making actual distribution in sixteen localities in the Kiaotung area, as well as in numerous new areas in the southern section and in areas along the railway."

The Communists successfully controlled the railway out of Shantung by having a company of workers remove nine miles of track, which mysteriously disappeared, and put the track back when required. It took less than an hour to do the job one way or the other.

General George G. Marshall was in the meantime doing his best to reconcile the Kuomintang and the Communists. The effort was doomed to failure because the Kuomintang would not concede to agreements such as distribution of UNRRA supplies into Communist areas.

It is my opinion that the Communists believed they would win the battle for China just by waiting for the Kuomintang to collapse. This seemed to be the feeling throughout China. Some of my missionary friends could not believe that such a change could take place, although a few missionaries had joined the Communists. I knew Anna Louise Strong when she studied the coal miners' problem in Colorado and later wrote a book about it. She was a loyal follower of the Communists to the very end. She provided a monthly publication entitled, "Letter from China," which kept her friends and others informed on what was going on in China.

Once I attended a cabinet meeting of the Kuomintang held in Nanking. Kizer had asked me to represent him. I had just returned from an area of mass starvation, and felt strongly that the government was to blame. It was in an area where the chief crop was rice. The farmers counted on two good crops, and a third, poorer crop if fortunate. The first and second crops were requisitioned by the military to support the local cadres and governments and the national government, leaving the poor third crop to the farmers. The governments expected UNRRA to supply the difference between subsistence and starvation. This was impossible for CNRRA-UNRRA to do because of lack of transportation and other problems. The people tried to survive on grass, leaves, bark, roots, and even certain kinds of soil which was mixed with what little rice was left to them. No compassion or understanding was shown by the governments or the military. Chiang Kai-shek did not attend the meeting, which was chaired by the prime minister. Nothing of importance was discussed, which seemed strange in so critical a time. They talked about the needs of the people and hoped that UNRRA could help. It was a listless and defeatist meeting in an atmosphere of doom. Nothing was said about the efforts of General Marshall.

China Lobby

The China Lobby was a propaganda organization for the Kuomintang and wanted to get rid of Kizer, because of his honesty and firmness about his UNRRA responsibilities, and his concern about the corruption evident in many areas of the Chinese government. A Mr. Olmstead was sent from Washington to investigate Kizer and his administration. Olmstead went to work for the Chinese government and asked me to be his assistant, an offer which for reasons of conscience was impossible to accept.

Kizer was asked to resign and was relieved of his position. The new director and I could not see eye to eye, so I gave him an involuntary resignation which stated my feelings. Kizer and I went home by a freighter, landing in Port Arthur, Texas and spent a few days with the Tennessee Valley Authority in which we were interested. When I reported to Washington, I was told that the new director of UNRRA in China had been relieved of his position and that Washington wanted me to return to China. But now I wanted to get back home to my family.

I heard from Sophia Chang after the Communists took over in China:

"There was great tension in Changsha near the end of July. On account of the effort of the Changsha people peace movement was promoted. The army announced its welcome of the Communists and stopped working for the Nationalists. Therefore there was no vacuum period. The YMCA is still going on. . . . We are doing our best to help the churches to adjust in the new environment. . . . There is a people's representatives' council in this city. . . . Ifan [her husband] was elected as one of the chairmen. . . . A Communist leader, secretary of the party in Changsha, is the chairman and Ifan is the secretary-general. . . . Ifan tried not to accept the post. But the mayor and others say that this will give the Y a greater opportunity to serve the people in this city. Ifan thinks too it is a challenge for the Y to show the Communist friends our Christian spirit of love and service. So he is working hard every day. There are quite a few committees such as "how to clean the city," "running water," "how to deal with beggars," etc. The mayor asks Ifan to sit in any of the city government committees."

Whenever I was in Shanghai I attended church in the Moore Memorial Church which was very much like Grace Church and Community Center in Denver, except that it was entirely Chinese. It was a mission church organized by the Methodist Church, south, with money from the United States, and was staffed by Chinese, except for one white missionary family. The men sat on one side and the women with their babies and young children on the other side. I could not understand the language, but the tunes of the hymns were familiar. The people joined in the services with great enthusiasm.

The church had ample facilities for religious and community activities; hundreds of children attended church school classes during the time of the services, which were quite long. There was no hurry to get through at any particular time, and many people lingered after the services to visit with each other. They were exceedingly friendly, and the few that understood English made it a point to get acquainted with me. One family invited me to their home for a meal and I accepted; they lived in a small two-room apartment with four children. They apologized that they didn't know about American food, so we enjoyed a simple Chinese dinner.

I visited the church during weekdays and discovered that among the many activities was the Soochow University. This university had had its own buildings but had abandoned them when the Japanese took over Shanghai and requisitioned the buildings. The students and faculty fled into the interior and continued their studies. They came back to Shanghai after the Japanese left, but the buildings could not be used until they were renovated, so the church invited them into the community building until their buildings were restored.

Rehabilitation and relief were already a part of their program; children from kindergarten up learned, played, and sang together, eating proper food and drinking powdered milk.

The Hoover Commission Survey

The highlight of my work in China was as a member of the ex-president Hoover's food and famine survey of China. President Hoover was chairman, and Col. R. L. Harrison was head of the mission. President Hoover was chairman of the first meeting, and I sat directly at his right. It was a lengthy meeting in which we discussed our mandate to survey the needs of the people of China. I had always liked President Hoover for his humanitarianism. He had been an engineer in China as a young man, so was somewhat familiar with the country. There were six members of the mission and eight observers; I represented UNRRA. We made an extensive tour of China by air, flying low enough to observe the farms, except when the weather was bad. We also surveyed the 1946 crop, which was slightly better than the crops of the war years but below the pre-war average; that meant that in 1947 there was a food shortage.

It was the unanimous opinion of all the members of the survey party that conditions in the interior were worse than formerly believed, either inside or outside China. There had been no comprehensive survey made of the areas visited, and for this reason Hoover was not completely informed of the seriousness of the situation or the extent to which starvation was occurring in the most deficient regions.

The members of the party unanimously believed that the UNRRA estimate of 7,000,000 facing death by starvation, and 32,000,000 living below subsistence level and attempting to survive by eating roots, bark, seeds, weeds, grass, etc., was if anything low. Practically all of these people were in rural areas or small towns, the areas to which the food received had not been moved.

Food obtained in provinces with a surplus was used mainly for support of the military; only small quantities were used to feed the civilian population. However, food imports helped, as it had been the practice of the military to live off the country, whether the area had a food surplus or not.

The worst situation was in Hunan province. In Hengyeng, and on the roads leading into the city, thousands of people wandered around in search of food, or lay comatose on the roads, sidewalks and in the gutters. Similar conditions prevailed in northern Kwangai province, Kwangtung province, Honan, and Hopeh. The amount of UNRRA food received in China from abroad was barely sufficient to combat malnutrition and starvation in the areas with the greatest food deficits.

CNRRA officials could not realize the magnitude of the food relief problem facing them (as many as 50,000,000 people affected) or the speed necessary to get food into areas to prevent actual starvation. There were no records of an official call on branches of the central government such as transportation, communications, or the military and provincial governments to assist in solving the distribution problem.

The large cities of China were somewhat better off than the rural areas, yet an entirely disproportionate amount of food was distributed and/or sold in large cities of China. An example is the city of Canton, which had 1 percent of the population of its distribution area but was allocated 20 percent of the food allowed to the entire area. Food was being sold to low income class people in Canton, to government employees in Nanking, and other favored groups. A substantial part of the food received was allocated to work projects not located in areas of greatest need. Something less than 10 percent of the food received in China was distributed in the areas of direst need.

We had some experiences en route that are memorable, such as visiting the ancient walled city of Peiping and the museum within. The various achievements of art were amazing. We saw the stone boat which an empress had made with money raised for a Chinese navy. We flew over the Great Wall of China built to keep out invaders, a massive structure curving up and down and around hills and mountains and valleys; like all military structures it served no useful purpose in protecting China. We had a near mishap on the way to Hankow. Since the weather was bad and we were approaching high mountains, we were flying high. One of the motors of our two-motor plane stopped operating and almost caught fire. We were loaded with supplies which had to be thrown overboard as the plane kept slowly going down; we were within 200 feet of the ground when we arrived in Hankow.

There were adults unpacking bundles of used clothing, probably sent from America, and distributing them to families of the church and others in need. The students were provided with clothing and food. There seemed to be thousands of inquiries about relatives, jobs, medical supplies, sickness and other problems. Many people were undernourished and some had contracted tuberculosis. The young people had various groups for music and entertainment. Men worked at repairs needed in the church, attending to the outside of the buildings and the landscaping as well. There was laughter and fellowship. The missionaries had left and this church and program were entirely Chinese.

I visited Bishop Ralph Ward, who had spent considerable time in a Japanese concentration camp. He would have suffered more than he had if it had not been for friends who brought him food and other essentials. I was a guest in a mission compound where foreign missionaries had some respite from their labors. The apartments were quite livable and servants took care of most of their needs.

Sophia Chang had attended missionary schools in her early years. She sent me her autobiography, and the following passage seems to sum up the China experience:

"In the evacuations from June 1944 to July 1945, a pretty hard life was our lot. I summed up my refugee life during that period in a letter to my friend: 'One year of unrest and wandering, the darker the way, the brighter the lantern of God's care for us, the kinder the sympathy of real friends, the closer our own folks become and the more thoughts of sharing with the less fortunate. Life is a sojourn and we are all travelers. Weep not for what is lost, for we have never owned any earthly things at all. But we must prepare ourselves in thought and actions so that there will be a world where people will have security and freedom, where each individual will be valued and developed in full potentialities, where everybody is happy and works hard, is taken care of and is nearer to truth, to beauty and goodness and is conscious of the presence of God.'"

General Aris Velouchiotis (left) of ELLAS, the military arm of the Greek resistance movement, is shown here with one of his aides. As the Germans withdrew from Greece in 1944 I had the opportunity to meet Velouchiotis at his headquarters in Lamia. He later died in the Greek Civil War.

We found most of the children of war-torn Greece in pitiful condition: malnourished, shoeless, and often dressed in nothing but rags.

One of the children's feeding centers in Greece.

Author is here pictured (sixth from right) with the first UNRRA shipment to Tsingtoa. Part of this shipment went to CLARA (Communist area).

Destitute Chinese near Lingling. We found that the diet of these people consisted mostly of weeds cooked with a small amount of watery rice—if it was available. The authorities and the military had requisitioned most of the available rice.

Delousing at the Hunan regional office of CNRRA.

8. MICHIGAN, 1947-1976

Mount Olivet, Dearborn 1947-1961

I returned to Colorado and was confronted with several opportunities. I called on my bishop, who could not offer me anything but a fledgling congregation meeting in a schoolhouse in a growing and affluent neighborhood, which I served for a few weeks while considering various proposals. The *Denver Post* offered me a position as youth counselor, which included radio and television time. The Rotary Club and the public schools offered me a chance to work in a delinquency area of Denver. To my surprise, the Small Loan Association wanted me to be their state secretary. I had been chairman of a state committee that had fought loan companies and succeeded in getting the legislation to pass a fairly decent law. Some of these people had become friends and sincerely wanted to change their image. I thought about going back to school to study law. The Democrats urged me to run for Congress.

My friend Owen Geer, who was planning to leave his church in Dearborn, Michigan, wanted to know if I were interested in succeeding him. Another friend, Dr. Henry Hitt Crane, minister of the Central Methodist Church in Detroit, urged me to consider Owen's church, the Mount Olivet Methodist Church in Dearborn. Then I received an urgent letter from the board of that church and a telephone call from Dean Tate, chairman of the board, who wanted me at least to go out to Dearborn and look at the church and its prospects. I agreed to do so if they could wait until Christmas week. I was bargaining for time to see what my prospects might be in Colorado.

I went to Dearborn as promised; Mr. Tate met me at the railroad station and drove me to his home. He placed his hand on my knee and said, "Dr. Wahlberg, I think it is the hand of God at work." I replied, *"I* am sure it is the hand of Mr. Tate."

I found that the congregation had built a gymnasium and community building in 1926 and had expected to erect a sanctuary, but the Depression had intervened. It was hoped that a church could now be constructed. The fact that this church was the Methodist church nearest to the largest factory in the world, the Ford Rouge plant, appealed to me.

Owen Geer had been the national youth director of the Methodist church and had organized an excellent youth program. There was a vigorous young couples club with a potential for leadership. These groups were disappointed when Owen Geer had left for a pastorate in California, and believed he was irreplaceable. The church board included mostly the people who had organized the church, but they were flexible and cooperative.

The church was interested in social issues and had a strong social action committee. Owen Geer had participated in the unionization of the auto workers and Local 600 of the UAW-CIO, the largest union in the world, and interracial. However, the church had fewer rank-and-file workers in its membership than I had hoped. Church members were mostly skilled and unskilled workers, professional people, school teachers, lawyers, businessmen, and dentists. Dearborn had recently united as one city, east and west Dearborn with a huge area in between entirely owned by the Ford Motor Company. A new charter had been adopted, and Dearborn had elected a strong mayor who was to hold his office for over thirty years.

Dearborn was racist, with a slogan "Keep Dearborn Clean"—meaning to most of its citizens, "Keep Dearborn White." Nevertheless, Mount Olivet Church was liberal. Its board passed an open housing resolution, thirty-three to three. The mayor was basically liberal and an excellent administrator, but became a well-known racist. Dearborn was threatened by the blacks from two sides, West Detroit and a neighboring community west of Dearborn called Inkster. The few blacks who dared buy or rent property in Dearborn were harassed by neighbors and city officials until they gave up and moved out. One family survived.

There were a number of other ethnic groups in Dearborn, Arabs, Polish and Italians, and one Jew. I was to discover that blacks traveling through Dearborn were often ticketed for alleged traffic violations, and few eating places would serve them. All this was to change for the better.

I met with the pastoral relations committee and the board and discussed various problems in detail. The church was surrounded by three Roman Catholic parishes and was financially embarrassed. A campaign to raise money for a new church had failed. The secretary and caretaker were underpaid and there was a current budget deficit. I preached on Sunday morning to a congregation of about 225 persons, and there were fewer than 100 at the Christmas Sunday evening program. I was offered the pastorate of the church, and after calling my family in Colorado, accepted. My family was reluctant to leave Colorado, but I felt a challenge.

My family and I expected to plan a five-year program, which we believed was sufficient time in which to build a new sanctuary, and then return to Colorado. However, we remained fifteen years, in spite of the fact that the new church was built on schedule.

Some of our neighbors were upset when they observed blacks entering our church, and sent anonymous letters to me and to the mayor. The mayor asked me to come to his office for a chat, following which he showed me a stack of anonymous letters about blacks being seen in and around our church (which wasn't often; nevertheless, one black constitutes a majority in the minds of some people). The mayor asked me what he should do with them. I said, "Tear them up and file them in the wastepaper basket, as I do with all unsigned letters." He said, "Okay, that is what I planned to do."

I was on a ministerial committee which included two blacks. When the meeting was over I suggested that we go up to Michigan Avenue and have a bite to eat. We entered a restaurant and sat down at a table. The waitress refused to serve us. We calmly remained in our chairs and waited to see what she would do. She called her boss on the phone and he told her to call the police, which she did. Three policemen rushed in. By this time the waitress was almost hysterical as she told the police her problem. One of the policemen knew me and came over to me and said, "She has to serve you. It is the law. Do you want to insist on being served?"

I replied, "No. I would be afraid that she would put strychnine in my hamburger. I wanted to know what you guys would do."

My friend informed me that we could press charges. The next morning Ralph Guy, the chief of police and a member of my church, called and said, "I hear you were embarrassed last night. If you ever get thrown in jail, let me know and I'll come and sit with you."

I joined the district metropolitan branch of the American Civil Liberties Union and was chairman during the McCarthy days (I had been chairman of the state organization in Colorado). This brought an endless stream of anonymous telephone calls and letters as we defended people on the right and on the left whose civil liberties were curtailed. Walter Bergman, Detroit public school administration, was the secretary. He participated in a bus demonstration in the South and was injured, spending the rest of his life in a wheelchair. Ernest Mazy became the director (brother of Emil Mazy, treasurer of the UAW-CIO), and formed a strong organization with branches throughout the state.

I had a front-page controversy with the mayor over the question of multiple housing. The John Hancock Insurance Company proposed building an extensive housing project in East Dearborn next to a building complex called the Ford Foundation. The mayor was emphatically opposed to any such multiple housing, for he believed that blacks might occupy some of the apartments. Housing in Dearborn was scarce so I was for it, and a heated debate ensued. The mayor called for an advisory vote on the part of the people, who, because they shared the mayor's viewpoint on racial matters, gave him a vote of confidence. The mayor in recent years changed his mind on the subject and is personally responsible for building four government-subsidized apartment houses for low income senior citizens. Other larger apartment houses were built with his approval.

There were a number of disagreements with the mayor. One had to do with a film produced by the UAW-CIO on brotherhood. We used it in our church school and found the film informative and helpful. Certain local pressure groups brought this film to the attention of the mayor, who promptly removed it from the city library. I was informed of this by the librarian, so I brought the matter to the attention of the pastors' union and urged the ministers to request the film; they were told why it was not available. I went to the mayor and urged him to return the film to the library. He said, "What film? Oh, you mean that 'nigger' film." I told him that he was not elected to be a censor of books or films or an agent of self-appointed censors—and if he didn't agree I could involve the American Civil Liberties Union, for which he had a profound respect. The film was returned.

Freedom Falters

The Denver Open Forum had been a success for over twenty years in Grace Church because people believed in free speech and provided a climate in which controversial subjects could be discussed. People also were committed to the principle that free speech meant that the most controversial subjects could be discussed and that it was un-American for anyone to infringe upon this right. Limitations on speaking developed with the Second World War, which meant that certain subjects were off limits, not only by the public but because superpatriots and government agencies disapproved. There is now no such thing as an open forum with no limitations on what can be discussed. We decided to drop our open forums until the climate of America would allow peaceful communication on controversial questions. (This time has not yet come.)

In 1949 we had a meeting in Mount Olivet Church to pursue the possibilities of public discussions of important questions. The response to the value of such a program was unanimous except when it came down to subject matter. There were topics that were off-limits—race, open housing and politics. There was a difference of opinion on peace, the United Nations, and anti-Semitism. We nevertheless decided to try a few meetings. One was on socialized medicine in England, and the meeting came off very well; my own doctor was present and later commented to me, "I liked that meeting. Hadn't even thought about it. I went into medicine to serve sick people. I guess there will be need for doctors in socialism. Sure got me to thinking. I don't always agree with the American Medical Association. I am a doctor to help people, not get rich."

We continued to provide forums on vital subjects—and then the roof fell in. The subject was "The Need to Prevent a Third World War." The participants were John Denman, representing the American Legion, serving on the public relations committee of the state organization; Dr. Russell Broadhead of Wayne State University; R. C. Lancaster, publisher of the *Dearborn Guide;* and me.

It seemed to be a successful meeting, except the Legionnaires were very unhappy about what the other three members of the panel said.

John Denman said, "The great fallacy of this forum here tonight is that it is delivered before the wrong audience. The question of whether there will be a third world war is not one that can be determined by anyone in this room, or even anyone in our national government. The bald truth of the matter is this: the power to launch or stay World War III is concentrated in the hands of a comparatively few cynical, amoral lusters after power: the men who make the decisions in the Kremlin. They, and only they, will decide the *when, where,* and *if* of World War III.

"What nature of men are these in whose hands the destiny of the world's peace rests? Do they measure up to the grave responsibilities that are theirs?

"The American Legion answers both questions with a flat unequivocal NO!"

There were other views expressed by members of the panel; perhaps I took the more optimistic position and reminded the audience that Americans had tremendous potential for helping to make and keep the peace. This meeting was held on January 31, 1951.

Repercussions of this meeting were not long restrained. John Denman, also chairman of the committee on un-American activities of the American Legion in Michigan, addressed a meeting of a women's conference at the Tuller Hotel in Detroit on February 20, 1951. His subject was "Red Conspiracy at Work." Part of his remarks were directed against Mount Olivet Methodist Church, and especially the minister. Violent charges poured into the phones of the parsonage and the church.

Audria Vogel and Charlotte Trubey, members of Mount Olivet Church, were at the meeting and were upset and alarmed by what Denman had said; they talked to him afterwards trying to understand his remarks. They reported as follows:

"Denman pointed out that Rev. Wahlberg was connected with several organizations which were cited as Communist front organizations, among which were Civil Rights Congress (Dec. 14, 1949) and Peaceful Alternatives; he was a signer of a peace petition, had signed a petition protesting the deportation of Harry Bridges, and belonged to the Methodist Federation for Social Service. Rev. Wahlberg circulated the Stockholm (Red Cross) petition and had a close relationship with Emily Green Balch publications. He told of petitions which were sent out with the Red Cross insignia at the top of them in regard to abolishing atomic war, and the return address of the petitions was the same address as the Mt. Olivet Community Methodist Church in Dearborn. The Red Cross, however, denied their association with this petition. Mr. Denman showed the audience a photostatic copy of the article as it appeared in one of the Detroit papers.

"Continuing, Denman stated that he accepted the invitation to take part in the forum discussion. He had planned on ten others attending with him and sitting at various places in the audience to bring up questions from time to time, to give him a chance to expose these people. He had a lady taking notes, but time would not permit him to go into detail, so he read a few of the questions and answers as they were written down, almost word for word. When he arrived with Lou Estes, they looked around and discovered a copy of *Soviet Russia Today* on the literature table, which was alleged to be a Communist publication.

"Mrs. Bernadine Becker, the chairperson, announced that the participants must adhere to the subject and at no time were personalities to be mentioned. He said that that pinned him down so that at no time did he have opportunity to bring out the points he had intended. At one point, however, a doctor in the audience asked him a question; Mrs. Becker prevented him from answering it, saying that she had not allowed Rev. Wahlberg to interrupt him when he was talking. The applause of the audience was a sign that the people were anxious to hear the answer, so Mrs. Becker finally gave her consent.

"One of the outstanding points that Mr. Denman emphasized was that 'Mt. Olivet Church has been converted, and stands as one of the most imposing Communist fronts.'

"After the Women's National Security Conference had closed its morning session to adjourn for luncheon in the Arabian Room of the Tuller, Mr. Denman and Mr. Estes were questioned by Charlotte and Audria and two or three women from Dearborn. They told us that they never spoke on these subjects until they were equipped with records and authentic information to back them up, and that at any time we wished to see these records, we were welcome to come to his office in the Veterans' Memorial Building on Jefferson Avenue.

"When asked if Mr. Wahlberg could have been or was being used as a tool by the Communist party without his knowledge, Mr. Denman said that that was a remote possibility. A man with his education could not help but see and know such things. Belonging to one or two of such organizations was excusable, but for a man or woman to be connected with so many of them, it didn't seem likely.

"When Rev. Wahlberg's war record and standing in the community was cited, the answer was, 'That is just the kind of people they select for this kind of work.'"

Mr. Denman concluded that he had a bombshell that he would release in a few days which would really stir things up.

It took time to regain my composure necessary to face the situation and provide perspective to deal with such nonsense. The experience was unbelievable and traumatic. I had to confront my congregation on Sunday.

I consulted Norris Porter, a lawyer in my congregation, for guidance. He told me to keep my shirt on and chin up and get all available facts. I called Mr. Denman. He said he could support his charges. I pointed out that he was party to misinformation and had created an intolerable situation; that I had no alternative but to get to the bottom of it, even to seeking justice before the law.

It was agreed that we have a preliminary meeting in the American Legion headquarters on February 27, with our lawyers present. I invited in addition my district superintendent, the officers of the church board, some minister colleagues, two Dearborn Legionnaires, and my wife.

I learned that the bombshell was that I was to be brought to trial by my Legion post for subversive activity and be expelled from membership. I made this farce unnecessary by sending a resignation "until the Legion could come to its senses and know the true meaning of freedom."

I requested a statement of the charges the Legion thought they had but was refused, "because if you knew the nature of the charges you could prepare a defense, and they want to get you." This infuriated my informer, who claimed it was unfair—that he would leave a copy of the charges on his dining room table and I was free to go into his house and copy them, which I did. It was a compilation of the citations by the Congressional Committee on Un-American Activities, statements related to Legion surveillance and newspaper clippings. I also discovered that the Legion had provided the Dearborn Police Department with this information.

My friend allowed me to read the current intelligence reports and statements of the State Department of the American Legion. It included a list of so-called subversive books which local Legionnaires were expected to weed out of school and public libraries; a directive on motion pictures directed to keeping local screens from "going pink," and an analysis of the activities of youth groups, ministers and organizations. It contained an especially vicious statement about a Jewish organization.

Sunday came before the Tuesday meeting. Excerpts from my sermon were: "Prepare yourselves for a shock. . . . Your minister has been accused by the American Legion as a subversive." I reviewed some of the charges. Fortunately, I had received prior permission from the board to attend several of the meetings, especially meetings on peace.

"I am completely fed up with these attacks. It is the problem of our congregation. There seems to be a lack of faith in Christianity—in Christian leadership.

"People are forced to trust only the military and pseudomilitary forces in America, and are acting much as Hitler and Stalin have acted in Germany and Russia. I am opposed to any group that uses the privilege of free speech to further their own objectives, if those ends are in conflict with our traditions of freedom and the best interests of our nation and the world."

I told my congregation that I did not want in any way to be an embarrassment, and then offered them my resignation. The whole congregation rose as a single person and gave me a vote of confidence. Furthermore, each family wanted Norris Porter to file a separate suit. Mr. Porter pondered the possibility of having to file 400 separate suits if it were necessary.

We assembled in the American Legion headquarters for a confrontation on Americanism. Mr. Denman called the meeting to order and in presenting its purpose spoke as if I were on trial and we were present to determine my guilt or innocence or at least the nature of my crime. Mr. Porter was immediately on his feet to declare that "Reverend Wahlberg is not on trial. He has committed no crime whatsoever. Mr. Denman is on trial for libel for intentionally injuring the reputation of a minister and his church."

The American Legion attorney apparently saw the point and had to admit that this approach was admissible. It was Mr. Denman who had accused me and Mt. Olivet Church of subversive activities. His approach was that no harm had been done, and the remarks by Mr. Denman were meaningless. He had meant no harm. I was promised a copy of his address but never received it.

Mr. Denman requested that my record be read. I agreed, inasmuch as I had nothing to hide. If I had made mistakes, they were at least honest. I was eager to get the whole thing into the open.

The statement directed against Mt. Olivet Church contained the panel address made by Mr. Denman in the discussion of "The Need to Prevent a

Third World War," and an analysis of the alleged subversive activities of Roy Lancaster of the *Dearborn Guide,* Prof. Russel H. Broadhead of Wayne University and myself—the three other participants in the panel. The basic issue was whether or not a Christian church had the right to discuss peace or any other subject—the right of free speech.

The charges already known to me in one form or another were as follows (about six of them came directly from the Congressional Committee on Un-American Activities):

Organization	Action	Source

1.
First Congress of Mexican and Spanish American Peoples of U.S. — Signer of call — Mimeograph release Mar. 24-26, 1939

(My comment: I do not recall the Congress of Mexican American Peoples of the U.S. During the thirties I was very interested in the problems of migratory workers. There were many activities in their behalf. I served in a number of areas related to human problems in Colorado from 1930 to 1944 and probably signed a number of petitions. I have learned that this particular congress never materialized.)

2.
Methodist Federation for Social Service — Member executive committee

(My comment: I have been a member of the Methodist Federation for Social Service [now Social Action] since 1920, and was at one time a vice president. It was organized in 1907 "to deepen within the church the sense of social obligation and opportunity, to study social problems from the Christian point of view, and to promote social service in the spirit of Jesus Christ." Harry F. Ward has been one of my most helpful friends.)

3.
Open letter on Harry Bridges — *Daily Worker* July 19, 1942

(My comment: Could very well be. I think this was the time that Harry Bridges was making a tour of the country in the interest of national unity. He spoke in a forum under the auspices of the University of Colorado. I was present along with prominent citizens. He made a favorable impression.)

4.
National Conference on American Policy in China and the Far East — Sponsor — Conference Call Jan. 23, 25, 1948 New York City

(My comment: I am interested in our American policy in the Far East. I did not attend this meeting. I probably felt that it was an important meeting and signed the call.)

5.
Civil Rights Congress
of Michigan   Sponsor

Call to Michigan
State Conference
April 1, 2, 1949

(My comment: My loyalty has always been to the American Civil Liberties Union. I don't recall that I was ever connected with Civil Rights Congress.)

6.
American Committee for
Protection of Foreign
Born

Signer of state-
ment against
denaturalization

Daily Worker
Aug. 30, 1950

(My comment: I am naturally for the underdog and the unjustly treated and am concerned about upholding their constitutional rights. If I signed this statement, it was for good reasons. The foreign born have not always been treated with dignity in America. Most foreign born would seem to love America. After all, my parents were foreign born.)

7.
Committee for Peaceful
Alternatives to the
Atlantic Pact

Signer of statement
for international
agreement to ban
use of atomic
weapons.
Signer of statement
on Korea

Statement attached
to press release
Dec. 14, 1949

July 28, 1950

(My comment: I attended, with the approval of my church, the Mid-Century Conference for Peace held in Chicago, May 1950. It did support the International Red Cross Appeal, which was to appeal to the governments of the world to come to some agreement on atomic weapons. The statement on Korea as of July 28, 1950, is no doubt one that was released by the National Council on Peaceful Alternatives. It called for the United Nations to do everything possible to mediate the Korean problem in an effort to save the lives of our boys in the service. My son was in that war.)

8.
The American Legion, Department of Michigan, has information that Wahlberg circulated, and caused others to circulate, the Stockholm Peace Petition, branded by the U.S. State Department as Communist propaganda device.

(My comment: There is some confusion in my mind about this and there must be some confusion in the State Department. This was a perfectly legitimate peace petition put out by the International Red Cross. I am certain that I signed the Freedom Crusade Petition.)

9.
Legion also records that Wahlberg served on reception committee for the Red Dean of Canterbury when that English clergyman spoke at the Music Hall in Detroit.

(My comment: I have never heard nor met Hewlett Johnson, but I understand

he is quite a gentleman. I was called about his appearance. I could not serve so was not on the reception committee.)

10.
Wahlberg quoted from a Communist in the panel discussion on Jan. 31, name of Communist, Sorokin.

(My comment: The person whose article I read was Dr. Pitirim A. Sorokin of Harvard University. The article was "Nine Theses on War and Peace," the last section of a book edited by Paul Poling, a brother of Dan Poling. The book was copyrighted and released in 1950 by the Board of Christian Education of the Presbyterian Church.)

11.
Close Association with Emily Green Balch publications.

(My comment: She and Jane Addams organized Women's International League for Peace and Freedom. Only two American women to have received Nobel Peace Prize. Never met Miss Balch. Knew Jane Addams.)

Mr. Denman was confronted by a group of people representing the church and the community of Dearborn who did not agree with him (including two members of his own organization). He could not believe it, accustomed as he was to the applause of his listeners in his alleged battle with Communism. It seemed incredible to me as I was conscious of a church that unanimously stood behind me and a community that had voluntarily come forward to defend me.

The meeting continued as long as anyone had anything to say. Mr. Denman inquired, "What now? What do we do to end this meeting?"

Mr. Porter turned to me and asked, "Wallie, what do you think? Do you want to sue for damages?"

Mr. Denman turned to the Legion attorney and asked, "What do you think? Have they got a case?" The attorney assured Mr. Denman that we had a good case and that it ought to be settled out of court.

I proposed that we did not want to be vindictive, that we would be satisfied with a retraction and apology from Mr. Denman in a letter addressed to me and printed in the state of Michigan publication of the American Legion.

Mr. Denman winced but the attorney recommended this solution as being quite generous, so Mr. Denman agreed.

He sent a letter which was printed in the *State Legionnaire*—but it was far from saying what he should have said. He worried himself into a bad case of ulcers. I made a hopsital call to assure him that I held no grudge.

Here is Denman's letter:

"Dear Sir: In the course of an address I delivered to the Michigan Women's National Security Conference at the Tuller Hotel in Detroit on February 10, 1951, I mentioned you and the church of which you are a pastor.

"Shortly thereafter, you informed me that two of the women in my audience of that date brought to you a report alleging my remarks imputed

Communist affiliations to yourself and the Mount Olivet Community Methodist Church.

"At my suggestion, you and a committee from your church met with me at state headquarters of the American Legion on February 27 to discuss what I actually said in the talk of February 20, and the construction placed on my remarks by the two women who reported to you.

"This letter will serve to clarify and to summarize the results of our conference.

"I categorically and emphatically state that neither by innuendo, direct statement nor connotation have I ever referred to the Mount Olivet Community Methodist Church in any manner as to reflect on its loyalty or its adherence to American ideals and principals. Nor did I, in my statements, charge or intend to impute any Communist party affiliations with reference to you. Impressions created to the contrary were without any intent on my part, and, in my personal capacity, I express my regrets for the misunderstandings that may have deleloped.

"Sincerely,

"/s/ John L. Denman"

And from Mike J. Sicle of Ford Post N. 173:

"Dear Reverend Wahlberg:

"Acting in the capacity as chairman of the Un-American Activities for the Ford Motor Post No. 173 American Legion in Dearborn, I presented a written report. This report was given to me by the State Department Un-Americanism chairman of the American Legion. I read this report on the floor at one of our regular post meetings.

"Since the presentation of this report, a retractive statement has been written by one Mr. John Denman, indicating that the charges and innuendos, as stated in the report, were baseless and not factual. This has placed me, as well as yourself, in a very embarrassing position.

"For the record, I wish to state that in presenting this report, I was only acting in the capacity of a chairman. I regret the incident very much and publicly apologize to you for the personal insults charged against you in the report.

"This report purported to affiliate you with some so-called Communistic organizations and activities. These false charges are both slanderous and libelous.

"I personally feel that a grave injustice was perpetrated on your character and integrity. This is not only unfortunate, but it is inexcusable. As an outstanding minister in our community, your American ideals and principles of Christianity are personified in your fine work in your church.

"This unfortunate incident of this erroneous report should be clarified. I feel that *you*, Reverend Wahlberg, are guilty *only* of being a fine Christian and a good American.

"Hoping to assist you in all ways possible, I shall always hold you in only the highest esteem.

"Yours, in apology,

"/s/ Mike J. Sicle

"Chairman, Un-American Activities Committee"

We have contended with falsehood and persecution throughout our history. There are closed minds on many subjects so that from time to time, it is difficult to discuss them in open forums or meetings. This became especially true in the fifties with the fanaticism of Senator Joseph McCarthy and a president who didn't approve of McCarthy but lacked the courage to dissuade him.

Is it any wonder that we built up a "silent majority" that tolerated the ruthlessness and scandal of an age of Nixon, in which traditional liberties eroded?

Committee on Un-American Activities

I believed that this experience was sufficiently serious to be communicated to my friends in Washington, as well as the Congressional Committee on Un-American Activities.

My friend Oscar Chapman, later appointed Secretary of the Interior, replied:

"Dear Wallie:

"Thanks for your nice letter received last week. I have had an opportunity to observe the Un-American Activities Committee at close hand, and want to say that your concern over the Methodist Federation of Social Action is only a small fraction of the fears of the danger to our freedom in this country which is being brought about by this committee. As you have known for more than twenty years, I have no sympathy for the Communists, as such; neither do I have any sympathy for the Fascists. I hate to see our very foundations of democracy destroyed by intemperate and immature approaches to the problem.

"Thanks also for sending me the copy of your letter to the president. I happen to know that he has a very deep sympathy for your interest in this matter, but this is something entirely in the hands of the Congress. You and every other Methodist interested in this matter should write to the Congress about this.

"Sorry I didn't get to see you this summer—better luck next time, however. Kind regards,

"Sincerely,

"Oscar"

This should have been adequate warning about the Methodist Foundation, but church people were already running for cover. The boom fell on the federation in the Methodist General Conference of 1952.

My friend Congressmen Wayne N. Aspinall wrote me:

"Dear Wallie:

"Yesterday afternoon I had a personal conference with Congressman John S. Wood, relative to matters which they have in the file about the charges concerning which you wrote to me the first of the month. Congressman Wood is going to answer your letter immediately, and he advised me that he would let you know what evidential statements they have. We talked at considerable length and he stated that in his opinion from the evidence which he has that you—like many other innocent people—in your desire to help the underprivileged people, were caught in an association with certain declared Communist groups without knowledge on your part of the fact that such organizations were controlled by Communists.

"After you have heard from Mr. Wood, if you have any further questions, Wallie, let me know.

"Sincerely,

"Wayne"

This letter is typical of many letters that I received from congressmen and senators. Some of them brought pressure on the committee. They reflected not only the mood and thinking of Congress but of people in general. It was a hot potato, and many people preferred to remain silent. The basic question was, why should there be such an organization whose main function was to keep files filled with clippings and alleged activities of thousands of citizens? I was offended by the statement "that you—like other innocent people—in your desire to help the underprivileged . . ." The problem has to do with the fact that there are underprivileged people. The implication was that if one was fool enough to work with the poor, this person was bound to be branded "red." The Un-American Committee ruined the careers of thousands of innocent citizens for no other reason than that they were not part of a "silent majority."

On March 16, 1951, I wrote to Congressman John S. Wood, then chairman of the Committee on Un-American Activities, sending copies to influential friends in Washington including Senator Ed Johnson, Oscar Chapman, then assistant secretary of the interior, and Congressman Wayne Aspinall. I suggested they bring pressure on the committee to release to me whatever the committee had in its files:

"Mr. John Denman, chairman of Un-American Activities of the American Legion, Department of Michigan, speaking on 'Red Conspiracy at Work' before the Sixteenth Michigan Women's National Security Conference, February 20, 1951, branded me as a subversive, using for his authority the Congressional Committee on Un-American Activities. He has made and is no doubt making similar statements on other occasions. He also issued a directive to have me tried in my own Legion post for subversive activity. He claims that he is equipped with records and authentic information to back him up, furnished by the Congressional Committee on Un-American Activities.

"This is a serious situation. It is of great concern to me, my congregation, and community, and we have a right to know what this is all about. My church has a distinguished record of Christian leadership and service.

"I would like for the Congressional Committee on Un-American Activities to send me a copy of the record which I assume has been given to the American Legion of Michigan, and to make whatever comments you feel justified. Mr. John Denman claims that the Congressional Committee on Un-American Activities has cited me for subversive activity. I am completely unaware of this and frankly I do not believe this is true. Would you be so kind as to do whatever is right in this situation? I am certain that it is the purpose of this and all congressional committees to protect the integrity and rights of American citizens. I cannot understand why loyal citizens should be smeared in this way. Would this not seem to be a type of subversive activity?

"I know that this matter is important and that you will regard it as such. I have a tremendous faith in the integrity of our congressional leaders and in our American government and our democractic spirit and desire for fair play."

I did not receive an immediate reply, so I wrote to him again and urged him to include my correspondence in his files. In the meantime, I received a forthright letter from Senator Edwin Johnson, which included the citations of the committee. About the same time the following letter came from Congressman Wood, nearly a duplicate of the letter from Senator Johnson.

"This will acknowledge your letter of March 16, 1951, regarding the remarks allegedly made by Mr. John Denman of the American Legion. You assume that the American Legion of Michigan was given a report on you by this committee and you requested a copy of the report be furnished you. You further state that we may make whatever comments we feel are justified.

"No record of you has been furnished the American Legion, but the files and records of this committee contain the following information regarding the Reverend Edgar M. Wahlberg.

"The *Daily Worker* of August 30, 1950, page 5, contains a statement issued by the American Committee for Protection of the Foregin Born against denaturalization, and the name of Edgar M. Wahlberg is listed as one of the signers. The attorney general of the United States has declared the American Committee for the Protection of the Foreign Born to be a Communist organization within the meaning and contemplation of Executive Order 9835, 'the authority for the Government Employee Loyalty Program.'

"A printed pamphlet entitled 'Call to Michigan State Conference' on April 1 and 2, 1949, sponsored by the Civil Rights Congress, contains the name of Edgar *N.* Wahlberg, Mt. Olivet Methodist Church, as one of the sponsors. The Civil Rights Congress has been designated as a Communist organization by the attorney general under the authority previously cited.

"The *Daily Worker* of July 19, 1942, reported that Edgar M. Wahlberg signed an open letter in defense of Harry Bridges. The Bridges' defense committees were cited under the authority previously cited.

"A 'Call for a Conference on American Policy in China and the Far East' reflects the name of Reverend Edgar M. Wahlberg, formerly with UNRRA in China, as one of the sponsors. This conference, as well as the parent organization, the Committee for a Democratic Far Eastern Policy, was cited by the attorney general as Communist under the authority previously stated.

"A mimeographed release dated March 24-25, reflects the name of Reverend Edgar M. Wahlberg, Grace Community Church, Denver, Colorado, as a signer of the 'Call to the First Congress of Mexican and Spanish American Peoples of the United States.' This committee cited the above named congress as a Communist front on March 29, 1944. [As I have mentioned this congress was never held.]

"It has never been the intention of this committee to smear anyone, and while information contained herein is from documents in our files, it is without comment or characterization. However, the information is factual insofar as our records are concerned, and if it is erroneous the error is not on the part of this committee.

"(Signed by John S. Wood, Chairman)"

It is interesting to note that the authority of most of these citations is based on an Executive Order 9835 "the authority for the Government Employee Program." I was not a government employee. I was a minister in the United Methodist Church. Mr. Wood stated in his letter that no information had "been furnished the American Legion," and yet duplicates were held by my own Legion post, the state Legion headquarters, the local police department, two Detroit newspapers and at least one Dearborn newspaper, a church official and others. Congressman Wood wrote, "It has never been the intention of this committee to smear anyone, and while the information contained herein is from our files, it is without comment or characterization." This did not prevent the American Legion from smearing me. This did not prevent the press from characterizing me as a "red" and making irresponsible and erroneous statements about me. This did not prevent church officials and groups from whispering these idiotic allegations about me.

I wrote a letter to the congressional committee in response:

"I am a member of the executive committee of the National Committee for Peaceful Alternatives, and a vice president of the Methodist Federation for Social Action. To my knowledge, there is no Communist infiltration of these groups. Would you be kind enough to give me any information that you may have on these organizations?"

They replied:

"Dear Reverend Wahlberg:

"This will acknowledge your letter of May 4, 1951. Enclosed herewith is a copy of the committee pamphlet on the Communist Peace Offensive, and you will find a reference to the Mid-Century Conference for Peace on pages 143 to 152. This conference was sponsored by the National Committee for Peaceful Alternatives.

"This committee has made no investigation of the Methodist Federation for Social Service or its successor, the Methodist Federation for Social Action, and therefore is unable to furnish you information in regard to that organization. [Emphasis mine]

"Sincerely yours,

"/s/ John S. Wood, Chairman"

I took the congressman at his word; nevertheless, I knew that the Methodist Federation for Social Action had been under fire for some time and many had fled its membership. This was good news, so I had the letter mimeographed and sent to many of my friends and other people concerned with the federation. I simply duplicated the letter to which Congressman Wood had signed his name. I attached this statement of my own to the letter:

"The following letter should be of interest to those who are interested in the Methodist Federation of Social Action. The Committee on Un-American Activities has not as yet investigated the federation. Press reports would indicate that the federation has been cited by the congressional committee."

I sent my release to Ralph Stoody, then in charge of Methodist information for the United Methodist church. He seemed to interpret the letter as I did.

This time, I received an unsolicited letter from our friend the congressman. It would seem that pressure had been brought upon him. He wrote:

"Reference is made to your letter of May 4, 1951, and my reply of May 10, 1951.

"You stated that the Committee on Un-American Activities had made no investigation of the Methodist Federation of Social Action or the Methodist Federation for Social Service, and therefore could not furnish you with any information of either organization.

"Although not spelled out specifically, my letter intended to convey the meaning that the committee could furnish no information developed as a result of an investigation because the committee had made no investigation.

"In view of the long period of time the federation has been in existence and its stand on many matters of a controversial nature, it hardly seems possible that you could believe that this committee was without information concerning the organization.

"It has come to my attention that you have given wide circulation to my letter of May 10, 1951, leaving the definite impression that the records of the committee were devoid of any information concerning the federation and its activities. This was an erroneous assumption on the part of you or someone else.

"Inasmuch as my letter of May 10, 1951, was given such wide circulation, I think it is only fair that this review of the Methodist Federation for Social Action, or the information contained therein, be given equally as wide circulation.

"/s/ John S. Wood, Chairman"

To which I replied:

"Enclosed is the release to which you refer which was circulated to a limited group of people.

"I have not intended to misrepresent you. I was quite certain that you had information on the Methodist Federation for Social Action, even though you did not so state. My release was a purely factual matter. Notice the heading, 'The following letter should be of interest to those who are interested in the Methodist Federation for Social Action. The Committee on Un-American Activities has not as yet investigated the Federation. Press reports would indicate that the federation has been cited by the congressional committee.' Note my wording with reference to 'not as yet investigated.'

"Your letter of February 18 says, in the second paragraph, 'You stated,' and then follows the wording from your own letter of May 10, 1951. I am sure that you meant, 'I stated,' as I am not responsible for such a statement. This certainly must be an error in your letter.

"I want to thank you for the review of the Methodist Federation for Social Action and the Methodist Federation for Social Service released by your committee as of February 17, 1952. I have never attempted to give the impression that the records of your committee were devoid of any information concerning the federation and its activities, nor has there been an erroneous assumption on my part. However, if you feel that I have in any way given the wrong impression, I shall be happy to give this letter of February 18, 1952, and your review of the Methodist Federation for Social Action, the widest possible circulation. If you want me to do this, kindly send me as many copies of the review you can spare.

"Thanking you for your kindly letter and interest, I am,

"/s/ Edgar M. Wahlberg"

Mr. Wood did not see fit to send me additional copies of the "Review." He had his own sources for distribution, as evidenced in the fact that a Roman Catholic church in my neighborhood received at least 200 copies. A member of the church came to talk to me about this. He gave me 20 copies and said, "I don't understand what is going on. We don't have any use for these pamphlets and don't mean to do anything about it. You can have all of them."

I thankfully accepted all of them and have distributed them through the years. Members of my church, including myself, received various so-called anti-Communist literature from a variety of groups and committees.

The fact is that the congressional committee never did investigate the Methodist Federation for Social Action. It did send out a pamphlet on the federation based on clippings and materials in its files of garbled information, misstatements, newspaper articles, innuendos, lies, false charges, some relevant and most irrelevant with no continuity or perspective. There were events and ideas that never took place except in the minds of paid informers, who disliked the facts of life as seen by the Methodist ministers who belonged to the federation.

Dr. Ralph Stoody of Methodist information was disturbed as he received feedback from various people including Bishop Oxnam, who later voluntarily appeared before the committee. I wrote to Ralph:

"I cannot explain to you just what is in the mind of Mr. John S. Wood of the Committee on Un-American Activities. All I can do is to give you a copy of Mr. Wood's letter to me and my answer to him. I take it that he means that the committee has not investigated the federation, but that the committee has considerable information on the federation, such as represented in their publication, 'Review of the Federation for Social Action.'

"The information about the federation is presented to confuse people and to condemn the federation. Take, for example, page 69 in the summary wherein the committee categorically states, 'The federation advocates the confiscation, without compensation, of private property from the present owners.' I am absolutely sure that the federation has at no time advocated such a proposition.

"The committee points up, in the summary, references from William Z. Foster, and Marx and Engels in the *Communist Manifesto,* to completely confuse the Christian outlook of the federation. However, this must be the information the committee has on the federation. It is presented, as I take it, without an investigation.

"Mr. Wood's letter to me contains some obvious mistakes, as I explained in his letter. In the second paragraph, he writes, 'You stated.' *He stated.* I am not responsible for the statement by the committee. I simply released a letter from Congressman Wood. If this business makes sense to you, you are a better analyst that I am.

"I cannot understand why the committee does not honestly investigate the federation in a way to present the truth about the federation. Why does it take rather lame and outworn techniques to embarrass the federation? It is a copout that is being sent all over the country to confuse the program of the Methodist federation. I hope that some of us will understand the situation.

"/s/ Edgar M. Wahlberg"

The *Detroit News* carried an editorial on Tuesday, July 7, 1953, which aptly describes the dilemma of those days:
"Like a scorpion, Mr. Mathews carries his sting in his tail. Having proved that Protestant clergymen are Communist in large numbers, he attempts to explain their full grace. He finds that explanation in the vogue of the 'social gospel' movement of the last sixty or seventy years. The movement was nothing more nor less than the awakening of the churches to their social responsibilities. Some liberal and Christian gentlemen were properly shocked at the extent to which the churches had become rich men's clubs dedicated to the blessing of the fortunate. They thought the church, as the followers of Christ, had at least an equal obligation to aid the unfortunate and work for a betterment of the community.

"If Mr. Mathew's reference to the social gospel means anything it means that a concern for social justice is basically subversive. The attempt to confuse liberalism with Communism is a Communist technique and a promising one. There is no quicker way to undermine our democracy than to sterilize it by silencing those who challenge the existing order in the interest of progress.

"On the record Mathews shows himself a bad American and a bad investigator. He has no respect for American traditions of freedom, and he has no respect for facts. The Senate investigating committee unfortunately cannot fire McCarthy, but it can fire Mathews."

The congressional committee had its channels of communication, and fed its information to all super-patriots who carried my skirmish with the committee in their publications—especially among the Methodists. I threw most of these references and articles in the garbage can where they belonged.

I rediscovered some of my old friends, such as Dr. John E. Bentley, dean of the college of arts and sciences of the American University, Washington, D.C., who wrote:

"A brochure has come to me from a group of Methodists in Texas entitled, 'Is There a Pink Fringe in the Methodist Church?' and since I saw your name on the list, and no reference to my own, I thought I would send you a greeting after so many years of silence. You will forgive me for butting in on this, but it looks to me like a bunch of nonsense. Why be afraid of a 'pink fringe'?

"Memory is a great thing, Edgar: I remember you and in my advancing 'youth' the old days in Denver crop up.

"This letter carries to you and Mrs. Wahlberg our fondest affection.

"Very sincerely yours,

"John E. Bentley"

Such letters were encouraging, but there were more of the others. I was cut off from many speaking engagements, but was not overly damaged in my own community of Dearborn. The Mount Olivet Church continued to grow.

Regardless of the merits or demerits of the clergy (or any citizen) there is no justification for dossiers and lists of citizens by paid informers of congressional investigation committees, and other private or public agencies who make it their business to meddle in the lives of people who have committed no crime except to think for themselves. Just as surely as a few ministers are intimidated, all ministers are intimidated. (Take a look at how church people have run for cover.) We are in danger of creating a religion without teeth and will be forced to gum our way through a meaningless life and world, without a faith of any consequence. Ministers will cease to preach truth that needs to be heard, answer questions no one asks. They will be cautious about the unchurched. They will no longer seek to be fellow travelers with the needy, the unjustly treated, and with the "least of these my brethren." Christianity will be churchianity and be no more than window dressing and a halo for the easy way of compromise and peace of mind.

The *Washington Post* had this to say in an editorial: "The committee apparently regards as 'subversive' any opinion of which it disapproves. The dossier compiled on Bishop Oxnam is the kind of dossier compiled by the political police behind the iron curtain.... It does not represent investigation. It represents a naked and ugly attempt at intimidation." Bishop Oxnam put it tersely: "This is not an investigation. It is intimidation. It is twentieth-century inquisition—an inquisition against people who deserve to be heard and for the lack of which we are in trouble."

Emil Lombardi

Emil Lombardi was born in Italy and worked years at the Ford factory in Dearborn. He went to the hospital for a simple operation and came out paralyzed from his waist down. He could no longer work for a living. He used all his savings to buy an old dilapidated building on the corner near his home, planning to renovate it and turn it into an apartment house. The building had had apartments on the second floor and an empty storefront on the corner. The city building inspector refused to give him a permit for the plans. Lombardi had a family to support. I somehow became involved, and asked an architect to draw official plans. I personally appealed to the inspector, who was adamant and recommended that the building be torn down. I went to the building board of appeals and was rebuffed. I went to the mayor and explained to him every detail and promised that the reconstructed building would be an asset to the neighborhood. He promised that he would look into the affair and for me to go back to the board of appeals. I did, and permission was granted. The place was turned into six livable apartments, and one of the concerns of Mr. Lombardi was alleviated. He and his family joined Mount Olivet Church. Our family ate many delicious Italian dinners in their home cooked by his wife Lena, who had also been born in Italy.

I talked to Emil about his physical condition and wondered if we ought to go to the Mayo Clinic and find out if something could be done for him. He agreed, and I accompanied him. After an exploratory operation on his brain, it was decided his physical condition would not improve.

Emil was exhausted and very depressed when he came home. I said, "Look Emil, all is not lost. You are physically impaired, but you can improve your mental activities—you know what I mean."

A light appeared in his eyes and he said, "I like birds, especially canaries." He turned his basement into a bird sanctuary and began studying and raising canaries of many varieties. His bird sanctuary was moved to the garage. Iron rails were installed from the house to the garage. He had a wheelchair in the garage so he could move from cage to cage. The garage was winterized and heat maintained at the right temperature. The birds sang and Emil smiled and laughed at his creatures of love.

We established the tradition of having canaries in our Easter services. Emil provided his best singers for these occasions. He picked his Enrico Carusos. People may not recall my Easter sermons, but they will never forget Emil Lombardi's canaries. When he died, I officiated. His canaries were present and sang their best for Emil.

Detroit

I had served Mount Olivet United Methodist Church for fifteen years, and expected to spend the rest of my ministry in that church until retirement. However, the district superintendent urged me to go to St. Mark's United Methodist in Detroit. I knew that the church was in a rapidly changing neighborhood with many problems, especially racial. The church building was of 1917 vintage, much like a tabernacle with a wide range of rooms not conducive to the supervision necessary to develop a community program. The church did have a gymnasium, bowling alley and parking lot as well as an elevator to take parishioners to the sanctuary. A number of eminent clergymen had served the church through the years. The time was long past for an integrated program related to the people in the neighborhood.

The church was located on Jefferson Avenue, one of the leading streets from the business area of Detroit to several affluent communities to the east. It was at the corner of Jefferson and Garland. Garland was famous or infamous, depending on one's viewpoint. Three short blocks away was the house which a black man, Dr. Ossian H. Sweet, had purchased and moved into with his family in 1925. He was not greeted with an invitation to attend one of the white churches in the neighborhood, but by a mob with threats and stones. It was "The Case of Dr. Sweet vs. Bigotry in 1925."

The *Detroit News* reported: "The woman who sold Dr. Sweet the house told him that she had been warned by a phone caller that if he moved in, she would be killed, the doctor would be killed, and the house would be blown up." Dr. Sweet later recalled, "I wasn't looking for trouble. I just wanted to bring up my little girl in good surroundings." He also recalled, "The street was a sea of humanity. The crowd was so thick you couldn't see the street or the sidewalk. Just getting to the front door was like running a gauntlet. I was hit by a rock before I got inside."

The *Detroit News* reported: "An organization called the Water Works Improvement Association was formed. During the trial a number of witnesses admitted under cross-examination that, despite its innocuous charter, its primary purpose was to keep Negroes out of the neighborhood."

A shot was fired from the house and a white man was killed. All the occupants of the house were arrested and charged with murder.

Clarence Darrow was the chief attorney for the defense. A few remarks to the jury are worth quoting.

"The Sweets spent their first night in their new home afraid to go to bed. The next night they spent in jail. Now the state wants them to spend the rest of their lives in the penitentiary. The state claims there was no mob there that night. Gentlemen, the state has put on enough witnesses who said they were there, to make a mob.

"There are persons in the North and South who say a black man is inferior to the white and should be controlled by the whites. There are also those who recognize his rights and say he should enjoy them. To me this case is a cross-section of human history. It involves the future and the hope of some of us that the future will be better than the past."

In his charge to the jury, Judge Murphy indicated clearly his belief that a man's home is his castle and that no one has a right to invade it. He left no question of the right to shoot when one has reasonable ground to fear that his life or property is in danger. The jury found the defendents not guilty. This was also true in a second trial of Henry Sweet, a younger brother.

Our first two years in St. Mark's Church were difficult. We lost one third of our membership, but gained as many more. The last two years were joyous. We raised some $60,000 and renovated the whole building. I would rather have torn it down and built a church that could have more easily served the needs of our people.

Conditions and programs at St. Mark's settled down to a subnormal tranquility. Artie White, our custodian, had had two years in college and was a natural leader of community activities. I proposed to the official board that he be made director of community services and we hire someone else for custodian, but the board and the church at large turned me down.

The response of the community to our activities was tremendous, but we lacked supervision and skilled leaders in a building that was hard to control; we lacked space for services to take care of special needs. We counted on volunteers from the community, but the problem of supervision was overwhelming. The church membership, by and large, had a dim view of a seven-day-a-week program. However, criticism had dropped to a minimum as whites and blacks got to know each other.

All the same, there continued to be uneasiness, probably a subconscious fear that a riot could break out at any time in the community at large—which it did a year after we left the church. I had hoped that a strong fellowship in the church might prevent this, but it was too little and much too late.

OEO

I was nearing retirement age and believed St. Mark's would benefit from younger leaders. At this time I was appointed the first director of the Wayne County Office of Economic Opportunity, which included all of Wayne County outside Detroit. I had reached the age of sixty-five and was eligible to retire from the church, which I did. I began my responsibilities March 1, 1965, and continued in this capacity for over two years.

The poor were entirely unrepresented in the planning and deliberations of a program meant to solve their problems. The federal act under which this office was created provided no specific direction. A four-day briefing session in Washington was a bedlam of confusion, dealing largely with the symptoms and ailments of poverty rather than remedies such as a guaranteed adequate income so that the people could live in decency and dignity. A fragmentation of services to the poor came with the creation of a new bureaucracy to do what other agencies were supposed to have been doing all along. It was urgent to provide as many programs as could be approved under the act so that the money appropriated by Congress could be spent before the deadline. The money was to be spent *for* the poor—not necessarily *by* the poor. I had hoped that this program might be administered by the poor, which is how it had been done in my days at Grace Church and Center during the Depression.

The real problem was to trust the poor and see what they could do if they had enough income on which to live. The cost would seem to have been staggering—more like $100 billion rather than the less than $2 billion appropriated by Congress. Such an appropriation would have gotten all the poor off relief and in the long run would have made them taxpayers and participants in the creation of society. Creating jobs would not have been an insurmountable difficulty. There were potentially thousands of jobs in replanting forests, building an adequate railroad system, clearing slums, providing youth programs, constructing new houses and recreational areas, cleaning up the environment, and on and on—work people would have been eager to do. Such a program would have paid for itself in the long run.

Our basic problem was that the poor lived in a hidden culture. Few knew them or even knew where they lived.

Wayne County had an administrative grant of $77,801—not a cent for the poor. I selected a small but well intentioned staff. There was no provision for office space or equipment. I was urged to get a downtown office where there were no poor people. We preferred to find space in the county hospital, some twenty miles from Detroit, that was crowded with the poor. Some of them did not know they were poor. We were directed to use the census tracts to determine the number of poor in any particular neighborhood. We spent the first month visiting areas of poverty and met with a number of groups who claimed that they were poor. Indeed many of them were, but they were not represented on the community action committees that had been appointed by official authorities throughout the country. Few of these committees could give much guidance on who were the poor in their own communities.

I learned that the well intentioned chairman of the board of supervisors had written the officials of the municipalities, townships, and school boards asking them to appoint committees to write programs to be processed by the newly appointed office of economic opportunity weeks before I was appointed. The poor were given no chance to plan or direct their own programs, in contrast to my work with the unemployed in the 1930s when everything was accomplished by the unemployed. Here no poor people were involved.

I learned that consultants approved by Washington had helped a number of groups to develop programs, now near completion, before the local office had materialized. Only one of these provided for direct services to the poor, except for a preschool program in Inkster costing $29,287. One program related to ten school districts provided for school-community agents, preschool nurseries, remedial reading and arithmetic, special education, and a minimum of health services and enrichment programs, at a cost of $1,081,272. This was an invaluable program providing for unmet needs in areas where school districts could not afford such services or thought they could not afford them. Some of these services continued under other educational appropriations after OEO expired. Nevertheless, the really poor hardly shared in the programs and were helped only slightly. Another project, costing $153,828, was planned by the county school district to teach teachers to work with the children of the impoverished. Our office had no alternative but to administer the programs, trying to bend them to serve the poor. Sumpter Township, the poorest of all, was bypassed. We had 126 townships and municipalities and almost as many school districts, most of them converging on our office. My primary questions had to do with the number of the poor and how to work with the poor in the planning stages. Some officials were confounded with working with the poor, even with knowing who they were and where they lived. The Wayne County Citizens Committee to which I was primarily responsible included in its membership of thirty, one third from the poor appointed by the poor. The number was finally extended to 50 percent of the poor.

We helped train the poor to organize neighborhood advisory councils made up entirely of the poor, and we assisted them in developing programs more responsive to the needs of the impoverished. Neighborhood centers staffed by the poor were developed.

The problem of a dual responsibility with the board of county supervisors was never entirely resolved. I had to report to my own committee and to the OEO committee of the board of supervisors. The first chairman, Roy Berger, was quite understanding and a pleasure to work with. Another chairman was less agreeable. He ordered me, on one occasion, to hire a certain individual whom I knew to be unfit for the position. I prevailed, but was shouted at in no uncertain language and told that I would be fired from my job. I finally retired at my own convenience and in my own time.

The neighborhood centers brought the OEO closer to the poor. The primary value was in the jobs provided for a limited number. It was the upper-class poor who were more aggressive who benefited most from the program; the lower-class poor benefited very little. Much of the work in the centers had no direct relationship with removing people from poverty and making them self-sufficient. Much of the energy expended in referring needy people to various agencies meant a duplication of effort; the agencies involved were not always cooperative, which led to misunderstanding and the dulling of motivation of center workers. When the poor tried to air their grievances through petitions and demonstrations, they were confronted with community pressures. OEO workers became locked into a subagency and an OEO system which offered neither dignity nor security; the results were fear, irritation, and inadequate performance. The best that can be said is that many OEO programs made poverty a little more comfortable for the relatively few that benefited in one way or another.

The Wayne County Work Experience Project was better. It was funded under Title V of the Economic Opportunity Act, initiated by the Michigan Department of Social Services, and carried out by the Wayne County Department of Social Services. The theory behind this program was to ascertain what persons on relief would do if provided with sufficient income to meet the minimum costs of living with decency. The goal announced was to make "taxpayers out of tax-eaters." I do not subscribe to the connotation of "tax-eaters." One thousand families were selected from the relief rolls. Each wage earner was required to participate in a work training program. Of those who completed the program, 94.9 percent secured employment and went off the relief rolls. Most significant is the fact that their 2,604 children were no longer stigmatized as "welfare children."

The decade of the 1960s will go down in history as the period when poverty was discovered in the United States. There is no justification for the assumption that the United States has solved or is on the way to solving its economic problems. There remains a growing culture of poverty, hidden from public understanding, within the larger culture of higher standards of living. The sheer tragedy and immensity of the problems are indicated in the statistics. More than 50 million of our population are poor, of whom more than 15 million are children. Michael Harrington in his book *The Other America* says: "They are at this very moment maimed in body and spirit, existing at levels beneath those necessary for human decency. If these people are not starving, they are hungry, and sometimes fat from hunger, for that is what cheap foods do. They are without adequate housing and education and medical care."

It could be argued that during the centuries of scarcity poverty was unavoidable. This argument is no longer valid in a time of abundance and the availability of goods and services.

The challenge to eliminate poverty may be one of the greatest in history. It is inherent in the traditions of democracy and "our way of life."

The financial deficit between poverty and an acceptable standard of living for all the people is about $14 billion a year (1970) which would mean a 3 percent adjustment in our national income. (Due to military expenditures, national debt, high prices, inflation, and manipulation of currency, the differential cost may be greater. Nevertheless, the solution of unemployment and poverty would stabilize our economy.) This is the financial loss that the poor are paying in substandard housing, living expenses, sickness, despair, filth, ignorance, and inadequate preparation for life. The $1.5 billion that was provided to fight the war on poverty was a beginning, but could not make a dent in the total war. That was asking the poor miraculously to pull themselves up by their bootstraps. Prosperity for many people often drives the poor deeper into poverty.

President Johnson's commission on income maintenance hit the nail on the head when it reported: "Many Americans wonder why the poor do not escape from poverty. The answer to this question is clear to us: they usually cannot, because most are already doing as much as can reasonably be expected of them to change these conditions . . . The simple fact is that most of the poor remain poor because access to income through work is currently beyond their reach . . . Society must aid them or they will remain poor."

A staggering problem related to the institution of poverty is the alienation of a large segment of the population, the white working men and women, especially that group that lives just above the upper poor class. It would seem that there are different classes polarized by the existence of poverty: the hardcore poor; the middle class poor; the marginal poor; and the marginal pensioner or worker who for the time being is not classified as poor. The latter group feels threatened from all sides. These people feel that they are discriminated against and no one is concerned about their welfare. They are financially hard up, and yet their children cannot go to a "Head Start" school and other programs. They feel that everything is being done for the poor and nothing for them. They are bitter when blacks are hired to conform to legal requirements. They are frustrated by taxes, payments, prices and inflation. They feel that they are being taxed to support the lazy poor.

The OEO experience should have taught us a few things. There is a need to eliminate the antiquated patchwork of public and private agencies. We must attack poverty by an adequate guaranteed annual income for everyone. It is no longer reasonable to believe that there are enough good paying jobs for everyone. The long held idea that only a worker is worthy of an income is no longer an ethical principle. We must have sufficient faith in each other to believe that a person is eager to work if a job is available. All persons deserve adequate support. It is a basic human and civil right.

Poverty in our society is a continuing and obstinate fact. Artificial respiration is useless as long as the patient is submerged in the sea of poverty. Poverty is increasing as high prices and inflation continue, fewer jobs are available as neighborhoods and houses deteriorate and more people are locked into their fears and frustrations. Alienation and violence are symptoms. Our peace is challenged by angry voices. It is better to be angry than dead.

One of the best OEO programs to my mind was the legal aid project; it helped a great many people and could have put before the public the real issues, but it was the most controversial. It might have given every person justice before the law, justice long overdue.

It is common knowledge that the poor do not have access to law and justice. They have no money to pay attorneys so many grievances are overlooked, many of which could be solved with competent advice. The poor cannot afford the cost of divorce, so go illegally from one miserable marriage to another. Small claims are forgotten because the poor have no way to fight for their rights. Jails are filled with poor people with alleged charges pending against them with only court-appointed attorneys to defend them. These are paid a minimum fee, and are loaded with cases with little time to investigate thoroughly each problem. Our legal aid project stimulated a new awareness among the poor that they could and should fight their legal battles rather than lose by default.

The Head Start programs proved to be the most popular. We had up to twenty such programs throughout our part of Wayne County. At intervals we provided evaluations of all our programs, and Head Start ranked the highest. Almost 90 percent of parents said the program helped their children.

We were also confronted with the problems of the aging, many of whom wanted something to do to escape the boredom of a limited existence, and many others who needed part-time work to buy the necessities of life. Over 20 percent were living in poverty, and the number was growing. Our projection was that 25 to 30 percent would be the victims of poverty by 1975-1980, due to higher prices and inflation. Older people were not eating proper foods and their interest in life was decreasing. I talked to a senior citizens group of over one hundred members and projected that they would live longer; I was amazed at a nearly unanimous, "What for?"

We organized several projects to provide some meager income for those over sixty-five. One was a grandparents' foster program in a handicapped children's institution. Our problem was to convince the authorities that such an idea was worthwhile. They harbored the stereotyped notion that retirees were over the hill and unable to cope with the problems of children. Furthermore, they were probably poor because they had been improvident in their working years. We countered these accusations by reminding them that these were people who had survived the Depression of the thirties when more than one fourth of the population was out of work through no fault of their own, had lost their homes and resources to survive. When times grew better they had worked and had partially recouped their status and raised their families. Many had even paid their longstanding debts. Now they were older and, if fortunate, were living on less than a minimum standard-of-living pension, unable to cope with the problems of maintaining their homes or renting adequate housing—which was unavailable. We forget that one whole generation of working people not only survived the Depression, but are now confronted with the devastation of inflation, which few were able to anticipate—especially when reduced to small pensions and fixed incomes which cannot cover their present needs. These are the people who paid for the staggering cost of the Depression in reverse while others prospered, and now are left out and discarded while many enjoy good incomes and huge profits.

The *Institution* agreed to cooperate with us on a minimal trial basis, providing for twenty-five foster grandparents to work three half-days a week on a one-to-one basis. The results were gratifying. These grandparents were not professionally trained for the job, but they had raised their own children;

their natural genius surfaced as they searched for stories long forgotten, retold their own childhood experiences, and talked about the world in which they had lived. Their special distinction was their love for children, often absent among professionals. There was a great warmth which only grandparents can provide. I have always said that the generation gap between grandparents and grandchildren is much narrower than between parents and their children. Parents have less understanding and time for children, and often, for their own parents. Grandparents have time and hunger for values that served them well with children. The program was a success, was continued, and did much good for the aging as well as the children.

Another program was a light in the dark if there ever was one. We organized a hundred older people to canvass their neighborhoods to search out other older people to inform them about their rights and available services. The director was an aging retiree who had been an employee in Wyandote. He was a crochety old man who didn't like me very well because I had turned down a program he had prepared for his town. I called him in to take charge. He was surprised and delighted. His heart was in it and his mind was more than equal to the task. He blueprinted the program, chose his people, trained them, and created an enthusiasm among them for helping people such as one does not often experience.

We discovered that many older people had never heard of Social Security, that many others were ashamed and afraid to come out of hiding to inquire about their rights. Our responsibilities were out-county, which did not include the city of Detroit. Many people were shy of bureaucracies. Many had never been in a bank and knew little about what was going on in their own comunities. Many had long since stopped attending church, and had little communication with their neighbors. A great many had never attended senior citizens' meetings, although in some instances such meetings were widely advertised and nearby. I came to the general conclusion that OEO was partially benefiting only the upper third of the poor.

Single older people, both men and women, lived in the most circumscribed conditions. There were more women than men, and it seemed that the women were slightly better off than many men. They lived in single rooms in cheap and rundown rooming houses. One man had not left his room for three weeks, according to the custodian, who said that it was not her business to know about the roomers—although she had knocked on the door several times without response. She explained that his rent was due. She opened the door for us and we were confronted with an unbearable stench and indescribable disorder of rags, old newspapers, empty cans, and half empty containers with rotting beans and soup and vermin. There were two uncashed Social Security checks on the floor for $87. The man was lying in his filth and stink with nails that had grown over his fingertips and toes. He was in a comatose condition. I called the visiting nurses who immediately sent him to the county hospital, a circumstance which he had obstinately refused. I learned that he was a member of Alcoholics Anonymous and for many months had prepared the coffee for the weekly meetings. Then he just didn't show up. He had no relatives and no one bothered to check on him. I called on him in the hospital in a ward with fifty or more men. He was defiant and depressed, and soon died. We found another man who lived under the back porch of a dilapidated rooming house. He had no means of support and lived like a furtive animal. I found that he had a son who had long since lost track of his father.

Nursing homes and convalescent homes presented us with another distressing plight of older people. I had been acquainted with this problem in my ministry. Presumably, people there are put away for good—meaning, waiting for the end. I called on one man, among many, who was lying in his excrement and so ashamed he cried. I called the head nurse and didn't have to say a thing. She ordered that the four beds in the small room be cleaned up. The only explanation was that they were short of help. I called weekly at varying times and the cleaning problem was eliminated. It wasn't many weeks before this friend of mine was sitting in a chair. Later he could walk to the visiting room, where we had a number of interesting conversations. Conditions in these homes vary from very bad to excellent, depending upon the monthly payments. The conditions of the patients, if such they can be called, vary accordingly. For a time I was a trustee of the Methodist Retirement Homes of the Detroit Conference. People receive adequate care in these homes, but they are out of reach financially for the poor—who by and large have lost their church connection, if they ever had any.

I was also a member of the Wayne County Committee on Aging, which makes a valiant fight to do a good job for the poor. One program provided for low cost meals in poverty areas for five days a week, not Saturday and Sunday. I wondered what some of these people did on the off days. There was a limited delivery program for those confined to their homes. Another program provided transportation for the poor so that they could get to medical and other services. However, I have a feeling that the lower third of the poor must continue in degradation and filth.

I must add that the larger percentage of the growing aging population is white, and the larger number of those who are poor are white, because they have a greater life expectancy. The average life expectancy of the American Indian is forty-seven, and few of them live long enough to share in benefits for the aging. Other minorities also have life expectancies less than that of whites. This may come as a surprise if not a shock to those who harbor images of improvidence on the part of minorities.

We discovered people who were poor by any standard of poverty but didn't know it. Some of them lived near an abandoned factory in company shacks which had been their homes when they had been employed in an ongoing enterprise. Most received small pensions of less than $30 a month. They had planted gardens in their back yards and raised garden staples such as potatoes, rutabagas, perennial winter onions, beans and other substantial vegetables. There were three cows in one such settlement, and one man tended three pigs. There was a warm sense of community, and a self-appointed preacher who held services in a small made-over barn. The women carried worn Bibles to and from the meetings, explaining that they did not attend the "proper churches" in the nearby village—which was self-explanatory as we observed their seedy and worn appearance. They just didn't feel at home anywhere else. As far as I could learn, there were no overtures from the "proper churches" to these people with their self-sufficient and peculiar ways. The defunct company made no effort to collect rents, so the people lived rent-free in the deteriorating shacks which they did their best to maintain. Their incomes did not provide for paint or screens and other conveniences. They drew their water from a few outdoor hydrants, and used outdoor privies. They wore made-over garments from a Salvation Army salvage store.

We talked to these people, who for the most part were not collecting Social Security and were probably not eligible. One family tenderly cloistered a retarded child. They made their own soap and prepared medical ointments and syrups for colds and other ailments. They had a midwife who gratuitously helped when needed. When asked about their needs, they would say, "I guess you cain't say that we are what you call poor; we just sort of make do."

The defunct company paid a lone guard to look after the grounds of the ailing factory. He related that they had started with three guards working eight-hour shifts, but now he alone remained. He explained, "There isn't much to look after, things breaking down like they have."

We discovered that he was quite generous with his former fellow workers and gave them whatever rotting timbers and wood they required for fuel and repairs. He said, "I guess no one cares; and anyway, it helps to keep things cleaned up a bit." He seemed to have little or no supervision, and was able to do as he saw fit.

The children were bussed to a nearby elementary school which had an ingenious and kindly principal of Polish origin. He had a nominal salary and owned a farm nearby. He was sympathetic and alert as to the needs of his pupils. I have rarely known a school man so universally loved. He started a school children's luncheon and paid for it out of his own funds and the produce of his farm. He appealed to his friends and various agencies for used clothing which he distributed to the neediest children. He served all the pupils in the luncheon because he had no yardstick as to who was poor, poorer, or poorest. "And anyway," he said, "they get so much fun out of it. I guess you might say I get a lot of satisfaction out of seeing it done." We worked out a program for this school, providing staff and provisions. We also had one of our Head Start programs in his school. He was so pleased and cooperative that you would think we were doing what we did for him personally.

The area is now bulldozed out of existence to make room for a new industrial complex. Few of the people were hired because they were regarded as unemployable. A nearby farmer told me that they "made do" with their own conveyances, piled on all their worldly possessions, and quietly moved away without a single protest. Where? I don't know, except now and then I would see a familiar but downcast face in the untidy slums of a small rural town. Perhaps a few made their way into the slums of Detroit.

Some of the poorest people in the out-county lived in the lower half of Sumpter County, a western township adjacent to Ann Arbor County. Many of these people had moved from the slums of Detroit hoping to escape the indignities and despair of the slums and improve their existence in a rural area. The land was marginal—largely wet and soggy with many swamps.

Rentals were low and the land could be purchased with almost any arrangement because the owners had not been able to make a reasonable living. The newcomers were blacks who took over the old farmhouses, and many lived in almost every conceivable type of shelter.

The schools were soon overcrowded in the poorest school district in Wayne County, which added to the difficulties of a fluctuating staff and the low quality and poor materials of education. Naturally the people were concerned about a less-than-adequate system of education for their children, which in this case was even lower than that provided in the slums of Detroit.

However, these people were vocal and represented by aggressive, militant and intelligent leaders. They believed in nonviolence, but nevertheless were alert to every possible way to help their communities. They appealed to our office for leadership and cooperation. Strangely enough, they wanted primarily a community facility for meetings and programs for human enrichment. They had learned to farm the higher and drier parts of their farms and to raise chickens, rabbits, pigs, and a few cows. They discovered that strawberries flourished in their soil and many customers were drawn to Sumpter County for the best strawberries in the county. They had learned to cooperate with each other to help all concerned as best they could, but they had no public facilities. OEO guidelines did not provide for building materials or construction costs.

They wanted a Head Start program for their preschool children, but explained that there was no facility available except an abandoned one-room school building which had served early settlers when the land was sparsely populated. We looked over this building and wondered why it had not been condemned and demolished. The foundation had partially settled so that the floor was uneven and rotting from the moisture that had seeped through the roof. Windows were broken and covered with makeshift boards. The doors were sagging so that they could neither be opened nor shut, and the building was raw from the lack of paint for many years. There was an ancient woodburning stove which could hardly warm the building in cold weather. Nevertheless, the building had been used until it was unsafe for any purpose. The committee elected by the poor was certain that we would agree that a community structure was the only alternative. They promised to provide all the labor if we could provide the materials.

We agreed that although it was not provided by OEO guidelines, we would provide the materials to renovate the old schoolhouse so that we could begin a Head Start program. Steps had to be built, as well as an outdoor privy. The committee felt that this was a mistake, and that what materials were required could be better utilized in the building of a modest community center. As it proved out, it *was* a mistake. The building could not be satisfactorily renovated. However, we went ahead and when completed we provided staff, who in turn selected thirty children to be served by Head Start. Water had to be brought in containers and food had to be prepared in a home nearby.

I shall never forget the cold and blizzardy day when we undertook to visit the Head Start programs in our responsibility. The wind chill was way below zero. Fortunately, an OEO official representing the Chicago Regional

Office was with us. We found the children bundled in their winter clothing huddled around the stove. The program of activities was at a standstill in the cold room, with the teachers doing their best to comfort the children. There was only one thing to do—close the school until the weather moderated. The children were delivered to their homes until further notice.

No one cried, "We told you so." Our alternative was to go ahead with the community center regardless of guidelines. The committee planned the building and gave us a list of essentials such as concrete blocks, cement, building materials, roofing, electrical wiring and essentials, plumbing, roofing, paint and other necessities. A piece of land had been donated in the center of the community around which a ditch had to be dug to drain off the moisture in the soggy soil.

The people were true to their word. They supplied all the labor, and in the course of a few months completed a modest building with indoor facilities, tables and benches. We donated a desk and a few chairs. Someone donated tin cups and pans and secondhand cooking ware. The dedication was a unique and festive occasion with singing and music and many speeches. The home talent was amazing. They even provided a home cooked luncheon, seemingly from nowhere.

The Head Start program was moved to the center, which became a busy place for meetings of all kinds including cultural and enrichment activities. There were no repercussions from OEO headquarters for misappropriating funds. How could there be? This was an adventure in helping people who wanted to help themselves.

On one red-letter day Mrs. Hubert Humphrey visited our Head Start program in Inkster, held in the black Episcopal church. Inkster was a gerrymandered city and community, robbed by adjoining communities of considerable territories to keep their communities white; Inkster was about two-thirds black. Head Start included black and white children who were bussed back and forth to the church. Hubert Humphrey was a friend of mine; I had come in contact with him in my work with Jim Patton of the Farmers' Union Cooperatives. He was campaigning for the presidency and intended to make some appearances in Michigan. We asked him to visit us and take a look at our program, which he promised to do; but his schedule became overloaded so he sent his wife Muriel in his place. She asked to spend her time in a Head Start school. She became so engrossed with the mothers and the children that she long overstayed her visit. She told the children stories, talked with them, questioned them, and turned to the mothers with her lovely and friendly spirit. The place was surrounded by local dignitaries and citizens, but she gave all her time to the school.

My Last Pastorate

A few months after I resigned my position with the Office of Economic Opportunity, I suffered a series of ailments and spent about four months in the hospital, including three operations. To make things worse my wife had a radical mastectomy a few days before I left the hospital. She had kept the knowledge from me as long as possible. We had rooms next to each other so we could see each other from day to day.

I went home to the most difficult job of my life—to be nursemaid, cook, housewife, delivery boy, food purchaser and many other things, since my wife was unable to care for herself or the household for several weeks. How I hated the supermarkets! Scott Nearing, in his book *Civilization and Beyond,* calls a supermarket an "embalming center." I didn't know anything about brands, quantities, qualities or prices or where I might look for various foods. Dry milk would be in one place, canned milk in another, and real milk would be somewhere on the other side of the store—and so it was with almost everything. I talked to men doing the same job and they invariable said, "I hate it." Then when you finally thought you might escape from the store, you had to stand in long lines to wait for your turn to pay for your purchases. I gave a lot of thought as to which line was the best, but I always lost.

In 1969 I received a call from the First Congregational Church of Dearborn asking me to help out for a few weeks. The few weeks turned into a seven-year pastorate, and a good one. The church had had two unfortunate experiences with ministers. The first one was a fundamentalist, a literalist, and sin-conscious. His sermons were all about sin. The people got weary of being reminded each Sunday about their sins. They figured that there was some good in everyone. The other minister was just the opposite—an extreme liberal with an excellent education. But most of his interests were outside the needs of his parishioners. Many people left the church, and those who remained took sides.

I knew a few members of this church and accepted the invitation to help out. I hadn't the slightest idea that there was anything amiss, except that they didn't have a minister. The church had enjoyed a good reputation for many years, and I had been personally acquainted with two of the ministers when the church was going strong. There were twenty-nine parishioners in the service that first Sunday morning, and I soon learned what was wrong.

On the second Sunday I spoke quite frankly to the congregation. I told them not to worry about their indebtedness; not to be angry with each other; that we would attempt to build a program, but we needed the help of everyone; that we would have fun together; that our main scripture for a while would be the Sermon on the Mount. Soon there developed the sweetest fellowship I had experienced in my long ministry.

One evening a trustee asked, "Is there anything we can do for you?" I replied, "No, not for me; but you can't do first class counseling in a basement atmosphere." That is all I said. Nevertheless, the men took time out to create one of the finest offices of my career. That was the beginning of a long series of improvements that gladdened the whole community. Furthermore, the outreach of the church into areas of greatest need grew to include a community center in the slums of Detroit. I developed a series of sermons on "We Don't Believe It Anymore." It was in this church where a young man said, "The trouble with preachers is that they preach on things we can't understand, and try to answer questions that no one asks."

We had a coffee klatch following every Sunday morning service in which people became acquainted. Our goal was to catch up on the finances and improvements and to save $12,000 so they could hire a full-time minister. By 1976 my old bones wanted to do less and less, while the church program demanded more and more. I knew the time had come to retire. Some counseled that I make it to eighty years of age and break a record. I think it dawned on everyone the time had come to make a change.

I can never repay this marvelous group of people for their kindness to our family, especially my wife and myself. It was a Congregational church with no bishops or district superintendents. I liked this very much; the laymen had the full responsibility.

Postscript

I have just finished reading Will and Ariel Durant, a *Dual Autobiography,* and have taken a few comments from its pages.

On page 186, I read from Ariel about Will: "Anticipating the theology of the 1960s, the 1933 article proposed that Christian churches should cease to require acceptance of the Christian theology, and should concentrate on the ethics of Christ; all persons should be welcome into church membership who accept the ethics of Christ as the goal—even if not the actuality—of their conduct."

I have wholly agreed with this position, except for the use of the name Christ instead of Jesus. I would have said, "the teachings of *Jesus*" with an understanding of the radical under- and overtones of Jesus as related to the closed society of the Pharisees and the power and monopoly wealth of the Sadducees who cooperated with the Romans. The use of the name "Christ" is related to Christology, which is part of the varied theologies of the Christian church, and there are numerous Christologies. Jesus is a name nearest to the man named Jesus.

Will says on page 213: "Every truth is tempted to expand until it becomes a falsehood. Every virtue is made a vice through excess, and nothing fails like excess. In all realms of our democratic life liberty has run its course from stimulus to disorder, from beneficence to disintegration.

"Freedom of thought, speech and press melted down old basic stabilizing customs, traditions and beliefs. Science, subsidized and hypnotized by its own mechanisms, turned biology into physics and chemistry and could see nothing else in the world except machines. Philosophy, divorced from the growth and miracle of the soil, capitulated to an enervating skepticism, a hopeless cynicism that found in completed rebellion the same absurdities and tyrannies, and in science the same incredibilities, as in the rules and faiths of older days."

What concerns me is the first sentence: "Every truth is tempted to expand until it becomes a falsehood." This is true of the Christian church. Christology and theology have overshadowed the teachings of Jesus. If the founding fathers of our nation had a glimpse of democracy and its implications as related to the common man (which I doubt), that vision has long since been lost in man's inhumanity to man—covered up with bureaucracies and vested interests. We have made exploitation legal while still brandishing the generalities and wordings of democracy, freedom and justice. It gets more and more difficult to draw out the specifics of human rights from the quagmire and complexities in which we find ourselves. At least, this is my conclusion after years of working with the American Civil Liberties Union—first in Colorado, where I was designated chairman by Roger Baldwin, and in the fifties as chairman for six years of the Detroit Metropolitan Branch of the ACLU. The common man fought for freedom and democracy in the Revolutionary War—only to place a property class in power to fully exploit a new land rich with resources to the point of ultimate destruction in the pollution of land, water and air. Man himself has become an endangered species. He is badgered by a military establishment which the world can no longer afford. He is bewitched by the myth that military strength is the chaperone of peace. It is treason to believe differently. If the resources now held by the military establishment could be rightfully returned to the people there would be no shortages, and mankind could cooperate together to solve the problems of inflation, poverty and hunger.

What Is God?

I am not certain. God could be an essence, an intimacy, a perfection, a process—an existence inherent in the timelessness of an unlimited universe in an immeasurable space, totally inside, infinitely outward. God is everything that has been, that exists, and what will be—limited by nature and the intelligence of man, who unfortunately uses only a small part of it. There seems to be a vastness and magnificence we may call God, in little things as well: beauty of all kinds, flowers, love, peace, justice, happiness, mountains, streams, oceans. There are experiences in which we may feel the presence of God, such as loving, affection, birth, children, joy of living, working with people and understanding them, healing, enjoying the silence, the night, moon and stars.

We do not need to know less about God, but much more about people and humankind. God will continue to be a gaseous nothing until we honestly and earnestly deal with our human confrontations and accept the implications and disciplines of our conduct. To be truly human is to be divine.

Finale—1982

My wife Jimmie (Eunice) and I retired to a mountain home in Estes Park, Colorado in 1978 at ages 79. We imagined that we had retired to complete leisure. It didn't happen that way. Jimmie is already widely recognized for her work with the American Cancer Society, and is involved in a number of church and community activities. Recently she organized two peace groups.

I acquired an adequate supply of fishing equipment and have used it with pleasure. I have officiated at several weddings, funerals, baptisms, and preached a few times. I have suffered physically, due to a few light strokes, several falls and broken bones. This has slowed me down a bit and made me more observant of the beauty of the mountains around us, and especially the wildlife—elk, deer, coyotes, rabbits, squirrels, chipmunks and thousands of birds.

Life has been good and we are thankful. We have a warm, loving family who visit us frequently, great grandchildren and all. We are approaching the age of eighty-four, and can say, "We are glad we are old, because if we were not we would be dead!" We are far from that. The same is true of our nation.

Governor Richard D. Lamm and Michael McCarthy have just released a profound book, *The Angry West—A Vulnerable Land and Its Future.* They described the exploitation of the West by the corporate East. Writing about former stainless skies, they say, "Now the blue dome is not so blue. And the purity is gone forever." Among their conclusions they write: "The West is angry, but it is not rebellious. It understands reality—the limit of power . . . but what it must do first is to work toward the restoration of federalism, toward reconstruction of a system—long in decay—where the states become equal partners with the federal government."

They speak passionately for the unemployed and dispossessed. I hear them as their thesis can be applied to society. In this context, individual citizens should seek self-respect rather than the respect of peers. Our nation is vulnerable, and there are many losers because of exploitation. We are now in a struggle for survival. None will survive unless all people can live with dignity.